Globalization *and* Firm Competitiveness

in the Middle East and North Africa Region

About the MDF

The Mediterranean Development Forum (MDF) partnership, which began in 1997, comprises Middle East and North Africa (MENA) region think tanks, the United Nations Development Programme, and the World Bank Institute. The partnership is dedicated to empowering civil society to participate in shaping public policy, making a contribution to the policy debate in key areas of regional interest, improving the quantity and quality of research on economic and social policy issues, and creating vibrant networks of development actors in the region. The partnership promotes activities supporting policy dialogue culminating in a Forum held approximately every two years: MDF1 in May 1997, MDF2 in September 1998, MDF3 in March 2000, and MDF4 scheduled for April 2002.

A crucial component of the MDF partnership is the Forum because it provides a rare opportunity for top-notch MENA experts, high-level government officials, and civil society representatives to meet and engage in a dialogue to help shape the region's development agenda. The significance of this opportunity to exchange ideas is reflected in the speech of World Bank President James D. Wolfensohn during MDF2: "Peace and opportunity and economic advantage to the broadest number of people comes with the sharing of knowledge, it comes with the sharing of experience, and it comes with a human commitment to make the lives of all of our people better and to give our children the opportunities that they deserve."

MDF1, MDF2, and MDF3 have already played a unique role in the region by providing a venue for open debate on new and cutting-edge issues and by breaking down national and country barriers through participant dialogue during the Forum. In addition, MDF has facilitated the publication of a number of books on issues discussed during the Forum and the creation and support of networks. MDF4 aims to increasingly focus on impact through MDF follow-up activities and networks.

Globalization *and* Firm Competitiveness
in the Middle East and North Africa Region

Samiha Fawzy
Editor

THE WORLD BANK
Washington, D.C.

ISBN 0-8213-4989-9

Cover design: Tomoko Hirata, GSD—Printing, Graphics, and Map Design, World Bank

Library of Congress Cataloging-in-Publication Data has been applied for.

Contents

FOREWORD   *xi*

PREFACE   *xiii*

ACKNOWLEDGMENTS   *xiv*

CONTRIBUTORS   *xv*

ABBREVIATIONS AND ACRONYMS   *xvii*

1   Overview   *1*
     Samiha Fawzy

Part I   Global Rules for Business

2   Challenges to Firm Competitiveness and Opportunities
     for Success   *13*
     Dorsati Madani and John Page

3   Global Competition and the Peripheral Player:
     A Promising Future   *45*
     Taïeb Hafsi

Part II   The Business Environment in the MENA Region

4   The Regional Business Environment in the Global Context   *63*
     Andrew H. W. Stone

5   Dispute Resolution and Firms' Competitiveness
        in the MENA Region   *76*
     Jeffrey B. Nugent

**Part III   Corporate Governance:
            Implications for the MENA Region**

6   Corporate Governance: A Framework for Implementation   *119*
     Magdi R. Iskander and Nadereh Chamlou

7   Transparency between Government and Business   *138*
     John D. Sullivan

Part IV   Sectoral Applications

8   Strengthening Small and Medium Enterprises
        for International Competitiveness   *157*
     Sanjay Lall

9   Support Services and the Competitiveness of Small
        and Medium Enterprises in the MENA Region   *187*
     Antoine Mansour

10   Beyond Credit—A Taxonomy of Small and Medium-Size
        Enterprises and Financing Methods for Arab Countries   *208*
     Mahmoud A. El-Gamal, Nihal El-Megharbel, and Hulusi Inanoglu

11   The Competitive Position of the Tourism Industry
        in the MENA Region   *233*
     Sahar Tohamy

Index   *261*

TABLES

2.1   Tariff Rates by Region   *14*
2.2   Middle-Income Countries: Speed of Integration   *17*
2.3   Tariff Bindings by Arab Countries Before and After the
        Uruguay Round   *19*
2.4   Bound Tariffs (Upper Ceiling) on Industrial and Agricultural Products
        Before and After the Uruguay Round   *20*
2.5   Extent of Commitments to Open Markets for Trade in Services
        by Arab Countries   *21*
2.6   Binding Constraints for Firms   *26*
2.7   International Country Risk Guide Indices for Bureaucratic Quality,
        Corruption, and Law and Order, 1998   *27*
2C.1 Infrastructure Indicators for Selected Fast Integrator
        and MENA Countries, 1996   *35*
2C.2 Main Indicators for Telecommunications Services
        in MENA Countries, 1999   *36*
2C.3 Information Infrastructure in Selected MENA Countries,
        and Others   *37*
3.1   Globalization of National Markets   *48*
3.2   Degree of Globalization of Industry and Competition   *49*
3.3   Degree of Globalization of Firms   *50*
3.4   Globalization and Strategy   *51*
4.1   Constraints to Enterprises by Region: World Business
        Environment Survey, 1999–2000   *67*
4.2   The Heavy State: Economic Activity of State-Owned Enterprises,
        1990–95   *68*
4.3   Average Import Duties in Selected Countries, 1997   *69*
4.4   Networking Indicators, 1997   *70*
4.5   Knowledge Indicators, 1997   *71*
5.1   Regional Comparisons of Indexes of Obstacles
        for Doing Business   *79*
5.2   Comparisons of the Responses Concerning Obstacles to Business
        Operations by Private Firms from the MENA Region with Those
        from SSEA and Developing Countries   *81*
5A.1 Alternative Aggregate Indexes of Economic Freedom   *102*
5A.2 Country Scores on the Components of the Index of Restrictions
        on Economic Freedom, 1998   *103*
5A.3 Country Scores on the Components of the Economic Freedom
        Rating for 1995   *104*
8.1   Role of Small and Medium Enterprises in Selected Countries   *160*
9.1   Distribution of Industrial Establishments by Size, and Contribution
        to Total Manufacturing Employment and Output   *189*
9.2   Role of SMEs in Some Developed and East Asian Economies   *190*

10.1 Small- and Medium-Enterprise Share in Total Establishments
        and Their Contribution to Employment   *211*
10.2 SMEs' Share in Total Establishments and Their Contribution
        to Employment   *213*
10.3 Small- and Medium-Enterprise Contribution to Output
        in Manufacturing, 1990s, and Exports, 1991–92   *214*
10.4 Selected Asian Economies: Inward FDI Flows with Respective
        Export and GDP Growth Rates, 1995   *217*
10.5 Credit Gap for Small and Medium Enterprises in the Arab World   *220*
10.6 Sources of Investment Capital for 173 Surveyed Egyptian Small
        and Medium Enterprises   *221*
10.7 Educational Level of Entrepreneurs of 173 Surveyed
        Egyptian SMEs   *221*
11.1 Importance of Tourism in World Trade, 1995–97   *234*
11.2 Top 10 Tourism Destinations and Earners, 1999   *235*
11.3 Tourist Arrivals and Receipts by Country in the MENA Region,
        1995–99   *237*
11.4 Travel and Tourism Economy, 1999   *238*
11.5 Share of MENA in Outbound Tourism, by Region, 1996   *240*
11.6 Physical Infrastructure: Power, Telecommunications,
        and Information   *242*
11.7 Education Participation and Youth Illiteracy in MENA   *243*
11.8 Labor Competitiveness Balance Sheet   *244*
11.9 Egypt and Jordan: Management and Labor Competitiveness, 1998   *252*
11.10 Quality Training Gaps at the Different Occupation Levels   *253*
11.11 Preferred Language Knowledge   *254*

FIGURES
2.1   Net Inflows of Foreign Direct Investment   *15*
2.2   Share of Merchandise Exports from Developing Countries,
        1965–2004   *16*
2A.1 Exports and Imports of Commercial Services   *32*
2A.2 Commercial Service Exports for Selected MENA Countries   *32*
2A.3 Trends in Exports of Goods for Selected MENA Countries,
        1985–98   *33*
2A.4 Trends in Imports of Goods for Selected MENA Countries,
        1985–98   *33*
4.1A Exports to Industrialized Countries: Change in Market Share,
        Manufactured Goods, 1990–96   *65*
4.1B Exports to Industrialized Countries: Annual Change
        in Merchandise Export Value, 1990–96   *65*
4.2   The Enterprise in the Business Environment   *66*

4.3   Time for Import-Related Processes: Algerian Enterprise Survey,
         1998   *72*
4.4   Constraints to Enterprises in Four Countries in North Africa,
         Based on World Bank Survey Data, 1998–99   *73*
6.1   Modern Corporations Are Disciplined by Internal
         and External Factors   *122*
8.1   Growth Rates of Total and High-Tech Production and Exports,
         1980–95   *162*
8A.1 Growth in Share of World Trade, 1980–96   *177*
10.1 Savings and Investment in Asia, 1980–2005   *210*
10.2 FDI Inflows to Emerging Markets by Region   *210*
10.3 Share of SMEs in Total Establishments vs. Growth Rate   *212*
10.4 Share of SMEs in Total Establishments vs. Growth Rate   *213*
10.5 Share of SMEs in Total Employment vs. Growth Rate   *214*
10.6 Small- and Medium-Enterprise Role in Promoting Export
         Growth (a)   *215*
10.7 Small- and Medium-Enterprise Role in Promoting Export
         Growth (b)   *216*
10.8 Small- and Medium-Enterprise FDI Inflows' Role in Promoting
         Growth   *217*
10.9 Small- and Medium-Enterprise FDI Inflows' Role in Promoting
         Export Growth   *218*
11.1 Regional Distribution of Receipts in 1998 and Arrivals in 1999   *236*
11.2 Share of Same-Region Tourism in Total Outbound, 1996   *238*
11.3 Areas of Knowledge Necessary for Tourism Human Resources   *251*

Foreword

Providing employment to a young and growing population is the major challenge faced by countries in the MENA region. Everywhere in the world, it is small firms that contribute most to job creation. Their ability to thrive and generate jobs is a function of the environment in which they operate and their capacity to deal with continuous change and build assets for the future. Hence firm competitiveness is high on the development agenda. In today's global environment, firms rather than nations have become the engine of growth, and competitiveness is the key for firms to survive.

On behalf of the Mediterranean Development Forum (MDF) partnership of 10 Middle East and North Africa (MENA) region think tanks, the World Bank, and the United Nations Development Programme, it is my pleasure to present the third book of the MDF publication series. This volume, titled *Globalization and Firm Competitiveness in the Middle East and North Africa Region*, is based on papers presented during the workshop on firm competitiveness held during the MDF3 conference in Cairo, Egypt, on March 5–8, 2000.

This book is devoted to the challenging environment in which firms operate, the tremendous opportunities globalization offers along with the risks it entails, and the partnerships required to build firm competitiveness in the MENA region. The clear message is that firms themselves, governments, business associations, think tanks, media, and universities all have a role to play in building firm competitiveness.

The MDF series hopes to capture some of the innovative and cutting-edge development issues being debated by over 500 of the region's most influential thinkers and practitioners ranging from high-level government officials and think tank representatives to private sector leaders, academics, and those in civil society. The series is based on papers presented during conferences organized by the MDF partnership approximately every two years: MDF1 in May 1997, MDF2 in September 1998, and MDF3 in March 2000. Following MDF2, books on public-private partnerships and trade and globalization were published. MDF4 will build on the wisdom of the previous conferences and highlight an emerging paradigm, the Nexus of Knowledge for Development and Competitiveness, and its importance for accelerating growth and reducing poverty.

We would like to express our thanks to Samiha Fawzy of the Egyptian Center for Economic Studies (ECES), as well as the authors who provided us with a unique perspective on firm competitiveness in the region. We hope that the papers presented herein contribute to the ongoing debate on the development opportunities and challenges facing the countries of the Middle East and North Africa.

Jean Louis Sarbib
Vice President
Middle East and North Africa Region, World Bank

Preface

In a world of 5.7 billion people, we at the Bank deal with 3 billion people who live under $2 a day and a billion 300 million people who live under $1 a day. A billion and a half of those people don't have clean water, and in this region of the world, you know full well the impact of not having clean water, an impact on the lives of families, an impact on the opportunities for women and girls, a destructive impact on the lives of our people. We are concerned with the issues of health and we are concerned with the issues of education. We have concluded in our institution that we cannot do this alone, and we have come to a . . . partnership around the world.

We've also learned that it's necessary in order to have growth, which is a prerequisite to human development, that we must be partners with business, with the private sector. Not just the private sector internationally, although that has grown enormously. To give you an idea, seven years ago, foreign investment in developing countries was $30 billion a year, and the loans from institutions like the World Bank were $60 billion a year, which means that the official institutions were twice the size. Today, the official institutions are around $45 billion and the private sector overseas investment is $260 billion. So from being half the size, it's now five to six times the size, and for every dollar invested from overseas, four or five dollars are invested locally. So the private sector is not a gloss, it's not an institutional group that we can forget, it's a group that is central to the activities of development.

—*Remarks by James D. Wolfensohn, President, The World Bank Group, at the Opening Ceremony of the Second Mediterranean Development Forum, Marrakech, Morocco, September 3, 1998*

Acknowledgments

We would like to thank the contributors to this volume for their dedicated efforts and responsiveness to suggestions. Our thanks also go to other participants at the Cairo workshop for sharing their insights and criticisms. In particular we would like to mention Taher Helmy, Jay Ganatra, Moataz El-Alfi, Ibrahim Shihata, Ahmed Galal, Sabry El Shabrawy, Atef Idriss, Mahmoud Mohieldin, Ziad Bahaa Eldin, Sherif Dellawar, Jeremy Coleman, Mahmoud El Afifi, Steven Keefer, Roberta Mahoney, Marcel Boyer, Gamal Atallah, Salama Fahmy, Elhamy El-Zayat, Gaith Zureikat, Mohamed M. Nasr, and Mohamed Bechri. Hisham Fahmy and his team at the Egyptian Center for Economic Studies, especially Nihal El-Megharbel and Alia Gamal, provided critical support, without which this volume could not have been possible. Last, but not least, we thank the World Bank's Office of the Publisher for editing, typesetting, and layout, and Janet H. Sasser of the World Bank's Office of the Publisher for production management.

Contributors

Nadereh Chamlou
The World Bank

Mahmoud A. El-Gamal
Rice University

Nihal El-Megharbel
The Egyptian Center for Economic Studies

Samiha Fawzy
The Egyptian Center for Economic Studies

Taïeb Hafsi
École des Hautes Études Commerciales

Hulusi Inanoglu
Rice University

Magdi R. Iskander
Formerly The World Bank

Sanjay Lall
Elizabeth House, University of Oxford

Dorsati Madani
The World Bank

Antoine Mansour
United Nations Economic and Social Commission for Western Asia, Industry Section

Jeffrey B. Nugent
University of Southern California

John Page
The World Bank

Andrew H. W. Stone
The World Bank

John D. Sullivan
Center for International Private Enterprise, U.S. Chamber of Commerce

Sahar Tohamy
The Egyptian Center for Economic Studies

Abbreviations and Acronyms

ABA	Alexandria Business Association
ABS	Asset-backed securities
ADR	Alternative dispute resolutions
AFTA	The Arab Free Trade Area
APEC	Asia Pacific Economic Cooperation
ASEAN	Association of Southeast Asian Nations
BDS	Business development services
BIS	Bank for International Settlements
BL	Business Link
CENTREX	Center for Export Requirements
CPC	China Productivity Center
DC	Developed country
DTI	Department of Trade and Industry
EDB	Economic Development Board
ERSO	Electronics Research and Services
ESCWA	Economic and Social Commission for Western Asia
EU	European Union
Euro-Med	Europe-Mediterranean
FDI	Foreign direct investment
FTA	Free trade agreement
GATS	General Agreement on Trade in Services
GATT	General Agreement on Trade and Tariffs
GCC	Gulf Cooperation Council

GDF	Global Development Finance
GDP	Gross domestic product
HKPC	Hong Kong Productivity Council
HS	Harmonized system
IASC	International Accounting Standards Committee
IFAD	International Forum for Accounting Development
IFC	International Finance Corporation
IHEI	International Hotel Environment Initiative
ILO	International Labour Organisation
IOSCO	International Organization of Securities Commissions
ISO	International Standards Organisation
ITC	Innovation and Technology Counselors
ITRI	Industrial Technology Research Institute
MENA	Middle East and North Africa
Mercosur	Mercado Común del Sur
MFA	Multi-fibre Agreement
MNC	Multinational corporation
NAFTA	North American Free Trade Agreement
NCB	National Commercial Bank (Saudi Arabia)
NGO	Nongovernmental organizations
NTB	Nontariff barriers
OECD	Organisation for Economic Co-operation and Development
PC	Peerless Clothing
R&D	Research and development
RTO	Research and technology organizations
SIEX	Electronic System for Exports
SISIR	Singapore Institute of Standards and Industrial Research
SME	Small and medium-size enterprises
SMR	Southern Mediterranean
SOE	State-owned enterprise
TDC	Technology Development Center
TRIPs	Treaty on Intellectual Property Rights
VAT	Value added tax
WTO	World Trade Organization
WTTC	World Travel and Tourism Council

CHAPTER 1

Overview

Samiha Fawzy

Globalization has increased competitive pressures on firms. Together with rapid technological change it has altered the environment in which firms operate. While globalization offers unprecedented opportunities for firms that act successfully, it heightens the foregone costs for firms that lag behind; those lagging firms thus risk becoming marginalized. The bottom line is that, in an open and liberalized world, increasing firm competitiveness has become a major challenge.

This challenge has recently attracted a great deal of concern in both industrial and developing countries, a concern that is debated at the firm level, in policymaking circles, and in the media. Parties to this debate have centered their discussions on crucial issues related to firm competitiveness, such as: What is meant by competitiveness? Why is it critical at this time? What are the rules and prerequisites to achieve competitiveness? What are the different roles of governments, firms, and other key actors in building firm efficiency?

The debate shows that while everyone seems to understand intuitively what competitiveness means, it does not have a universally accepted definition. Some economists define competitiveness as "the combination of favorable trade performance." The most popular definition is the one given by Laura D'Andrea Tyson: "Competitiveness is the ability to produce goods and services that meet the test of international competition, while the citizens enjoy a standard of living that is both rising and sustainable" (Tyson 1993). The Organisation for Economic Co-operation and Development (OECD) also offers a definition along the same lines: "Competitiveness should be understood as the ability of companies, industries, regions, nations and supranational regions to generate, while being and remaining exposed to international competition, relatively high factor income and factor employment levels on a sustainable basis" (OECD 1998). Others, like Krugman (1994), argue that competitiveness is nothing but a different way of saying "productivity," taking into account the rate of growth of one firm relative to others. Despite this ambiguity, it is clear that competitiveness matters. As Reinert (1995) said, "Although often misused and mostly ill defined, the term competitiveness properly used does describe an important feature in the world economy."

Some participants to the debate agree that while the terminology comes from the business literature, where it has a clear meaning, transferring the concept to a whole economy, or even to one sector, is not straightforward (Lall 1999). For example, Krugman confirms that this term is applicable only to firms and not to countries. Countries do not compete with each other the way corporations do. First, when a company is more competitive than its rivals, it tends to gain at their expense. However, when a country does well in the international markets, its success is not necessarily at the expense of other countries. International trade is not a zero-sum game. When firms are noncompetitive, they go out of business and disappear, while countries, obviously, do not (Krugman 1994).

Despite these different interpretations, there is a growing consensus about the importance of firm competitiveness. The argument is that firms, not nations, are the agents of growth—firms, not nations, shape the global economic order. In a global world, a world "without borders," competitiveness has become the key to firm survival.

The discussions have also helped to identify new global rules for business: In today's race for efficiency, firms cannot acquire a competitive edge through pricing alone. To be successful they must also demonstrate a strong commitment to quality, flexibility, design, reliability, accessibility, and networking. Furthermore, competitiveness increasingly depends on the way firms combine technology, managerial entrepreneurship, employee skills, business organization, and software to service markets and to interact with customers and suppliers (OECD 1998). In addition, competitiveness depends on the extent to which firms adopt the international standards for corporate governance.

Finally, the debate also reveals that firm competitiveness has become a national concern, which requires concerted efforts from different actors in the economy. Although firms' economic strengths and successes are primarily determined by their internal management, the characteristics of the national business environment can substantially influence, both positively and negatively, firms' abilities to compete. The debate has also made clear the crucial role that other key actors in the society (including business associations, think tanks, universities, and the media) have to play in building the competitiveness of firms.

In the Middle East and North Africa (MENA) region, competitiveness has yet to take center stage. Evidence indicates that firms have not restructured their businesses in ways that enable them to deal with the new challenges. Many firms in

MENA continue to be dominated by individuals, they lack good corporate governance, they compete based on price alone, and they lack up-to-date managerial and
technological resources. Recent competitiveness indicators show that MENA exporters have not made significant progress to better position themselves in the
global market (Madani and Page 2000). Briefly, this is the overall challenge now
facing firms in the MENA region.

This volume discusses the competitiveness of firms in MENA. It addresses
key issues for the future of the region, including: What are the real challenges
facing firms' operations and efficiency? Can MENA firms compete in global markets? Which are the key institutional constraints that they face? What are the standards of good corporate behavior that they should follow? How can small- and
medium-size enterprises (SMEs) play a more effective role as an engine of growth
in the region? What are the reasons behind the observed gap between the actual
and potential performance of the tourism sector in MENA? How can MENA's
potential in this sector be achieved? Finally, how can governments, firms, business
associations, the media, think tanks, and universities participate in building firm
competitiveness in the MENA region?

The remainder of this chapter provides an overview of this volume and concludes by offering a number of broad conclusions inspired from the chapters
themselves.

Overview of the Volume

This volume contains a set of interesting papers, presented as chapters, which
provide a thorough analysis of firm competitiveness from different perspectives, as
well as insightful information on the MENA region. It is organized into four parts,
each of which will discuss a different issue related to firm competitiveness. These
four parts are global rules for business; the regional business environment; corporate governance; and a final part on two important sectors in most MENA countries: the SME and tourism sectors.

Part I: Global Rules for Business
While rapid changes in the global economic environment have brought new opportunities for firms in the MENA region, they have also generated risks. Multinationals are ready to face these challenges and to grasp opportunities, but the situation
is different for small firms in less developed countries. In part I two chapters address the following questions: What are the most important changes shaping the
global economic order? What are their implications for MENA firms? How can
firms cope with these changes? Do SMEs in MENA have a chance for survival?
How can they best survive? Finally, how can MENA governments help to ensure
survival of their SMEs?

In chapter two Dorsati Madani and John Page offer a comprehensive overview
of the global challenges and opportunities for firms in MENA, and discuss how

firms can meet these challenges. They argue that the implementation of the Uruguay Round and the aftermath of the Seattle meeting in 1999, as well as the Europe-Mediterranean (Euro-Med) agreements and other regional agreements—such as The Arab Free Trade Area and the Gulf Cooperation Council—will affect market access and import competition across a wide range of manufacturing, agricultural, and services sectors. The liberalization of trade under the auspices of the World Trade Organization has provided the basis for what they call the "rule of law" in international trade. Although the Seattle meeting failed to launch a new agenda of negotiations, Madani and Page suggest that MENA firms can benefit from further liberalization through the "built-in agenda" on agriculture and services.

The Euro-Med free trade area is expected to generate significant long-term economic benefits for the region, but it will also involve transitional costs. Several studies estimate the effects of these agreements on MENA countries. All show that free trade agreements (FTAs) between MENA countries and the European Union will generate welfare gains to these countries, albeit at different scales. The size of these gains depends on the efforts made by MENA governments and firms to prepare themselves to cope with trade liberalization. Governments should work on improving the institutional set-up, especially on trade-related infrastructure, and on improving the business environment in general. Firms should immediately start by internal restructuring, to avoid falling into the trap of transitional periods allowed in regional agreements. Industrial restructuring will require changes in products, standards, and business lines.

In chapter 3 Taïeb Hafsi starts by discussing the concept of globalization, then deals more specifically with the situation of small firms in less developed countries. He argues that globalization is a new version of an old game. In the past, firms such as Exxon could not consider its market as anything but international. Globalization does not refer to the decision of a firm to go abroad—rather, it is the willingness of all firms to enter each other's markets. This means that even when a firm does not go abroad to do its business, it must anticipate that others, from all over the world, will come and challenge it on its own territory.

Hafsi also distinguishes differences among the globalization of national markets, of industries, and of firms. He argues that markets are global if they are open enough to international competition. As for the globalization of industries, he maintains that it occurs when firms attempt to relate their activities across countries in order to achieve a competitive advantage, while the globalization of a firm relates to the decomposition of its value chain and its dispersion around the world. Hafsi concludes that a global strategy does not exist. Rather, it is a strategy that accounts for the globalization of one or several markets, or the globalization of an industry, or the globalization of the firm. In light of this distinction, he discusses the role of both firms and governments.

Hafsi argues that understanding laws and regulations in target markets is necessary to improve the competitive position of firms. Globalization certainly gives more opportunities for larger firms, yet it concurrently creates numerous chances for smaller firms, while leaving unattended and unsatisfied market segments in all industries. Therefore, smaller firms have to use their flexibility to respond better to the more neglected markets. Globalization also generates new threats for these firms, which intensifies the need for designing appropriate strategies. He argues that free competition does not exist, and that the role of governments is indispensable. Governments create the enabling conditions that lead firms to implement their goals without implicitly directing them to do so. Governments can help by providing market and consumer needs studies, making information available, and by facilitating alliances for smaller competitors. Hafsi concludes by emphasizing that governments should pay more attention to small firms.

Part II: The Business Environment in the MENA Region

With globalization, the distinction between international and domestic policies becomes less relevant. As a result, sound domestic business environments acquire a fundamental importance. It is critically important to know which domestic policies to adopt in order to cope with the realities of change. To this end, part II starts by indicating how the business environment in MENA compares globally, and highlights the institutions that most impede firms' competitiveness in the region. It also presents best practices in dispute-resolution mechanisms, which is known as one of the most severe institutional constraints in MENA.

In chapter 4 Andrew H. W. Stone provides a detailed analysis of the business environment in the MENA region. Based on survey results and on international competitiveness indicators, the author shows that the region compares poorly with international standards, with respect to enterprise impediments. Although the business environment surveys highlight considerable similarities and differences among MENA countries, some regional features are clear. The most obvious are weakness between government and the private sector, fear of instability of economic policies, high red-tape costs, and high tax levels and cumbersome tax regulations. Finally, the author suggests a substantive policy agenda that places a priority on the following reforms:

- Improving policy stability

- Enhancing transparency and accountability

- Reducing the size of the state

- Eliminating transaction costs, especially those arising from tax administration and customs

- Revising inadequate conflict-resolution procedures.

Jeffrey B. Nugent, in chapter 5, deals specifically with dispute resolution impediments in the region and their implication for firm competitiveness. While the chapter focuses on MENA countries, it also draws on the experiences of some

Latin American, Eastern European, and East Asian countries. Based on this international experience, he offers three approaches for reforming and improving conflict resolutions: legal reform, judicial reform, and alternative dispute resolutions (ADRs). The first two deal with the existing formal system, while ADRs introduce new approaches to reform. Nugent concludes that since each approach has its own advantages and disadvantages, each country should carefully consider the benefits of each approach relative to its own conditions before choosing a reform strategy.

Part III: Corporate Governance

Both firms and countries increasingly recognize that good corporate governance is important for broad economic progress. With globalization, firms must tap domestic and international capital markets to satisfy their financial needs. Increasingly, financiers not only base their decisions on a company's outlook but also on its reputation and governance structure. Part III of the volume deals with some critical issues related to corporate governance, such as: How can we achieve sound corporate governance? What are its prerequisites? How can we learn from best international practices in corporate governance?

Despite the fact that corporate governance and its analytical tools are still emerging, Magdi R. Iskander and Nadereh Chamlou provide, in chapter 6, a comprehensive framework to identify the major determinants of good corporate governance structures. According to Iskander and Chamlou, it is the interplay between internal incentives and external forces that governs the behavior of the firm, its performance, and its value. Internal incentives (which define the relationships among key players in the corporation) can be viewed as a set of arrangements internal to the corporation that define the relationships between managers and shareholders. The role of external forces (notably policy, legal, regulatory, and market competition) is to provide firms with the discipline to minimize the difference between private and social returns, and to protect the interests of stakeholders. Iskander and Chamlou suggest an ambitious agenda for reforming corporate governance in developing countries based on a combination of regulatory and voluntary private actions.

In chapter 7 John D. Sullivan complements the work of Iskander. He first explains how societies benefit from a strong system of corporate governance, then he summarizes the corporate governance principles adopted by the OECD, and gives examples of good corporate governance practices and models. The value of his chapter lies in the fact that Sullivan goes beyond the economics of corporate governance to discuss its political dimensions. Corporate governance is not only a prerequisite for economic development and growth, but also of importance to democratic development, especially the rule of law. Sullivan provides an explanation of the slow process of corporate governance reform in developing countries. He notes that although corporate governance ultimately depends on public-private cooperation, the private sector in countries with protected markets and a large state sector tends to put off reforms until privatization and other public reform take place.

Sullivan concludes by indicating in a precise way the role of policy research centers, national business associations, and civil society organizations that work together to design corporate governance systems in a country's best interests.

Part IV: Sectoral Applications

SMEs and tourism have great potential for growth in the MENA countries—but their growth has been modest. Part IV of this volume investigates how SMEs and tourism can live up to their potential.

Through chapters 8, 9, and 10, Sanjay Lall; Antoine Mansour; and Mahmoud A. El-Gamal, Nihal El-Megharbel, and Hulusi Inanoglu discuss how SMEs can play a more dynamic role in enhancing economic growth and improving welfare in the region.

In chapter 8 Lall shows that most SMEs in industrial and developing countries face three sets of problems. The first set is inherent in being small, the second is a reflection of distortions in the markets and institutions, and the third is caused by policy intervention. Drawing on the experience of industrial and newly industrialized countries in providing support systems for SMEs, he concludes that while conducive business environments and private support mechanisms are necessary conditions for SME promotion, they are not sufficient. Proactive policies are also needed, including those that will make SMEs aware of the challenges they face. Equally important is to help SMEs prepare to meet the challenges by understanding their strengths and weaknesses and by providing the inputs that they need in order to upgrade. Experience also suggests that the best way to help SMEs is by combining support in an attractive package, rather than by delivering support piecemeal.

After giving an overview of the relative importance, characteristics, and main problems of SMEs in MENA, Mansour, in chapter 9, focuses on assessing the existing schemes for supporting SMEs, which he judges to be ineffective. Consequently, he offers a set of recommendations to enhance the role that SMEs play in enhancing economic growth by following the approach of clustering and networking. According to the author, benefits from clustering derive from external economies, while networking improves firms' competitiveness as it prepares them for globalization through opening up new markets for new products. Mansour also stresses the importance of specialization and sector-specific support programs. Finally, he suggests that business support programs must be demand-driven, responding to real needs, in order to be more effective.

In chapter 10 El-Gamal, El-Megharbel, and Inanoglu deal with the issue of financing and offer fresh insights. They argue that SMEs should not be dealt with as one homogeneous group. Rather, we need to distinguish between SMEs in traditional production areas, SMEs in emerging market niches, and SMEs in avantgarde (high technology) industries. Although the three groups of SMEs share some common characteristics, there are fundamental differences among them, which render certain alternative sources of financing appropriate for some but not for others. El-Gamal, El-Megharbel, and Inanoglu argue that the best vehicle for funding traditional SMEs is group lending through conventional banks and nongovernmental organizations. For market niche-seeking SMEs they suggest that lease—and lease purchase—financing can be a very successful source of funding. The ideal financing method for the avant-garde SMEs is venture capital financing. The preceding taxonomy of SME types and appropriate financing methods reflects the main message that El-Gamal, El-Megharbel, and Inanoglu deliver. The authors suggest that the government role in financing SMEs should be less direct than it seems in the MENA region. This implies that governments should concentrate more on creating an enabling environment for private financial institutions to take the lead.

With the view of exploiting the productivity of firms operating in the tourism activity in MENA, Sahar Tohamy, in chapter 11, starts by analyzing the mismatch between the potential and actual revenues of the tourism sector in MENA (and the modest competitive position of the region in the world market for tourism), its strengths, and its weaknesses. Recognizing that increasing the competitiveness of tourism needs a host of short- and long-run reforms, Tohamy selects two main reform areas for further discussion: marketing and human resource development. The reasons behind this selection are twofold: first, these areas need constant efforts for reform to succeed, given the increasingly contested international tourism market; second, initiatives in these areas are likely to produce short- to medium-term results. The author concludes by highlighting some areas for reform including information; marketing research and surveys; promotion campaigns, fairs, and training; and skills up-grading programs.

Conclusions

Three broad conclusions can be drawn from this volume. First, firms in the MENA region have no other choice than to join the race of competitiveness. Any other alternative would be extremely costly. The MENA region has the resources and means to join this race, and to play a more effective role on the global scene. Whether the future will be "good" or "bad" depends on how shrewdly firm competitiveness is enhanced. Second, meeting this challenge is a shared responsibility on the part of firms, the government, and other actors, such as business associations, think tanks, universities, and the media.

The Role of Firms
Firms must improve their ability to deal with continuous change and to build assets for the future. Firms need to work on building competitive edges rather than depending on inherited or comparative advantages. They must base their competition on quality, flexibility, design, reliability, and networking. Creativity, specialization, and diversification are key for firms to gain competitive positions in the global market. Dealing with global new rules also requires investing in improved

productivity, adding more credibility to products by using internationally accepted certification methodologies, seeking new product lines (especially in the areas of services and agricultural products), and trying to diversify markets by penetrating new markets, such as those in East Asia and Latin America.

Greater investments in new kinds of assets are crucial for flexibility and long-term competitiveness. Probably the most important change in firms' strategies to improve competitiveness is their emphasis on investment in intangible assets (research and development; technology, managerial, entrepreneurial, and employee skills; business organization; market development; and software). Intangible assets provide firms with the capabilities and flexibility needed to survive and prosper. In addition, firms must move from family-owned or sole proprietor businesses to more formal governance structures, which guarantee the balance between the interests of shareholders and other stakeholders such as employees, customers, suppliers, and communities. This kind of governance structure will lead to better and more sustainable performance.

The Role of Governments

Firms must improve their competitiveness. However, the government should guide their efforts in this respect. Because most developing countries suffer from market failures, governments' remedial actions can improve the distribution of resources, be cost-effective, and benefit long-term aggregate growth. Firms need clear rules, a stable macroeconomic environment, efficient institutions, access to imports, and elimination of red tape. Governments also need to provide a better framework for good corporate governance, including greater competition, stronger banking and capital markets, and better rules to protect minority shareholders. More attention must be paid to economic interdependence in policy design and implementation.

In addition, globalization demands more of governments. Policies should not gratuitously restrain globalization by attempting to shield domestic firms and markets from competition, or by applying protective mechanisms. In its broadest sense, the challenge for governments is to pursue policies whereby the benefits of globalization are fully realized and widely shared by all of society. Finally, public-private partnership should become a reality if the region seeks competitiveness in a changing and dynamic global market.

The Role of Other Actors

Different actors (including business associations, think tanks, universities, and the media) are considered to be the third partner in development, along with the business sector and the government. Without their effective participation, the road to global markets would be difficult. In this regard, business associations should try hard to deepen public-private partnerships. They can communicate, analyze, and explain the implications of public policy to their members; increase their members' awareness of global competitive challenges; and assist with the development of cooperative policies to help firms cope with new realities. Think tanks and universities should direct their research concerns to help firms and governments improve productivity. The media should undertake intensive public awareness campaigns so that firm competitiveness becomes a real national concern; the media should also work on promoting the concepts of participation and inclusion. All actors are called on to play an active role in building an excellent image for firms in MENA.

Finally, it is of crucial importance to remember that today's windows of opportunity are extremely promising—but it is equally important to remember that windows do close. With these three conclusions, this volume offers some insights, but insights are just a beginning. The next step is action.

Bibliography

Krugman, Paul. 1994. "Competitiveness: A Dangerous Obsession." *Foreign Affairs* 73(42, March/April).

Lall, Sanjaya. 1999. *Promoting Industrial Competitiveness in Developing Countries: Lessons from Asia.* Commonwealth Economic Paper No. 39. Oxford: Queen Elizabeth House.

Madani, Dorsati, and John Page. 2000. "Global Rules for Business: Challenges to Firm Competitiveness and Opportunities for Success." *Working Paper Series* 43, The Egyptian Center for Economic Studies, Cairo, October.

OECD (Organisation for Economic Co-operation and Development). 1998. "Industrial Performance and Competitiveness in an Era of Globalization and Technological Change." Directorate for Science, Technology and Industry, Industry Committee, Paris, June.

Reinert, E. 1995. "Competitiveness and Its Predecessors—A 500 Year Cross-National Perspective." *Structural Change and Economics Dynamics* 6: 23–42.

Tyson, Laura D'Andrea. 1993. "Who's Bashing Whom: Trade Conflict in High-Technology Industries." Institute for International Economics, Washington, D.C.

PART I

Global Rules for Business

Challenges to Firm Competitiveness and Opportunities for Success

Dorsati Madani
John Page

Rapid changes in the global economic environment have brought new challenges and opportunities to firms in the Middle East and North Africa (MENA) region. In response to these recent developments, this chapter begins by briefly reviewing how MENA countries have fared in the global economy. The study then outlines the challenges and opportunities arising from the changing global economic environment, and follows with an evaluation of how firms in MENA are currently facing these challenges. Finally, the chapter suggests private and public actions that will be necessary in order for the MENA region to take advantage of the opportunities offered by the global trading system, and then offers its conclusions.

How Do MENA Countries Fare in the Global Economy?

The goods and services feeding into production processes have become increasingly geographically delinked and internationalized. This phenomenon has been facilitated by the decreasing cost of doing global business, resulting from reduced uncertainty in foreign direct investment (FDI), declines in traditional transport costs, and remarkable technological improvements in communications.

MENA countries are now faced with transformed and more competitive economic environments in other developing countries. The East Asian economies—followed by most Latin American countries in the late 1980s and 1990s—liberalized

---

their economies and adopted more outward oriented policies. This process has not yet fully taken place in MENA, putting MENA producers and exporters at a cost disadvantage and reducing their competitiveness. Although most MENA countries have undertaken tariff and tax reforms since the 1980s, progress has been slow and uneven (table 2.1).

The impact of these developments has resulted in three distinct patterns. First, international production sharing between industrial and developing countries has increased substantially during the past two decades. Production sharing is partially reflected in the substantial increase in FDI flows from industrial to developing countries, with the majority directed to East Asian and Latin American economies.

TABLE 2.1 TARIFF RATES BY REGION
(percent)

Exporting region				Importing regions			
	High income	East Asia	South Asia	Latin America and the Caribbean	Middle East and North Africa	Sub-Saharan Africa	Rest of Africa
Manufactures							
High-income	1.1	10.7	56.4	8.9	12.3	12.4	17.3
East Asia	4.6	12.7	62.4	14.6	12.2	18.0	28.6
South Asia	7.8	7.9	62.9	13.9	12.1	23.8	17.7
Latin America and the Caribbean	1.9	6.4	58.3	11.1	12.1	13.9	15.2
Middle East and North Africa	4.3	6.7	63.9	11.0	11.4	13.1	18.5
Sub-Saharan Africa	2.7	9.1	58.4	12.1	11.6	18.4	6.6
Rest of Africa	5.9	4.6	62.3	14.9	9.8	15.1	19.6
Agriculture							
High-income	15.9	31.9	26.1	2.9	15.1	16.2	16.0
East Asia	13.3	16.9	55.0	4.4	17.6	9.0	18.1
South Asia	10.5	18.9	21.5	8.6	21.0	3.2	15.9
Latin America and the Caribbean	14.3	16.8	49.7	8.1	10.5	7.5	15.3
Middle East and North Africa	10.8	14.3	58.0	8.5	15.5	22.1	23.4
Sub-Saharan Africa	13.7	28.3	62.2	7.4	12.1	12.8	12.2
Rest of Africa	31.9	17.7	16.5	9.9	19.1	5.8	13.8

Note: The tariff rates do not reflect the General System of Preferences rates.
Source: General Tariffs Application.

The output share of multinational affiliates in developing country gross domestic product (GDP) increased from 4.4 percent in 1982 to 6.3 percent in 1995.[1] MENA countries have fared poorly in comparison (figure 2.1).

Intra-industry trade—often a measure of increased production sharing and specialization—also highlights this underperformance. Between 1985 and 1997 MENA countries had relatively low levels of intra-industry trade and show little change compared to Brazil, the Republic of Korea, Malaysia, and Taiwan, China (Yeats and Ng 1999).

Second, there has been a substantial increase in manufacturing exports from developing countries since the mid-1980s (figure 2.2). In addition, manufactured goods trade among developing countries has increased from just over 30 percent to over 70 percent (Hertel and Martin 1999). This increase in importance is widely distributed among developing countries, but MENA and Sub-Saharan Africa have lagged, with 40 percent or less of manufactured exports.

Third, the services trade has grown substantially, and industrial countries are increasingly outsourcing services activities to developing countries. Jamaica, for

FIGURE 2.1 NET INFLOWS OF FOREIGN DIRECT INVESTMENT
(millions of U.S. dollars)

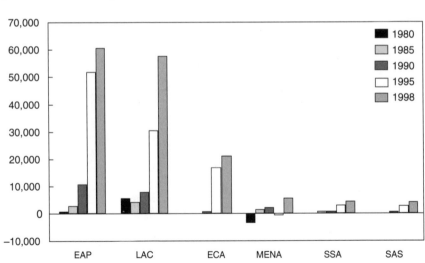

Note: EAP = East Asia and Pacific; LAC = Latin America and the Caribbean; MENA = Middle East and North Africa; SSA = Sub-Saharan Africa; SAS = South Asia.
Source: World Bank, Statistical Information Management Analysis (SIMA) Database; World Bank 1998b, 1999b.

FIGURE 2.2 SHARE OF MERCHANDISE EXPORTS FROM DEVELOPING
COUNTRIES, 1965–2004

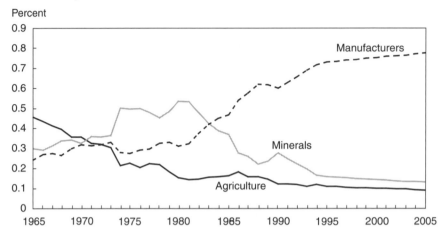

Source: Hertel and Martin 1999.

example, has been highly successful in attracting billing and back-office activities
to its Montego Bay export-processing zone, and India has grown famous for its
software clusters in and around Bangalore. Once again, the majority of the expansion of trade in services has accrued to East Asia, Eastern Europe, and Latin America,
with the MENA region as a distant fourth (see figure 2A.1, in appendix 2A). While
the MENA countries have historically provided labor to each other and the European Union (EU), and have exported some construction services, they have not
really exploited opportunities in alternative services exports. Recent indicators show
that with the exception of the Arab Republic of Egypt's commercial services exports, trade in commercial services is generally lacking in MENA countries (see
figure 2A.2, in appendix 2A).

MENA's speed of integration with the global economy has lagged behind
other regions. Only one MENA country—Morocco—is a fast integrator. All other
MENA countries are moderate, weak, or slow integrators (table 2.2). Examining
the MENA region's lackluster period of 1985–98 shows that while there has been
some growth in exports (notably a threefold increase in the case of Tunisia),
exports from Egypt and Jordan stagnated in the 1990s (see figures 2A.3 and
2A.4 in appendix 2A). The trends do not match the sharper increase in imports
and exports in other regions.

A review of cross-regional trade patterns over the past 10 years reveals some
interesting trends. Some major Latin American and East Asian economies (Argen-

TABLE 2.2 MIDDLE-INCOME COUNTRIES: SPEED OF INTEGRATION

Fast integrators	Integration pace	MENA integrators	Integration pace
Argentina	0.59	*Fast*	
Chile	0.65	Israel	0.66
Costa Rica	0.73	Morocco	0.97
Czech Republic	0.46	*Moderate*	
Hungary	0.95	Iran, Islamic Republic of	0.20
Jamaica	1.19	Syrian Arab Republic	0.42
Korea, Rep. of	0.63	Tunisia	0.16
Malaysia	1.80	United Arab Emirates	−0.18
Mauritius	2.35	*Weak*	
Mexico	1.44	Egypt	−0.19
Morocco	0.97	Jordan	−0.39
Philippines	0.99	*Slow*	
Poland	0.58	Algeria	−1.51
Sri Lanka	0.95	Iraq	−1.68
Thailand	2.12	Oman	−1.00
Turkey	1.87	Saudi Arabia	−3.40

Note: The speed of integrator index is derived from changes between the early 1980s and early 1990s in four indicators: (a) the ratio of real trade to GDP, (b) the ratio of FDI to GDP, and (c) institutional investor credit ratings, and (d) the share of manufactures in exports. The speed of integration index is the simple average of changes in the four indicators over the period (each expressed as a standard deviation from its average). *Source:* World Bank 1996, pp. 24–25.

tina, Brazil, China, Indonesia, Korea, and Taiwan [China]) have made consistent inroads into leading MENA markets. However, the MENA exporters have not made significant inroads into the major Latin America and the Caribbean and East Asian economies. Furthermore, no major links to the rest of Africa (especially with its major economies—South Africa and Nigeria), or to South Asia (India) are evident for any of the MENA countries.

Global and Regional Rules: Challenges and Opportunities for the MENA Region

Firms in the MENA region will face significant new challenges as multilateral and regional agreements governing international trade come into play. For the region as a whole, three important rule-setting processes are taking place simultaneously. First, the implementation of the Uruguay Round agreements and any follow-up to the Seattle meeting of the World Trade Organization (WTO) held on November 30,

1999, will affect market access and import competition across a wide range of manufacturing, agricultural, and services sectors. Second, agreements with the EU (for example, Europe-Mediterranean [Euro-Med] agreements) are being concluded by an increasing number of MENA governments. Third, regional trading blocs with other Arab States (the Arab Free Trade Area [AFTA] and the Gulf Coopera-tion Council [GCC]) are entering the picture. Each of these poses a potential com-petitive challenge—and offers substantial new opportunities—to MENA producers.

The World Trade Organization Uruguay Round Agreement

MENA countries are recent arrivals to the WTO.[2] Algeria, Lebanon, Oman, Saudi Arabia, and the Republic of Yemen are currently WTO observer governments, and all of these countries have applied to join the WTO, apart from the Republic of Yemen. With the exception of Egypt, MENA countries did not actively participate or engage in setting out the agenda for the Uruguay Round, and not all MENA WTO members may be fully able to do so in the new round.

The Uruguay Round commitments have clarified the liberalization of trade regimes in agriculture and manufacturing products, and have provided a basis for the rule of law in international trade. MENA WTO members are committed to binding agricultural and industrial tariffs (see table 2.3).[3] While their binding com-mitments covered 100 percent of agricultural products and 75 to 98 percent of manufactured goods (except for Tunisia's 53 percent), many chose binding tariff ceilings much higher than their applied rates (see table 2.4), providing discretion-ary power to policymakers to protect subsectors and special interests.

Yeats (1996) notes:

> The Uruguay Round made major progress in removing nontariff barriers (NTBs) facing Middle Eastern exporters—especially in agriculture, tex-tiles, and clothing. As a result of what was achieved, the average OECD [Organisation for Economic Co-Operation and Development] NTB cov-erage ratio for Middle East exports should fall from 10 percent to be-tween 1 or 2 percent. The decline in the coverage ratio for Egypt is dramatic. Prior to the [Uruguay] Round, 32 percent of Egypt's exports to the OECD faced NTBs—this share should fall to about 2 percent after the Multifibre Arrangement (MFA) and agricultural restrictions are removed.

There were also reductions in tariffs facing Middle Eastern exporters. In manu-factured goods there was a 40 percent cut in industrial countries' tariffs, with an increased binding coverage from 94 to 98 percent of all imports. This translates into an average tariff reduction of approximately 2.4 to 4 percent. However, the reduc-tions in major sectors of importance to the developing countries, such as textiles, clothing, footwear, and transport equipment, were lower than average.

Yeats's (1996) analysis suggests that, overall, Middle East exports should increase by $800 million[4] to $900 million because of the Uruguay Round. How-ever, the positive impact may be uneven across MENA countries, because the removal of MFA restrictions will render the textiles and clothing markets much

TABLE 2.3 TARIFF BINDINGS BY ARAB COUNTRIES BEFORE AND AFTER THE
URUGUAY ROUND
(percent of total tariff lines in country's tariff schedule, harmonized system basis)

	Agricultural products[a] (share in total)		Industrial products[b] (share in total)		Total (share in total)	
	Before	After	Before	After	Before	After
Bahrain	—	100		70		75
Egypt[c]	3	100	3	80	3	97
Kuwait	—	100		95		98
Morocco	—	100		95		98
Qatar[d]	—	—	—	—	—	—
Tunisia[e]	10	100	16	45	15	53
United Arab Emirate	—	100		95		98

— Not available.
a. The product coverage comprises the products defined in Uruguay Round Agreement on agriculture (harmonized system [HS], chapters 1–24, excluding fish and fish products).
b. The product coverage is as defined in the Uruguay Round Agreement (HS, chapters 25–97, including fish and fish products, and excluding crude petroleum).
c. Egypt's pre-Uruguay Round rates of binding are from the General Agreement on Trade and Tariffs (GATT) 1992.
d. The list of Qatar's concessions was not included in the Final Act of the Uruguay Round Agreement.
e. Tunisia's pre-Uruguay Round bindings are from GATT 1994.
Source: El-Naggar 1996.

more competitive. On the other hand, net food importers (for instance, Egypt) could be adversely affected by the higher international food prices that may result from the Uruguay Round.

In the General Agreement on Trade in Services (GATS), Arab countries generally granted concessions to foreign service suppliers in sectors where they held a comparative advantage, such as tourism. Opening markets to foreign service suppliers also occurred in sectors where Arab countries could acquire technology and knowledge transfers and efficiency gains could be made. In the sectors where domestic markets were opened, explicit limitations were detailed. Specifically, limitations were applied to the supply of foreign services through commercial presence and entry and stay of people supplying services and to equity participation by foreign investors (see table 2.5).

The Post-Seattle World Trade Organization Environment
While the Seattle WTO ministerial meetings failed to launch a new round of negotiations, MENA firms can benefit from further liberalization possible through the "built-in agenda" on agriculture and services. Most MENA countries show a strong

TABLE 2.4 BOUND TARIFFS (UPPER CEILING) ON INDUSTRIAL AND
AGRICULTURAL PRODUCTS BEFORE AND AFTER THE URUGUAY ROUND
(percent ad valorem)

	Applied tariff rates before Uruguay Round		Bound tariff rates after Uruguay Round	
MENA countries	Industry	Agriculture	Industry	Agriculture
GATT members				
Bahrain	20	20	35	35
Egypt, Arab Rep. of	100	153	60	80
Kuwait	4	4	100	100
Morocco	45	45	40	289
Qatar	—	—	—	—
Tunisia	73	73	90	200
United Arab Emirates	4	4	40	40
Non-GATT members				
Jordan	150	150	—	—
Saudi Arabia	30	30	—	—

— Not available.
Source: El-Naggar 1996.

comparative advantage in fruits and vegetables. Greater access to markets will present them with substantial opportunities to expand production and exports. Furthermore, greater access to other developing countries' markets (both regional and worldwide) will provide for a more differentiated export market. Further liberalization of services can provide opportunities for the MENA countries to become back-offices to European firms (especially—but not limited to—France). Ireland and Jamaica have successfully developed this service sector based on low-cost English language clerical and information processing skills. Construction services also hold potentially significant gains for MENA, especially if progress is made to ease the movement and temporary employment of workers in other countries.

Regional Agreements: Europe-Mediterranean, the Arab Free Trade Area, and the Gulf Cooperation Council

The revival of regional arrangements such as the Southern Common Market (Mercado Común del Sur [Mercosur]), the Gulf Cooperation Council (GCC), the Arab Free Trade Area (AFTA), the Association of Southeast Asian Nations, the North American Free Trade Agreement (NAFTA), and the Asia Pacific Economic Cooperation, together with the proliferation of bilateral free trade areas such as Euro-Med agreements, has changed the pattern of preferential market access, in-

TABLE 2.5 EXTENT OF COMMITMENTS TO OPEN MARKETS FOR TRADE
IN SERVICES BY ARAB COUNTRIES

Country	Commitment within sector or subsector	Number of service activities within sector or subsector
Bahrain	Insurance and re-insurance	4
Egypt	Construction and engineering, tourism and travel services, banking, insurance and re-insurance, maritime transport, and auxiliary services	28
Kuwait	Business, construction and engineering, environmental services, health-related and social services, tourism and travel, recreational and sporting services	44
Morocco	Business, telecommunications, construction and engineering, environmental services, banking, insurance and re-insurance, tourism and travel services, air and road transportation	41
Qatar and United Arab Emirates[a]	—	—
Tunisia	Banking, insurance and re-insurance, tourism and travel services	11

— Not available.
a. Qatar and the United Arab Emirates had not submitted their schedules of commitments as of April 15, 1994.
Source: El-Naggar 1996.

vestment, and, consequently, of trade.[5] The emergence of Eastern Europe and the rather rapid integration prospects of some Eastern European economies into the EU may herald the rise of potential competitors to the MENA countries for EU markets and FDI.

The EU is a major trade partner throughout the MENA region. Neighboring and regional trade partners are not a significant factor, except for Jordan and Syria. In fact, for many MENA countries the EU has continued to be the only major trade partner. This trade dependency (on both export and import sides) is especially evident in the cases of Tunisia and Algeria, with their obvious EU partner, France. Morocco's dependence on the EU is a bit more attenuated, though distinct, and is bound to increase with its recent signing of a bilateral free trade agreement (FTA) with the EU.

THE EURO-MED AGREEMENTS

Unlike past arrangements, the current Euro-Med agreements initiated in 1995 require reciprocity in matters of trade liberalization. They set a well-defined time frame (12–15 years) and intermediate steps leading to a free trade area between each of the southern Mediterranean (SMR) countries and the EU for nonagricultural products. Elimination of NTBs is set to take effect upon signing of the agreement, while tariffs are to be removed within 12 years. The EU continues its policy (in existence since the early 1970s) of granting free access to virtually all manufactured products exported by these countries, and of providing limited preferential access for their agricultural exports. There is reciprocal right of establishment for investors. Morocco, Tunisia, and Jordan have already agreed to adapt their regulatory framework to approximate that in the EU in the areas of competition, government procurement, subsidies, and technical standards, and to strengthen cooperation on migratory issues.

The free trade area is expected to generate significant long-term economic benefits for the region, but it will also involve transitional costs. Over time, welfare gains will accrue as trade liberalization reduces the anti-export bias present in many of the SMR countries' trade regimes, and incentives for industrial restructuring increase. SMR countries may become more attractive to foreign investors if there is a positive credibility effect associated with being "locked into" a liberalization schedule with a major regional trade grouping.

Gains in the manufacturing sector will be limited, because most SMR countries' manufactured goods already have free access to the EU. However, if the agreements were to allow substantially increased access to European markets for agricultural products and for those manufactured products currently subject to barriers—products in which the SMR countries have a comparative advantage, such as textiles and clothing—the benefits to the SMR countries would be substantially higher.

Efficiency improvements will also accrue to the SMR countries from harmonizing standards and measures, and regulations in areas such as subsidies, competition policy, and public procurement. Further productivity gains may result from the increased competitive pressures that will reduce monopolistic rents.

The size of welfare gains will be related to the extent to which the SMR countries implement trade reform with non-EU countries. If they do so, given the fact that the EU is already their dominant trade partner, one could anticipate that trade creation will outweigh trade diversion.

Accurate country-specific estimates of costs and benefits of the Euro-Med agreements depend on the variety of factors described above. Jbili and Enders (1996) provide an indicative analysis for the Tunisian case. They note that Tunisia has a large dependence on European trade and investment, tourism, and workers' remittances.[6] As of 1996 effective protection remained high in a number of sectors (such as textiles). Domestic industries, composed mostly of family-owned small- and medium-size enterprises, remained fragile and overly dependent on trade protection and government support.

While labor costs are relatively low, the lack of adequate infrastructure, high energy costs, the shortage of industrial land, and distortions related to both remaining price controls and cumbersome administrative regulations all hinder competitiveness.

Jbili and Enders conclude that under this agreement, Tunisia gains little additional access for its exports, except for a few agricultural items, and that the expected growth of exports will result mostly from a reallocation of resources from import-substituting production into export industries, increased investment, and productivity gains. Tunisian gains would be higher if its agricultural products obtained better access to European markets during the transition period.

A number of simulations have been undertaken to estimate the impact of the Euro-Med agreements on MENA countries. They seem to indicate that generally multilateral liberalizations have slightly better welfare effects on MENA countries than adoption of an FTA. However, in the longer run, FTAs may yield significant welfare gains.

Rutherford, Ruström, and Tarr (1995) provide a simulation for Tunisia's FTA with the EU. They estimate that Tunisia's welfare would increase by 3.11 percent in the short run (with sector-specific capital) and 4.65 percent in the long run (with mobile capital). By comparison, a multilateral liberalization would increase Tunisia's welfare by 3.71 to 5.33 percent. A second estimation by Brown, Deardorff, and Stern (1997) finds that if we assume FDI and sector-specific capital, Tunisia will experience a decline in welfare. Once capital mobility is allowed, welfare improves by 3.3 percent.

For Morocco, authors Rutherford, Ruström, and Tarr (1993) suggest that unilateral liberalization would be more welfare enhancing than an FTA with the EU, bringing about a 2.06 to 3.12 percent increase relative to 1.70 to 2.38 percent, respectively. Konan and Maskus (1997) find that for Egypt unilateral liberalization relative to formation of an FTA with EU may have the same approximate welfare effects (2.7 percent as opposed to 2.4 percent).

Will Martin (1997) finds that Lebanon would suffer a small welfare loss from eliminating its tariffs against the EU. A Euro-Med agreement reduces the risk of losing the access to EU markets provided under the 1977 agreement; however, the potential gains are small because Lebanon sends only 17 percent of its exports to the EU and the margin of preference is small. Freeing trade with other SMR countries[7] would generate significant welfare gains while the barriers against the outside world remain high in these countries. Nondiscriminatory liberalization by Lebanon would be beneficial both for welfare and, by reducing the costs of exporters, for developing competitive export sectors.

Given the asymmetry of access offered by the Euro-Med agreements, the major short-term challenge faced by SMR firms derives from the increased import penetration of European products into traditionally protected manufacturing sectors. While the FTA does not require that prices in MENA countries fall to international levels (hence the small welfare gains from the liberalization outlined above), the decline to European price levels and the increased quality and variety of goods will significantly increase competitive pressures faced by a number of existing manufacturing sectors.

It is difficult to estimate precisely the impact of the relative price change that MENA firms will face at the sectoral or individual firm level. At the aggregate level, the protection from European producers could ultimately be reduced by more than 10 percent (table 2.1). It will be substantially larger in specific lines of production in which tariffs and quantitative restrictions offer significantly greater nominal protection.

The simulation exercises for Egypt, Morocco, and Tunisia outlined above give some indication of the sectors most likely to be affected by the Euro-Med agreements. In general, there are output gains in consumer products and light intermediates, particularly clothing. Wood products and footwear are also positively affected in the Tunisian case. Medium and heavy industries, such as machinery and chemicals, are generally projected to be negatively impacted. Petroleum refining—and in the case of Tunisia, electrical machinery—seems to be the exception to this trend.

Overall, agricultural output would tend to fall. In Morocco, where more disaggregated data are available, the model predicts that citrus fruits and vegetables output will grow because of the Euro-Med agreement. The general trend in services points to gains in Egypt (transport, tourism), Morocco (transport, construction), and Tunisia (financial, personal).

The transitional arrangements embedded in the Euro-Med agreements acknowledge this presence of increased competition. The protective structure applied to noncompeting manufactured imports is the first to be liberalized in all cases, while the liberalization schedule applied to final goods is extended to the end of the 10- to 12-year implementation period. This pattern of liberalization, while providing a longer adjustment period for MENA firms, actually raises effective protection and potential profits for import-competing industries during the implementation period. Unless these excess profits—and the time provided—are used to improve the competitive position of MENA firms, the resulting adjustment to increased competition may prove even more difficult than originally foreseen.

THE ARAB FREE TRADE AREA

The Arab Free Trade Area (AFTA) was established in January 1998 with 18 member countries[8] with the goal of eliminating import duties and other barriers to trade on goods of Arab origin by 2008. One of the most innovative features of the program is the involvement of the private sector in monitoring the implementation of different stages of the program (including difficulties that traders encounter with customs administrations and other regulatory agencies of member countries). The implementation of the AFTA will reduce high tariffs and NTBs, increase transparency of member countries' trade policies, and lead to significant trade creation (Zarrouk 1998). The consequence will be improved intraregional competitiveness and expanded product coverage of intraregional exports (Devlin, Guerrieri, and Page 2000). This process will be further stimulated by the growing intra-industry specialization in the region. There is also improved potential for attracting FDI while becoming less reliant on EU markets for exports.

THE GULF COOPERATION COUNCIL

The Gulf Cooperation Council (GCC) was established in 1981.[9] The Unified Economic Agreement, ratified in 1982, specifically aimed to promote economic cooperation among its members. The Agreement's goal was to establish a common market. Following the Agreement, GCC countries removed customs duties on intra-GCC imports. The adoption of a common external tariff has been delayed and has now been postponed until 2005.[10] This reduces their chances of entering into a free trade area with the EU, which had placed such a uniform tariff as a key precondition for negotiations.

There are three concerns regarding the effect of the GCC on member countries. The first is the similarity of comparative advantage among member countries and the resulting small benefits of integration. The second concern is that larger firms from more developed members will benefit from the enlarged markets, taking over the markets of smaller firms and gaining more economic (and political) power over smaller or weaker members. GCC membership also includes several potential benefits. By far, the most important of these is the effect of increased political and economic bargaining power in the world economy. As a unit, the GCC will have better access to world markets with better negotiating and bargaining power. The larger internal market allows an expansion or diversification for local exporters to export non-oil product, achieving economies of scale, and decreasing production costs and prices to consumers. The standardization of regulations and practices will facilitate trade. The larger market may therefore attract both more intraregional investment and FDI.

Meeting the Competitive Challenge: How Is MENA Stacking Up?

In an increasingly competitive global trade environment, the timely and competitive production and delivery of goods is of critical importance. Trade logistics can enhance or hamper the competitiveness of producers and exporters. In this regard, institutional facilities and services, and trade-related infrastructure, become necessary but not sufficient for global success.

Customs Administration and Reform

Most MENA countries have undertaken tariff and tax reforms since the 1980s, but progress has been slow and uneven. Egypt, Jordan, Morocco, and Tunisia have made the most progress. Nevertheless, tax and tariff systems in MENA are complex and difficult to administer. Most countries are still using NTBs such as quantitative restrictions and surcharges.[11] Furthermore, while effective tariffs are not excessively high compared to the average of non-OECD countries, their variance adds to their discriminatory effects.[12]

Reform of border measures, however, does not address fully the institutional reform needed for effective trade integration. Table 2.6 provides insight into the work still needed in this area. Importing firms find customs procedures (inspection, valuation, and quality control) very binding. This in turn affects costs and competitiveness of domestic producers and exporters. MENA countries need to rationalize their imports and export procedures to reduce traders' uncertainty, costs, and delivery time (see appendix 2B).

Many Asian and Latin American countries have made great progress in implementing procedures that require filing one form and minimize the time spent going through customs. El Salvador's reform efforts illustrate one successful approach. It established the Center for Export Requirements (CENTREX) in 1987 to centralize all permit requirements for imports and exports. Before CENTREX, the preparation of documents took from 8 to 10 days, and sometimes as many as 15 days. In 1995, CENTREX established the Electronic System for Exports (SIEX) to speed up export formalities. This has allowed companies to obtain automatic export permits on-line seven days a week. Sanitary certificates, certificates of origin, and other documentation are processed the same day. The introduction of SIEX has reduced the time for preparation of export documentation to less than one day.[13]

TABLE 2.6 BINDING CONSTRAINTS FOR FIRMS

Firms	Score	Ranking
Importing		
Customs procedures (inspection, valuation, and quality control)	0.85	1
Port services (formalities, discharging, handling, storage, and high fees)	0.75	2
Freight transportation regulation (road and maritime)	0.59	3
Import policy uncertainty	0.54	4
Exporting		
Competition rules in importing countries (anti-dumping actions)	0.95	1
Standards and quality control requirements (in importing countries)	0.72	2
Freight, insurance, export financing services	0.64	3
Customs procedures (in importing countries)	0.52	4

Note: Traders were asked, in a questionnaire, to rank the severity of a set of obstacles on a scale of 1 to 5. The score results were normalized to a scale of zero to 1, where zero means that the constraint is not binding at all and 1 means that the constraint is prohibitive. Regulatory constraints with a score equal to or greater than 0.5 were retained in the final results.
Source: Zarrouk 2000.

Governance Issues

Transparency, impartiality, and predictability of rules in taxation, ownership, labor, and investment provide a business-friendly environment by reducing the potential for discretionary actions and corruption. Table 2.7 provides information on how the MENA countries rate in three governance aspects. In all three categories (law, corruption, and quality of bureaucracy), the MENA region compares favorably to East Asia and Pacific, as well as Latin American countries.

On an individual basis, however, all MENA countries ranked a marginal two on the quality of bureaucracy index, below Korea and Malaysia. Egypt and Algeria rank poor (2 out of 6) on the corruption ranking, while the others rank average to above average (3 or 4 out of 6). These two constraints are identified in surveys as a source of great concern for producers and exporters (Zarrouk 1998). The costs of corruption and the uncertainty correlated with opaque bureaucratic processes reduce profitability and incentives for expansion of production and exports.

Trade-Related Infrastructure

Development of physical infrastructure to reduce the costs of doing business and foster trade is key to a competitive productive chain and arms-length delivery. This

TABLE 2.7 INTERNATIONAL COUNTRY RISK GUIDE INDICES FOR BUREAUCRATIC QUALITY, CORRUPTION, AND LAW AND ORDER, 1998

Countries and regions	Quality of bureaucracy[a]	Corruption[b]	Law and order[b]
Morocco	2	3	6
Tunisia	2	3	5
Egypt	2	2	2
Algeria	2	2	4
Jordan	2	4	4
Bolivia	2	3	3
Costa Rica	2	5	4
Korea, Republic of	3	4	4
Malaysia	3	3	5
East Asia and Pacific	2	3	4
Latin America and the Caribbean	2	3	3
Middle East and North Africa	2	3	4
Sub-Saharan Africa	2	3	3

a. For bureaucratic quality, the index runs from 0 (bad) to 4 (good).
b. The corruption and law and order indices run from 0 (bad) to 6 (good).
Source: World Bank, Statistical Information Management Analysis (SIMA) database; World Bank 1999a.

infrastructure base includes roads, ports, airports, corresponding handling (loading and unloading) and storage facilities, electricity, water, and telecommunication.

The MENA countries still face a panoply of infrastructure constraints. Tables 2C.1–2C.3 in appendix 2C highlight this fact by comparing MENA's infrastructure (telephone lines per 1,000 people, electrical power production, and roads) with fast integrators such as Argentina, Korea, and Malaysia. Importers rank port services (formalities, discharging, handling, storage, high fees) and freight transportation regulations (road and maritime) as serious constraints. Exporters consider freight issues to be a barrier to trade.

Malaysia's approach to improving trade facilitation has involved the private sector in managing port facilities since the mid-1980s at Port Kelang (leasing containers to private consortia). Starting in the early 1990s, Malaysia expanded this approach to cover more local ports and maritime transport–related services. In each port, productivity has increased between 15 and 20 percent. The Philippines also had a very successful experience with reform in this area. In 1988, the government contracted with the private sector for the operation of the Manila International Container Terminal. The impact was immediately felt: ship turnaround time was reduced by 60 percent, and the increase in productivity was between 15 and 20 percent.

Tables 2C.1–2C.3 in appendix 2C provide further information on telecommunication and computers. While local businesses rate telephone services as fair to good, the wait for a new telephone line is on average over a month and in several cases over a year (table C2.2). Furthermore, fewer telephone main lines and personal computers are available in the group of MENA countries than in their East Asian counterparts.

Clearly, communications facilities need further, rapid enhancement. Privatization and private sector involvement have been successful in alleviating this constraint in Latin America and the Caribbean and East Asia and Pacific. Latin America and the Caribbean has been leading all regions in private participation in this sector. Total investment in telecommunications projects with private participation in Latin America and the Caribbean from 1990 to 1998 was about $110 billion, followed by East Asia and Pacific at about $40 billion, while MENA has a meager $2 billion to $3 billion. The Philippines has the most liberalized and privatized telecommunications market among Asian economies. In reforming this sector, the Philippines followed the common Asian approach: a shift from public to private ownership, increased scope for foreign ownership (or control, or both), and liberalization of entry into the industry. The number of main lines grew 21.3 percent per year from 1990 to 1995.

What Needs to Be Done? Private and Public Action

A post-Seattle round of the WTO may increase both export opportunities and domestic competition. The Euro-Med agreements will also soon bring European competitors into Arab domestic markets. Are Arab producers ready to compete with them? Seeking further protection only delays the inevitable. Investing in improving productivity, in new products, and in market analysis by business associations and individual exporters will become progressively more important for MENA firms.

Standardization of Products

Producers and exporters can add a great deal of qualitative information and credibility to their products by using internationally accepted certification methodologies. By ensuring that they match these standards, they minimize importers' uncertainty regarding product quality. For instance, in the Kaohsiung Export Processing Zone (Taiwan, China), many of the firms and their domestic suppliers are voluntarily adopting ISO 9000 certification to ensure buyers of the quality of products.

SEEKING NEW PRODUCT LINES

Services outsourcing decisions are based on four factors: adequate labor skills, common language, lower labor costs, and the technological and communications network necessary to allow timely processing of documents. In MENA, and more specifically in countries such as Tunisia, the first two factors are fulfilled. Improvement of the communications network will open up the field to rapid expansion of services exports.

As discussed previously, better market access for agricultural products to both the EU and the markets of other developing countries will allow MENA countries to develop and reap the benefits of their comparative advantage in fruits and vegetables. In this light, their active participation in international negotiations (such as the WTO) is critical.

SEEKING NEW MARKETS

Since the EU is the main trade partner of most Arab countries, Arab exporters are directly affected by the EU economic conditions. Exporters should seek to spread their business risks by diversifying their buyers. MENA countries have very little import penetration in East Asia and Latin America, not to mention the rest of Africa. Intraregional trade may offer opportunities for MENA exporters.

Trade Facilitation

Implementation of trade facilitation measures in MENA economies should be accelerated. One such activity is a project being launched in Tunisia with the assistance of the World Bank that aims at unifying and computerizing export requirements.

The examples of the Philippines and Malaysia discussed in this chapter provide good illustrations of productivity gains and cost reductions arising mainly from transportation facilitation, end of monopolies, and privatization. We provided striking examples of improvements in telecommunications in East Asia. Many MENA countries (including Algeria, Tunisia, and Syria) are still very cautious in undertaking reforms in this area. Morocco started this process with the

August 1999 award of a second mobile telecommunications license through an international tender. All bidders had made commitments on quality, coverage, and tariffs that would significantly expand and improve services. The winning bid went to Medi-Telecom, a consortium of Telefonica of Spain, Portugal's Telecom, and Moroccan investors. The new license has already prompted the existing service provider to improve services and reduce prices.[14]

Minimization of red tape, discretionary rules, and regulations for exports remains a top priority. The administrative set-up of export processing zones is a good example of a hands-off regulatory regime. MENA governments have not used free trade zones to the same extent as Latin American and East Asian governments as devices to streamline institutional and infrastructure services to exporters. Mexico, the Dominican Republic, and Malaysia are notable for the variety of quasi free trade environments established—from duty free zones, to export processing zones, to bonded warehouses, to duty free factory sites—to facilitate export transactions. Recent reforms of public sector free zones in Egypt, Jordan, Saudi Arabia, and Yemen point in the right direction, but implementation of the institutional and regulatory changes will be the key to success. There are very few examples of successful private development of export processing zones in the region.

INDUSTRIAL RESTRUCTURING

The Euro-Med agreements include very substantial resources for industrial sector adjustment to the increased competitive challenge of European imports. Egypt and Tunisia have begun to implement industrial restructuring programs, designed to assist firms to upgrade technology, improve product quality, and diversify product lines. These programs are based on public-private partnerships, and often include access to investment capital at subsidized interest rates for "approved" restructuring plans.

The existing programs in Tunisia and Egypt have met with some skepticism on the part of firms. Latin American governments (including Argentina, Colombia, and Mexico) pursued similar restructuring programs in the late 1980s and early 1990s during their trade liberalizations (see appendix 2D). In general, those programs were most successful when they exhibited a number of common attributes:

- A public-private partnership, organized along specific sectoral lines, that defined the nature of the restructuring program and the approach to be followed.

- A restructuring program focused on providing information on the types of changes that would be needed to meet increased competition, as a public good to all firms in the sector.

- Financial institutions brought into the process at an early stage so they understood the "bankability" of proposed projects. Interest rates were not subsidized and investment decisions were left to the market.

- Substantial effort given to learning and follow-up.

Importers are assigned to a verificateur and a chief inspector to inspect the goods and assign appropriate tariffs. Problems arise from this system because the importer lacks the ability to request another verificateur or chief inspector in case of a dispute. If there is a dispute, the importer can use an expert to assess the value of a good. This is often avoided by the importer because the expert is often a competitor and can request a large fee for assessing the good, delay the release of the good, or increase the value of the good, resulting in higher tariffs for the importer. This system gives the verificateur and the chief inspector enormous power over the importer, and makes the customs procedures in Lebanon highly prone to corruption.

Appendix 2C. Indicators—Telephone and Computer Infrastructure

TABLE 2C.1 INFRASTRUCTURE INDICATORS FOR SELECTED FAST INTEGRATOR AND MENA COUNTRIES, 1996

Country	Telephone main lines (per 1,000 people)	Paved roads (percent)	Electric power production (kilowatt hours per person)
Fast Integrators			
Argentina	174	29	1,993
Chile	156	14	2,199
Korea, Rep. of	430	73	4,849
Malaysia	178	75	2,447
Mexico	93	37	1,747
Morocco	46	50	457
Thailand	70	98	1,457
Average	161	52	2,306
MENA			
Iran, Islamic Rep. of	95	50	1,514
Syria	80	23	1,133
Tunisia	64	79	837
Egypt	50	78	975
Jordan	62	100	1,514
Algeria	44		712

Sources: World Bank, Statistical Information Management Analysis (SIMA) Database; World Bank 1998b, 1999b.

TABLE 2C.2 MAIN INDICATORS FOR TELECOMMUNICATIONS SERVICES
IN MENA COUNTRIES, 1999

Country	Waiting time for installation of direct line	Local business evalua- tion of telephone services	Internet avail- ability	Annual sub- scription fees (dollars)	Users' fees (dollars)	Party offering Internet services
Algeria	1 yr +	Fair	Yes	—	$172/mth	Government
Egypt	1 yr +	Good	Yes	260	Open	Private
Jordan	1 mth	Good	Yes	—	$20/mth	Private
Lebanon	1 mth	Good	Yes	1,000	$45/mth	Private
Morocco	1 mth +	Fair	Yes	750	Open	Private
Qatar	1 wk	Good	Yes	55[a]	$17/mth	Government
Syria	2 yrs +	Fair	No	—	—	—
Tunisia	1 mth +	Fair	Yes	600	Open	Private
Yemen	1 yr +	Fair	Yes	335	0.10/min	Government

— Not available.
a. Registration charge.
Source: Partial reproduction from tables in Zarrouk 2000.

TABLE 2C.3 INFORMATION INFRASTRUCTURE IN SELECTED MENA COUNTRIES, AND OTHERS

Country/region	Telephone mainlines		Wait (years)	Personal computers		Paved roads (percent)		Paved roads in good condition (percent)
	1990	1997	1997	1990	1997	1990	1996	1994
Algeria	32	48	8	1	4	67	69	40
Tunisia	38	70	1	3	9	76	79	40
Morocco	16	50	0		3	49	50	50
Egypt, Rep. of	30	56	4		7	72	78	43
Jordan	58	70	5		9	100	100	72
Syria	40	88	10		2		23	—
Taiwan	310	500	0	34	118	85	89	—
Korea	310	444	0			72	73	—
Malaysia	89	195	0	8	46	70	75	—
East Asia and Pacific	16	60	1	2	11	24	12	—
Europe and Central Asia	125	189	3			77	83	—
Latin America and the Caribbean	64	110	1	6	32	22	26	—
MENA	37	71	5		10	67	50	—
South Asia	6	18	6	0	2	38	41	—
Sub-Saharan Africa	10	16	4		7	17	16	—

— Not available.

Note: Telephone main lines (per 1,000 people), personal computers (per 1,000 people), and wait refer to time in years to get a telephone main line.

Source: World Bank, Statistical Information Management Analysis (SIMA) Database; World Bank 1998b, 1999b; World Road Statistics; and MENA Region Live Data Base (MENA LDB).

Appendix 2D. Industrial Restructuring

Mexico Industrial Restructuring

Following the 1982 debt crisis, Mexico began a process of economic reform, under the De La Madrid administration (1983–87), which included macro reforms, such as liberalization and stabilization, and structural reform—deregulation, industrial restructuring, and eventually privatization. Rapid trade liberalization, including Mexico's entry into the GATT, the dismantling of most NTBs, and a deep reduction, across the board, in tariff levels, was designed to open the Mexican economy to competition in world markets. This process culminated with Mexico's adherence to NAFTA.

Structural reforms, under De La Madrid, were initially focused on industrial restructuring and complementary deregulation. Eventually, during the Salinas administration (1988–93) privatization became the focus of structural reform. Industrial restructuring was essentially bifurcated between restructuring and eventual privatization of state-owned enterprises (SOEs) and support for private sector restructuring, in the wake of market failure during the debt crisis.

Industrial restructuring support for the private sector consisted primarily of deregulation and a substantial effort by the government to assist sectors that needed to adjust in the wake of liberalization. With respect to deregulation, at the beginning of each administration (sexeino—six-year term), the government traditionally prepared plans for each industrial subsector, supported by a comprehensive system of licensing for firms seeking to enter the sector. There was also strong control over FDI, generally restricting majority foreign ownership. Therefore, many large domestic groups, with close ties to the government, generated profits through rent-seeking activities, for example, exclusive licenses to enter particular market niches or through large government contracts to provide goods and services to the SOEs. Not surprisingly, pervasive corruption further distorted the market. Starting in 1986, the government began to dismantle its central planning system and to deregulate. In addition, the government began to promote FDI, and to lift ownership and other adverse restrictions on FDI in all but a few strategic sectors, primarily oil, gas, and electricity.

For example, in the automobile industry, the government revamped a series of regulations governing the auto parts sector that eliminated a domestic "must buy" list, reduced domestic content regulations, and generally reduced a host of restrictive regulations. In its place, the government created a number of incentives supporting exports of both auto parts and assembled vehicles. In just a few years, the government was able to induce some $10 billion of FDI into the sector as U.S. automakers, fearing Japanese competition, began to assemble cars for export from Mexico into the United States. This was followed by investments from foreign auto producers, and a critical cluster of activity was created in the sector. Similar deregulation occurred in electronics, attracting major producers such as IBM and Hewlett Packard, that eventually exported a majority of their production from

Martin, Will. 1997. "Assessing the Implications for Lebanon of Free Trade with the European Union." DECRG-Trade, World Bank, Washington, D.C.

Nabli, Mustapha K., and Annette I. De Kleine. 1998. "Managing Global Integration in the Middle East." Paper presented at the conference "Benefiting from Globalization." The Mediterranean Development Forum, Marrakech, Morocco, Sept. 3–6.

Nsouli, Saleh, Amer Bisat, and Oussama Kanaan. 1996. "The European Union's New Mediterranean Strategy." *Finance and Development* 33 (3, September).

Rutherford, T., E. Rutström, and D. Tarr. 1993. "Morocco's Free Trade Agreement with the European Community." Policy Research Working Paper 1173. World Bank, Washington, D.C.

————. 1995. "L'accord de libre-échange entre le Tunisie et l'Union Européenne." Confidential final report. March. Tunis.

Stern, Robert M. 2000. Forthcoming. "Dynamic Aspects of Euro-Mediterranean Agreements for the MENA Economies." In Devlin, Julia, Raed Safadi, and Sebastian Dessus, eds., *The Dynamics of New Regionalism in MENA: Integration, Euro-Med Partnership Agreements and After.* Paris: OECD.

United Nations. 1999. World Integrated Trade Solution: Trade Data Warehouse, Comtrade.

Wellenius, Bjorn, and Carlo Maria Rossotto. 1999. " Public Policy for the Private Sector." Note no. 199. Finance, private sector and infrastructure network. World Bank, Washington, D.C. November.

World Bank. Statistical Information Management Analysis (SIMA). Database. Washington, D.C.: World Bank.

————. 1996. *Global Economic Prospects 1996.* Washington, D.C.: World Bank.

————. 1998a. "Colombia Industrial Restructuring and Development Project (Loan No. 3321-CO)." Implementation Completion Report. World Bank, Washington, D.C. November.

————. 1998b. *Global Development Finance.* Database.

————. 1999a. Live Data Base (LDB).

————. 1999b. *World Development Indicators (WDI)*. Washington, D.C.: World Bank.

WTO (World Trade Organization). 1995. The General Agreement for Tariffs on Trade, Uruguay Round.

Yeats, Alexander. 1996. "Export Prospects of Middle Eastern Countries." Policy Research Working Paper, No. WPS-1571. World Bank, Washington, D.C.

Yeats, Alexander, and Francis Ng. 1999. "Beyond the Year 2000—Implications of Middle East's Recent Trade Performance." DECRG-TRADE, World Bank, Washington, D.C. Processed.

Zarrouk, Jamel. 1998. "Arab Free Trade Area: Potentialities and Effects." Presented at the Mediterranean Development Forum, September 3–6, 1998. Marrakech, Morocco. Arab Monetary Fund.

Zarrouk, Jamel. 2000. "Regulatory Regimes and Trade Costs." In *Catching Up with the Competition: Trade Challenges: Trade Opportunities and Challenges for Arab Countries*. Studies in International Economics. Ann Arbor: University of Michigan Press.

CHAPTER 3

Global Competition and the Peripheral Player: A Promising Future

Taïeb Hafsi

Globalization is both an old and a new phenomenon. In the past, a firm such as Exxon (or its predecessor, Standard Oil of New Jersey) could not consider its market anything but international (Chandler 1962). Its strategy—and that of its competitors—to build a new and interconnected vision of the world is not substantially different from today's concept of a global village. Yet while adopting a global perspective may have distinguished companies 50 years ago, today "going international" is considered a natural phase in the development of all firms (Chandler 1977, 1990; Vernon and Wells 1976). This does not mean, however, that globalization is no longer an innovative and important aspect of competition.

As the standard practices of the world's markets have changed, so have the definitions of what it means to globalize. The market to which most modern firms refer is a wider market—even when the firms decide to concentrate only on a small part of it. Thus, the concept of globalization is no longer related to the decision of a firm to go abroad as much as it is to the willingness of all firms to do the same. This means that even when a firm does not intend to go elsewhere, it must expect others, from all over the world, to come and challenge it in its own territory. In other words, globalization, which was once considered a firm's specific strategy, has become a structural element that has dramatically changed competition dynamics in many industries.

There are many issues related to such a situation. As competition is becoming much more sophisticated, traditional industrial organization concepts have simultaneously become more relevant, such as when economies of scale dominate an industry (Caves 1980), and challenging, as when increasing returns to scale create new monopolistic or oligopolistic situations (Arthur 1993). Governments, as much as firms, are also being put to the test. They are expected to manage competition within their sovereign boundaries in order to avoid predatory behavior and restraint of trade or commerce. Such management is generally as much formal as it is informal, involving negotiations among all parties concerned, including competitors, customers, suppliers, and so on. In global competition, the overall logic evades any government's willingness to intervene. It requires that all governments act in concert—which is hard to envisage and would be even harder to organize. Governments are therefore obliged to think more in terms of national competitiveness to fit their logic into the firms' logic when involved in global competition, which means that they have to understand better the global competitive game and work at bending the firms' competitive logic to take into account the country's interests.

Globalization is therefore a new version of an old game that opens up the field, involves all relevant players—local, international, private, public, and governmental—and transforms completely their traditional behavior. Such a game generates not only incredible threats but also amazing opportunities, the stakes of which are the prosperity not only of firms but also of nations. How can different players deal with globalization and the resulting competition? What choice does each player— in particular the smaller and weaker player—have? Which of these choices is best? These are the key questions dealt with in this chapter.

We intend to provide an overview of the realities and challenges of today's globalization and of the responses that firms and governments have developed or are implementing. First, we define "globalization" and propose that there are various levels of globalization. Next, we describe firms' strategic responses to the realities they are now facing, then show how governments can get involved, and how they are responding. We next address more specifically the situation of smaller firms based in smaller countries, and suggest that their strategies need not be the same as those of larger firms in larger countries. Finally, we conclude with a discussion of what the future holds, both for firms and for governments, in smaller and developing countries.

Globalization: Multiple Realities

The word globalization is often used to describe differing realities. For example, we can speak of the globalization of markets or industries, as if it were imposed on the actors and unrelated to their actions (Porter 1986). In this way, the television market and the piano market are said to be global. We can also speak of the globalization of the firm and of its strategy (Doz 1986; Porter 1986). Clearly, International Business Machines Corporation (IBM) and Ford are global, but what about

TABLE 3.4 GLOBALIZATION AND STRATEGY

Degree of intervention	Degree of competition		
	Low	Average	High
Low	Opportunism	Differentiation or integration	Integration or differentiation
High	National responsiveness	Focus or mixed strategies (including alliances)	Mixed (including alliances) or focus strategies

Source: Author.

As shown in table 3.4, when government has a hands-off policy and competition is local, the main actors are in a situation where opportunistic strategies are appropriate. They tend to use their local position to strengthen their global position, but have to be cautious to avoid retaliation that could increase global competition.

When the government follows a hands-off policy, but competition is becoming more globalized, the most common strategies are those that take advantage of the global dynamics to justify integration. This includes specializing plants and integrating their activities across countries. As long as the globalization is incomplete, firms proceed cautiously, because integration leads to major commitments and rigidities. The best strategy in situations of transition to a global industry is differentiation. It does not require integration and allows more flexibility.[2]

When governments intervene a little and global competition is strong, we have an accentuation of the preceding trends. Global competition justifies and facilitates integration. In fact, cost (thus, economies of scale) is a critical advantage in generalized globalization. Cost-effectiveness is important, regardless of whether a firm is able to concentrate on a specific segment or is compelled to deal with the whole industry.

Again, the auto industry is a good example. In such an industry, economic scales for components are so huge that no national market is sufficient to justify a plant of the right economic size. One is compelled to build plants for several national markets. Yet one has to take into account the pressures exerted by governments through the laws and regulations they set. This has led Ford to build a Gear box plant in France, an engine plant in Germany, a small pieces plant in Spain, and assembly plants in many locations. As we see in this example, despite competitive dynamics that favor integration, most automobile companies do not fully integrate. They integrate within the limits of the constraints, formal and informal, exerted by governments. In some cases, when the fashion or status content is high, differentiation is dominant and firms tend to produce in one location to serve a global segment. This was the case with German and Japanese automobile firms in the 1980s—again, to satisfy content requirements or because this is the fashion.

When government pressures are strong, and legitimately so (that is, the governments must have strong reasons to support the pressures resulting from new laws or so), the most appropriate strategy is a national responsiveness strategy. This happens in industries where national stakes are high and international competition is low, with firms mutually adjusting to each other. This was the case in the oil and tobacco (especially cigarettes) industries until the mid-1980s.

When government pressures are strong but competition is intense and increasingly globalized (as was the case in the computer and telecommunications industries until the mid-1980s), the best strategy is either a focus or a multifocal strategy mixing integration and differentiation. Doz (1986) has described the 1980s telecommunications industry in Europe as multifocal, responsive to government demands, yet giving attention to the technological development imposed by competition all over the world. Multifocal strategies may involve alliances with varying degrees of involvement among the partners.

When a government's stakes in a global industry are high, strategies are unclear, thus necessarily multifocal, with multiple alliances and concentration strategies whenever possible. The clothing industry provides a good example, especially in Europe, where firms have developed alliances with their governments and other important actors of the industry. Similarly, the two major aircraft manufacturers (Airbus and Boeing) are increasingly made of many firms related on a permanent or semi-permanent basis.

Competition among Nations: The Formal Diamond

The globalization of markets, industries, and firms has considerably reduced the ability of governments to directly influence the behavior of firms. They are now obliged to act indirectly by trying to create the conditions that lead firms to favor their policies, such as creating employment, developing local technology, and so on. As a result, firms become the government's "critical customers," and they compete to attract their favors. It is therefore useful for us to consider the competitive advantage of nations.

To measure the competitiveness of nations, Porter (1990) proposes first to do an industry-by-industry evaluation using the simple model known as the "diamond of national competitiveness." This method defines the competitive capacity of a nation in a specific industry as its capacity to entice firms to use the country as a platform from which to conduct business. The diamond describes the four major factors that affect firms' decisions:

- Demand characteristics, keeping in mind that a demanding and sophisticated local market attracts firms

- Factor characteristics—including quality labor, cheap capital, and advanced technology in the country—which attract the leading firms of the industry

- A competitive structure that promotes robust and healthy competition, and thus contributes to the competitive strength of firms

- Support industries, which, when dynamic and innovative, are also an attractive factor.

Porter argues that after assessing the strength of the diamond for each industry, governments should concentrate their efforts on boosting the industries in which the diamond is strong rather than weak. This is a highly controversial argument and, as we shall discuss later, is more appropriate for large, rather than small, industrial countries and firms. In the areas where a country has a strong diamond, thus a strong national advantage, governments tend to think in terms of a set of interrelated sectors called clusters—a concept typically used by European economists. The idea behind clusters is that the health of interrelated sectors is dependent on the health of each individual in the cluster. In Canada, for example, the Province of Quebec's government identifies all the interrelated sectors and develops a strategy to help them develop jointly.

While competing governments are all in the business of finding ways to improve the nation's competitive advantage, some have been more successful than others. Kenichi Ohmae (1985), who has suggested that the world competition is gearing up for a confrontation among a triad made up of Asia, Europe, and the United States has also shown that the Chinese government has invented a new way to attract foreign firms and investment through the concept of regional or city-centered development. According to him, the more relevant scale for national strategy is the one suggested by the Chinese experiments: the city or the region.

The diamond concept, and the related idea of cluster, is arguably more useful for dominant countries that are in the business of world-scale competition, such as those included in Ohmae's triad. For smaller economies, however, it is either irrelevant or hardly credible. For example, in his study of Canada's industries, Porter has found that there is no industry, with the possible weak exception of the forest industry, in which Canada had a strong diamond. Yet, as argued by many scholars (Rugman 1990), Canada is a thriving country, doing well by all standards and recognized as one of the more dynamic countries of the Organisation of Economic Co-operation and Development.

Dominant and Peripheral Games: The Successful Small Firm in a Global Dynamic

Despite Porter's argument, in most Canadian industries there are dynamic and successful firms. In particular, there are several firms in the clothing industry (in which Canada has not traditionally been a powerhouse) that, despite being small and apparently insignificant, are competitive in a market where Asian and European competitors are strong. A small $100 million[3] company called Paris Star, for instance, regularly beats the Southeast Asian giants for famous designers' contracts. Similarly, Peerless Clothing (PC) in Montréal is the world's largest exporter of high quality men's suits to the United States, competing successfully with such well-known U.S. firms as Armani and Hugo Boss.

This suggests that Porter's diamond analysis (as well as all the industrial organization-based theories that he and others have proposed, including the traditional competitive analysis and value chain manipulations) is better suited to firms or countries that compete for a dominant position in an industry. All the firms or countries that happen to be in a more peripheral situation have to conceive the world, and the market in which it works, differently. In particular, using the idea of the diamond, we could suggest that firms that are not in a dominant situation have to think in terms of a "virtual diamond" rather than the more formal Porterian diamond. Such a diamond would be built by the firm and could involve elements spread all over the world. For example, for a Canadian clothing firm, the relevant demand may be the American demand, the relevant factors (capital, technology, and labor) may be Canadian, while the supporting industries and the industry dynamics may be worldwide. In a sense, the virtual diamond is not a feature of the country—rather, it is built by the firm.

The idea of a virtual diamond reveals that the firms' managers play a critical role in conceiving and building the bases on which their competitiveness will rest. Building the virtual diamond means not only understanding clearly the dynamics of the industry, but also identifying the forces that can help in developing an advantage. This indicates that alliances and cooperative strategies are at the heart of the virtual diamond. For example, PC had to compete against Hugo Boss and Armani in the United States, but it could obviously not do it in the traditional distribution channels. The large chains had a clear bias in favor of the better-known competitors. They could invest a lot in advertising and storage to respond to their market. In contrast, the smaller retail chains needed responsiveness to appeal to quality and price-sensitive customers. They needed to develop a quality image and house brand at a reasonable cost. They needed to reduce their suit stocks, while responding to their customers' demands for quality name-brand men's suits. Their products had to be of a quality similar to that of the competition, yet a little less expensive, in order to provide a better value. An alliance with a small, responsive, and cost-effective supplier was bound to provide results.

To respond to such a market, PC built storage facilities close to the customers. Sophisticated intelligence of the market and a high-technology production system allowed the firm to produce stock and respond quickly to customer orders. The smaller chains could also have their own private brand on the products, delivered on request, and they could return any unsold suits. By offering these benefits to its customers, PC demonstrated the value of understanding the specific needs of cus-

Porter, M. E. 1986. *Competition in Global Industries.* Boston: Harvard Business School Press.

————. 1990. *The Competitive Advantage of Nations.* New York: Free Press.

Prahalad, C. K., and Y. L. Doz. 1987. *The Multinational Mission: Balancing Local Demands and Global Vision.* New York: Free Press.

Rugman, A. M., ed. 1990. *Research in Global Strategic Management*, Vol.1. Greenwich, Conn.: JAI Press.

Vernon, R., and L. Wells. 1976. *Economic Environment of International Business.* Englewood-Cliffs, N.J.: Prentice-Hall.

PART II

The Business Environment in the MENA Region

FIGURE 4.1 EXPORTS TO INDUSTRIALIZED COUNTRIES

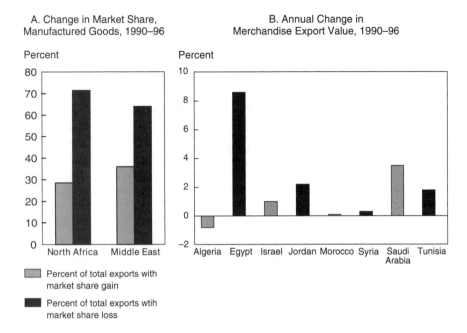

A. Change in Market Share,
Manufactured Goods, 1990–96

B. Annual Change in
Merchandise Export Value, 1990–96

Percent of total exports with
market share gain

Percent of total exports wtih
market share loss

Note: North Africa includes Algeria, Egypt, Libya, Morocco, and Tunisia; the Middle East includes Bahrain, the Islamic Republic of Iran, Iraq, Israel, Jordan, Kuwait, Qatar, Saudi Arabia, the Syrian Arab Republic, the United Arab Emirates, and the Republic of Yemen.
Source: United Nations, Trade CAN/Comtrade Database 2000.

How does the region compare internationally with respect to enterprise impediments? With Asia as our first source of information, we can compare regional data from the surveys carried out as background for the *World Development Report 1997* (World Bank 1997).[2] These enterprise surveys highlight similarities and differences among countries, especially with regard to governance conditions. The responses about the MENA region that emerged from the (relatively small) sample of firms surveyed, placed against the broader context of other regions of the world, suggest the following regional features:

•   There are weaknesses in the relationship between government and the overall business community, as reflected in:

1.   An above-average fear of retroactive changes in laws and legislation

2.   A decline in the predictability of laws and policies over the previous 10 years.

FIGURE 4.2 THE ENTERPRISE IN THE BUSINESS ENVIRONMENT

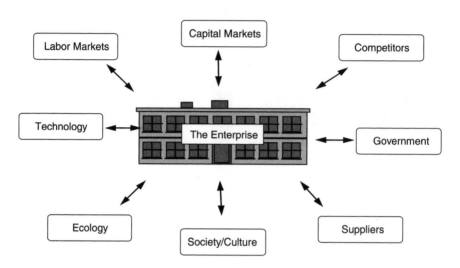

Source: Author.

- There is above-average fear of instability, as reflected in concern over unconstitutional changes in government.

- There is an imperfect rule of law in the region, as reflected in firms' identification of:

    1. Unpredictability of the judiciary—that is, the outcome of judicial systems is not regarded as consistent and reliable.

    2. An above-average ranking of the corruption constraint, meaning that corruption impeded firm operations and growth more in the region than occurs as the global norm.

- Taxes and regulations impose substantial constraints to regional businesses.

    1. Taxes and regulations are a leading concern of businesses, as they are in other regions of the world.

    2. In MENA trade regulations rank higher than in many other regions.

    3. A higher proportion of firms in the region, contrasted with firms in other regions, report that they did not invest due to government regulations.

    4. Firms' senior management spends a high percentage of time on regulatory and legal compliance activities.

The recent surveys carried out as part of the World Business Environment Survey[3] in 1999 and 2000 highlight, through three observations, some of the same differences between MENA countries and countries in other regions that host firms with which MENA firms will likely have to compete. MENA firms rate relatively poorly with regard to the constraints imposed by policy instability, corruption, exchange rate uncertainty, anticompetitive practices by other enterprises and government, taxes and regulations, and the judicial systems[4] (see table 4.1).

MENA firms may take comfort in the fact that the region rated relatively better than South Asia, developing East Asia, and even Latin America (in some respects)—if those are the regions from which they expect the greatest competition. As MENA firms integrate into Organisation for Economic Co-operation and Development (OECD) markets, however, the superior conditions in China and newly industrialized East Asia, as well as OECD countries, may provide competitive challenges.

MENA International Competitiveness: Selected Indicators

Aside from original data gathered through surveys, another way to diagnose the business environment in MENA is to look at official statistics and other comparative data sources. Some of these are particularly useful in benchmarking competitive conditions in the national business environment. What do competitiveness indicators tell us about business environment constraints?

TABLE 4.1 CONSTRAINTS TO ENTERPRISES BY REGION: WORLD BUSINESS
ENVIRONMENT SURVEY, 1999–2000
(percent of enterprises in regions identifying constraint as "major" or "moderate")

Constraint	Africa	MENA	East Asia NIC/China	Latin America	OECD
Policy instability	45.3	69.1	26.4	70.2	36.9
Financing	65.6	50.0	50.8	63.6	39.2
Inflation	59.8	55.7	31.1	63.1	33.2
Corruption	64.1	66.2	20.4	58.2	17.4
Taxes and regulations	32.8	54.1	20.1	72.6	61.7
Exchange rate	35.4	54.9	25.4	62.6	24.8
Anticompetitive practices	n.a.	54.2	29.0	48.1	30.7
Street crime	56.1	43.2	14.1	66.1	22.1
Infrastructure	63.0	42.3	20.5	45.6	21.7
Organized crime	52.8	26.4	14.7	51.1	13.4
Judicial system	n.a.	42.9	14.5	45.4	20.9

Note: NIC = Newly industrialized country. OECD = Organisation for Economic Co-operation and Development.
Source: World Bank 2000, *World Business Environment Survey 1999–2000.*

First they tell us that the state in the MENA region is simply more engaged in economic activities than in the advanced industrial economies, hence more likely to impose a burden on private firms by crowding out activity or financing, monopolizing or protecting the production and distribution of certain goods or services, or inefficiently supplying vital upstream or downstream goods and services. While, again, figures are not available for all countries in the region, for the North African countries for which these data are collected, it is clear that the state is heavier than in any other country for which these data are available (with the exception of the economies of the former Soviet Union). During the early to mid-1990s state-owned enterprises accounted for between 17 and 58 percent of GDP in these economies, as opposed to an average for developing countries of only 11 percent (table 4.2). Clearly, for the leading industrial economies, this figure was even lower. A second indication of state heaviness in some of the economies of the region is the major role played by trade-related taxes and protectionist policies that impede the growth of trade. One indication of this is the level of import duties which, in economies such as the Syrian Arab Republic, Tunisia, Algeria, and Egypt, exceed the standards of rapidly industrializing economies (table 4.3).

A second question we can ask in the age of globalization, where economic success increasingly relies on rapid exchange of information, is how well the economies of the region are networked. How linked are the economies of the region to the rest of the world through foreign direct investment (FDI), which can bring with

TABLE 4.2 THE HEAVY STATE: ECONOMIC ACTIVITY OF STATE-OWNED
ENTERPRISES, 1990–95
(percent of GDP)

Ranking by share of public enterprises in GDP	Country	Indicator
1	United States	1.0
2	Argentina	1.3
4	Mexico	4.9
15	Turkey	5.1
26	Brazil	8.0
34	Korea, Rep. of	10.3
42	India	13.4
43	Tanzania	13.7
52	Morocco	17.2
56	Egypt	30.0
57	Tunisia	30.2
58	Algeria	57.6

Source: World Bank 1999a, World Development Indicators 1999 (available for 58 countries).

TABLE 4.3 AVERAGE IMPORT DUTIES IN SELECTED COUNTRIES, 1997
(percent of imports)

Country	Import duties
Korea, Rep. of	4.3
Malaysia	0.5
Jordan	12.4
Lebanon	14.9
Turkey	1.8
Syrian Arab Rep.	29.7
Morocco	14.8
Yemen, Rep. of	9.7
Tunisia	19.9
Egypt	18.8
Oman	2.5
Algeria	24.2

Source: World Bank 1999a, World Development Indicators 1999.

it not only financing, but market access, technology, management know-how, and other linkages? Several East Asian economies achieved sustained periods of high levels of FDI before (and after) the financial crisis of the late 1990s. A number of Latin American economies have attracted more FDI in recent years, as well. For the economies of the MENA region, the record is mixed—some are quite linked through FDI, others less so (table 4.4). Clearly, there is room for improvement.

Based on a number of indicators, some of the countries of the region appear to have serious impediments to information networking. Two are presented in Table 4.4. First, in several countries in the region the delays in accessing a new telephone line are extraordinarily lengthy, led by Yemen (5 years), Jordan (4.8 years), Egypt (3.9 years), and Tunisia (1.3 years). While some might argue that the advent of cellular telephone technology obviates the need to improve access to fixed lines, this ignores the higher expense (hence competitive disadvantage) imposed by current cellular phone services as well as the current (though diminishing) limitations in this service in terms of fax and Internet connectivity. Second (and perhaps related to the issue of connectivity), penetration of the Internet and computerization more generally is very limited in the region. Computer access is extremely low on a per capita basis throughout the region (except in Lebanon, where it is 318 per 10,000; and in Turkey, where it is 207 per 10,000), and the density of the Internet network measured through Internet hosts is exceptionally low. When compared to the rapid-growth economies of East Asia such as Malaysia and Korea, this contrast becomes especially stark.

TABLE 4.4 NETWORKING INDICATORS, 1997

Country	Gross FDI (percent of GDP)	Years wait for a telephone line	Personal computers (per 10,000 people)	Internet hosts (per 10,000 people)
Korea, Rep. of	35.00	0.0	151	37.66
Malaysia	30.87	0.4	461	18.38
Argentina	18.93	0.0	392	5.92
Mexico	15.92	0.8	373	8.75
Poland	17.98	2.8	362	25.55
India	16.77	1.0	21	0.11
Jordan	24.65	4.8	87	0.79
Lebanon	21.16	n.a	318	3.33
Turkey	20.75	0.4	207	0.43
Morocco	14.56	0.2	16	0.05
Yemen, Rep. of	13.40	5.0	12	0.01
Tunisia	12.09	1.3	86	0.06
Egypt	12.06	3.9	73	0.33

Source: World Bank 1999a.

A final area that lends itself to international benchmarking is that of knowledge—are the economies of the region prepared to compete in a world economy that increasingly relies on the knowledge of workers and technicians more than it does on the low cost of unskilled labor? Even comparing within the region (and vicinity), vast differences in levels of education and the density of skilled scientists and technicians become evident. Literacy rates, for countries available, vary from a high of 100 percent in Israel to a low of 44 percent in Morocco, while tertiary school enrollment varies from a high of 44 percent to a low of 4 percent. A third indicator is the number of scientists and engineers per capita (a figure available for, unfortunately, only a few countries). Nonetheless it is clear there are wide variations (see table 4.5).

Internationally comparable benchmarks of business environment conditions are highly desirable but often not available. Surveys can sometimes supplement official statistics. One field where surveys are becoming more detailed and sophisticated is in documenting the costs of administrative and regulatory procedures. For example, port and custom-related processing times impose important constraints on the competitiveness of internationally trading firms in several countries in the region. One Moroccan exporter complained to the World Bank during a private sector assessment: "Although Europe is geographically near, in time and money

TABLE 4.5 KNOWLEDGE INDICATORS, 1997

Country	Literacy rate (percent)	Tertiary school enrollment (percent)	Scientists and engineers in R&D (per million population)
Algeria	62	13	—
Egypt	51	23	458
Israel	100	44	—
Jordan	87	—	106
Kuwait	79	27	—
Lebanon	—	27	—
Morocco	44	11	—
Oman	—	6	—
Saudi Arabia	63	16	—
Tunisia	67	14	388
Turkey	82	18	261
Yemen, Rep. of	—	4	—

— Not available.
Source: World Bank, *World Development Indicators 1999.*

terms for exporting my goods I am farther away than an Asian firm." Figure 4.3 shows the survey-based figures regarding delays of goods during importation to Algeria. While the 39 days total required for industrial firms to import goods seems unreasonably high, it is hard to place the overall figures, or the time taken by each step in the importation process, in context without a more complete international dataset. This emphasizes the importance of countries in the region collaborating and coordinating their policy research efforts to leverage their limited resources.

The Business Environment in Selected MENA Countries: Survey Evidence

Unfortunately, detailed, comparable survey data are not currently available for all the countries in the MENA region. However, recent survey work in North Africa shows both similarities and differences between the countries of the region. Figure 4.4 shows the results from four countries in North Africa in roughly parallel World Bank surveys of private enterprises carried out in 1998 and 1999.[5]

The first and most noticeable similarity among the countries is that taxes and tax administration impose the leading constraint to firms in all four of the North African countries surveyed. A second similarity is that inflation worries figure

FIGURE 4.3 TIME FOR IMPORT-RELATED PROCESSES: ALGERIAN ENTERPRISE
SURVEY, 1998

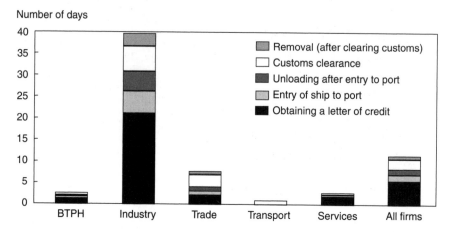

Number of days

Legend:
- Removal (after clearing customs)
- Customs clearance
- Unloading after entry to port
- Entry of ship to port
- Obtaining a letter of credit

Categories: BTPH, Industry, Trade, Transport, Services, All firms

Note: BTPH = bâtiment, travaux publics, et hydrauliques (construction, public works, and hydraulics).
Source: World Bank 1999b.

high among firm constraints in all the countries. However, important differences
appeared as well. For example, the severity of corruption as a constraint appeared
to vary substantially between countries. The level of constraint imposed by crime
and safety concerns also varies substantially between countries—from Algeria,
where it is among the most important constraints, to Egypt, where it ranks last
among firms' identified constraints. A final key finding is that businesses in some
countries appear to feel generally better off than those in others. The average constraint score assigned by Tunisian firms is simply far lower than that assigned by
firms in the other countries. It cannot be judged without a more detailed contex-
tual analysis whether this is due to better long-term economic and institutional
conditions, or temporary market or policy conditions benefiting local businesses.

Conclusions

What can we conclude from this diverse set of comparative indicators of the business environment? First, although each presents a partial and incomplete picture
of business environment constraints in the region, taken together the evidence produces a substantive policy agenda that places priority on the following reforms:

FIGURE 4.4 CONSTRAINTS TO ENTERPRISES IN FOUR COUNTRIES
IN NORTH AFRICA, BASED ON WORLD BANK SURVEY DATA, 1998–99

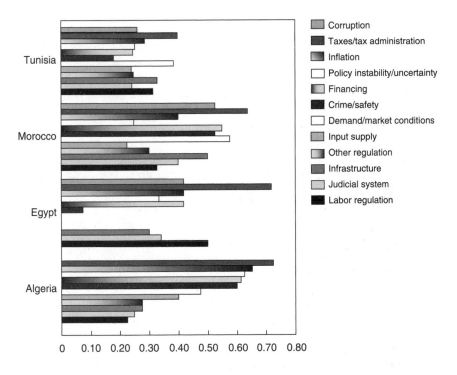

Source: World Bank 1999b, World Business Environment Survey 1998–99.

- At a general level, there is a need for governments to improve policy stability, increase transparency of policy formulation and implementation, and improve public accountability at multiple levels of government. It is clear from the uncertainty about policies and their implementation faced by businesses that one fruitful approach is better consultation between business and government on market-oriented policy reforms.

- In spite of significant progress in several countries of the region, there remains a substantial task in reducing the size of the state, its involvement in productive sectors, and its interventions in markets.

- There is a general need to reduce transaction costs, especially those arising from the administration of taxes and customs, as well as those arising from inconsistent or discretionary administrative practices or inadequate conflict resolution mechanisms.

- Clearly, many parts of the region suffer from elevated costs of moving goods and information in and out. Governments need to act to reduce these costs, if only by establishing the conditions for competitive market development in such critical services as ports and telecommunications.

- There is a regionwide need to strengthen investment in human capital, and to improve the incentives for private firms to invest in worker training. There is also a need to rationalize incentives for capital investment.

- Finally, governments need to work to strengthen the rule of law (and combat corruption), strengthening the administration of justice and the judiciary.

Beyond these policy observations, the chapter points to the need for more parallel empirical work. The regional policy institutions participating in the Third Mediterranean Development Forum have a strong potential role in coordinating their work and sharing information so that countries can better benchmark their current performance, gauge progress over time, and leverage limited local resources by linking national to international policy research initiatives. The World Business Environment Survey presents one opportunity for countries to link to a growing database of measures of business environment conditions. Extending its coverage to more direct measures of firm-level productivity would enhance the direct link of business environment constraints to competitiveness. More detailed surveys of administrative and regulatory costs pose a second opportunity to relate firm-level costs to performance, and to compare costs across countries. These results would be more than intellectually interesting—they could point to the business environment reforms that yield the greatest benefit for firm-level competitiveness.

Notes

1. Based on the presentation at the Third Mediterranean Development Forum in Cairo, Egypt, March 2000. The views expressed here are those of the author and do not reflect those of the World Bank Group, its management, or its directors. The author wishes to acknowledge the assistance and encouragement of Drs. Ahmed Galal and Samiha Fawzy of the Egyptian Center for Economic Studies, and R. Shyam Khemani of the World Bank.

2. Based on Brunetti, Kisunko, and Weder 1997.

3. The World Business Environment Survey (WBES) is an initiative of the World Bank Group that, in partnership with other institutions, has assessed the state of the enabling environment for

private enterprise in 80 countries and one territory, to date. The WBES uses enterprise-level surveys (usually administered through personal interviews) to assess how conditions for private investment are shaped by local conditions. It establishes the basis for internationally comparable indicators that can track changes over time, and can stimulate public-private dialogue on business perceptions. The per country sample size was generally a minimum of 100 firms. The WBES builds on the survey for the *World Development Report 1997* (World Bank 1997), but substantially broadens the issue coverage, expands the sample, and harmonizes the methodology.

4. As the table makes clear, inflation was the third ranking constraint for the region, identified by 56 percent of firms as a major or moderate constraint, but compared to other regions, this rating is not exceptional.

5. Some of the surveys in Tunisia were carried out in a group setting, and it may be assumed that this reduced the severity assigned to some constraint rankings. In Algeria the surveyors were not allowed to ask the question on corruption. The author acknowledges the work of the Egyptian Center for Economic Studies and Dr. Samiha Fawzy in carrying out the Egypt survey, and the consulting work of Dr. Saad Belghazi regarding implementation of the other three studies.

Bibliography

Brunetti, Aymo, Gregory Kisunko, and Beatrice Weder. 1997. "Institutional Obstacles to Doing Business: Region-by-Region Results from a Worldwide Survey of the Private Sector." World Bank Policy Research Working Paper No. 1759. World Bank, Washington, D.C.

World Bank. 1997. *World Development Report 1997*. Washington, D.C.: World Bank.

———. 1999a. *World Development Indicators 1999*. Washington, D.C.: World Bank.

———. 1999b. *World Business Environment Survey 1998–99*. Washington, D.C.: World Bank.

———. 2000. *World Business Environment Survey 1999–2000*. Washington, D.C.: World Bank.

CHAPTER 5

Dispute Resolution and Firms' Competitiveness in the MENA Region

Jeffrey B. Nugent

Despite the considerable progress of the Middle East and North Africa (MENA) region toward peace and political stability, the real gross domestic product (GDP) per capita has at best remained constant since 1985. This lack of economic growth is expressly due to population and labor force growth rates, which are the highest of any region in the world. The MENA region's performance has been no better than that of Sub-Saharan Africa and worse than that of all other regions except Eastern Europe.[1] Furthermore, with both the population growth momentum and the female labor force participation rate on the rise, rapid increase in the labor force is expected to continue for some time. As a result, MENA countries will have to substantially accelerate their economic growth rates if they are to avoid dangerously large increases in unemployment rates and further deterioration in labor productivity. Adding to this dilemma is the paradox that while the agricultural and service sectors of MENA economies are currently suffering from extreme underemployment, the open unemployment rates are by far the highest of any region in the world.[2]

Furthermore, despite a decade of talk about privatization, the MENA region also leads the world in the amount of wealth that remains in the state sector. Even at the margin—in terms of change in the stock of capital—more than half of the region's investment is still undertaken by the government. Yet, because of high debt to GDP ratios, on-going reductions of tariffs and other taxes, and the realization that the government cannot and should not extend its functions beyond the administrative capacity, it is the private sector that will have to provide both the impulse to that growth and the employment opportunities for the region's rapidly growing labor force.

There are, of course, two main strategies for achieving a transformation from state to private sector domination. One is privatization—yet in many countries this process has proved problematic because workers, managers, bureaucrats, and politicians often offer strong resistance. Even when privatization is not blocked in this way, it can occur only where the viable enterprises to be privatized will be of interest to the private sector in the end.

The other strategy is to create an attractive environment within which new private sector activities can develop. If MENA countries are to grow rapidly in the near future, it will require considerable structural change. Keeping in mind that even large privatized firms could play only a minor role in the future economy of the country,[3] the creation of an appropriate environment for nurturing private sector activities is likely to be far more important than privatization.

The creation of such an environment, however, requires a substantial change in the role of the state. As Page, Saba, and Shafik (1997) so aptly put it, the role will have to change "from player to referee." Only by withdrawing from the role of player in favor of the role of referee, which means getting the institutions "right," will MENA countries have a chance of developing the kind of environment that is conducive to a competitive, flourishing, and rapidly growing private sector. Getting institutions right means identifying, creating, monitoring, and enforcing the kinds of rules by which markets for new goods and services and productive factors can be created, nurtured, and made keenly competitive. Essentially, solid institutions will enable private firms to undertake the activities necessary to become internationally competitive.

Contrary to the assumption of traditional neoclassical economics, such institutions are vital to the efficient performance and growth of the economy. The creation of these institutions and their maintenance through monitoring and enforcement activities are by no means without cost, however. Indeed, these "transaction" costs can be sizable, in spite of the fact that each agent in the economy may be motivated to minimize them. In a primitive economy dominated by subsistence activities largely carried out within individual households, these transaction costs may be very low. As the volume and complexity of exchanges and contractual relationships (including those with governments and foreigners) increase, the importance of transaction costs increases substantially.[4] One component of these costs that grows especially rapidly in proportion to aggregate economic activity is the cost of dispute resolution.

As will be demonstrated below, MENA countries vary significantly in the extent to which they have made the necessary transitions in the role of the state and in identifying, implementing, and enforcing the rules that can reduce transaction costs and encourage private sector development. Some have made commendable progress in the last decade or so, especially in macroeconomic reforms—reducing budget deficits, stabilizing the money supply, and reducing inflation. Some have also liberalized regulations, especially those on trade and capital flows, lowered tax rates, and introduced new laws for investment and other activities of relevance to private sector development.[5] In general, however, we shall see that the costs of dispute resolution have become an increasingly serious problem throughout the MENA region, according to the entrepreneurs interviewed.

This chapter is organized as follows: first, we compare the relative importance of different constraints on private sector competitiveness both in individual MENA countries and between MENA and other regions, as reported by the entrepreneurs themselves. Next, we provide background on the evolution and characterization of dispute resolution mechanisms in the MENA region. Finally, we identify the benefits and costs of each of these dispute resolution systems, different ways in which the costs can be reduced, and best-practice examples wherever possible.[6]

What Firms Say about the Constraints on Their Competitiveness

Because of the aforementioned success of most MENA countries in controlling inflation and fiscal deficits and in liberalizing trade, it might not seem that institutions and rule setting would be a crucial problem. Indeed, government officials and international agencies have often used certain MENA countries, such as Jordan and Tunisia, as examples of how reforms should be undertaken. Consistent with this view, table 5.1 shows that businesspersons in the MENA region are the only ones who say that the most serious obstacle to doing business in these countries is an "inadequate supply of infrastructure," rather than "unfriendly regulations." Indeed, regulations on foreign currency, safety and environment, prices, and even labor were found to be among the least important constraints by MENA businesspersons. At first glance, therefore, institutional factors would not seem to be an important constraint on business activities.

If we dig a little deeper into these survey results, however, a different picture emerges—indeed, one in which institutional constraints in the MENA region are very important. For example, corruption was ranked the second most serious obstacle, tax regulations third, trade regulations fifth, and uncertainty of regulations sixth. For most of these categories, the MENA region's rankings of these obstacles were near the highest of all seven regions identified in the survey. Note also that "regulations on starting new operations," even though placed lower down in the rankings, are viewed in MENA as a stronger obstacle to doing business than in any other region except South and Southeast Asia. However, it is important to note that Jordan, Morocco, and the Palestinian territories of Gaza and the West Bank, which all have relatively strong institutions, represented the MENA region in this survey. Had the sample been more representative of the region, regulations would undoubtedly have been rated as considerably greater obstacles to doing business than indicated by the scores reported in table 5.1.

TABLE 5. 1 REGIONAL COMPARISONS OF INDEXES OF OBSTACLES
FOR DOING BUSINESS

Obstacle	World	MENA	DC	SSEA	LAC	SSA	EE
Financing	4.06	3.87	3.43	3.60	4.38	4.17	4.22
Labor regulations	3.50	3.22	4.17	3.83	3.98	3.47	2.95
Foreign currency regulations	3.16	2.50	2.50	3.58	3.01	3.47	3.31
Tax regulations	4.65	4.17	4.39	4.12	4.38	4.65	5.04
Policy instability	3.68	3.54	2.55	3.32	4.22	3.63	4.15
Safety or environmental regulations	3.24	2.93	3.52	3.32	3.46	3.36	2.90
Inflation	3.83	3.51	2.50	3.87	4.02	4.30	3.95
General uncertainty on costs of regulations	3.75	3.60	3.13	3.63	3.68	3.84	4.05
Crime and theft	3.88	2.19	2.76	3.37	4.45	4.27	4.13
Terrorism	2.38	1.68	2.17	1.76	2.86	2.28	2.58
Inadequate supply of infrastructure	4.02	4.55	3.11	3.91	4.47	4.31	3.94
Corruption	4.21	4.27	2.76	3.64	4.70	4.67	4.35
Regulations for starting new operations	3.22	3.38	3.34	3.67	3.22	3.24	3.05
Price controls	2.67	3.12	2.20	3.13	2.82	2.63	2.78
Regulations on foreign trade	3.45	3.78	2.67	3.54	3.64	3.57	3.61

Note: The MENA sample is rather small (109 firms) compared with 254 for developed countries (DC), 139 for South and Southeast Asian countries (SSEA), 474 for Latin American and Caribbean countries (LAC), 1,288 for Sub-Saharan African countries (SSA), 1,321 for Eastern European countries (EE), and 3,685 for the world as a whole. The MENA sample was confined to three entities (Jordan, Morocco, and the Palestinian territories of Gaza and the West Bank) believed to be among the most private business–friendly in the region.
Source: Brunetti, Kisunko, and Weder 1997.

Evidence in support of this point is provided in tables 5A.1–5A.3 in appendix 5A, which compare the scores of two well-known institutional indexes: the Fraser Institute's "Economic Freedom Rating" for 1975–95 and the Heritage Foundation's "Index of Economic Freedom" for 1998. The ratings generally indicate that MENA countries face more severe restrictions than countries in other regions. However, because the deeper level of analysis provided by these two indexes allows us to gauge the relative severity of specific constraints, it is possible to observe that while some are much more cumbersome in the MENA region than in other regions, others are actually significantly less binding. MENA countries demonstrated greater restrictions for capital flows, restrictions on banks, wage and price controls, property rights, regulations, and black market activities (serving as a proxy for foreign exchange regulations). However, in terms of inflation, rights to have currency abroad, government transfers, the top marginal tax rate, trade openness, and government consumption as a percentage of total consumption, many MENA countries have scores comparable to their non-MENA counterparts. The scores of several specific countries (Bahrain, Djibouti, Kuwait, and the United Arab Emirates) indicate lower restrictions in the form of tax rates and trade protection.

Table 5.2 presents the average scores on each of the components of the "obstacle to business operations" scores from firms in the same three MENA countries used in table 5.1 as well as those for the SSEA and DC samples. Clearly, even in this rather favorable sample of MENA countries, entrepreneurs are much more likely to feel disadvantaged with respect to the cost of doing business than their counterparts in the SSEA or DC samples. Indeed, 70 percent or more of sample MENA firms indicated that "unpredictability of the judiciary presents a major problem for my business operations" and that "it is never, seldom, or only sometimes true that, in the case of changes in laws or policies affecting my business operation, the government takes into account concerns voiced either by me or my business association." These responses make it clear that businesspersons in the MENA region feel that laws and regulations, and the processes of making, changing, enforcing, and applying them, are quite unfavorable to successful business operations.[7]

Although they are not done systematically across countries, there are some single-country surveys that give even more attention to the legal and administrative impediments to firms' competitiveness. For example, Lahouel's (1998) study of Tunisia found that 68 percent of the firms said that rigidity of administrative procedures represented a "fairly or very serious obstacle to their business." In Egypt the introduction of new products or changes in production techniques were reported to require the submission of both establishment and operation licenses, which both require much time to obtain (Anderson and Martinez 1996). Kanaan (1998) reported the results of a survey of businesspersons in Jordan in which 83 percent agreed that "bureaucratic impediments were very important obstacles to their business operations" and 68 percent agreed that "legislative and legal obstacles were very important." Included among the latter were the multiplicity of laws, frequent changes in and amendments to these laws, and their inconsistent application.

In an unusually detailed single-country study, Fawzy (1998) reports the results of a 1998 survey of Egyptian firms showing tax administration and commercial dispute settlement to be the two most severe constraints on their operations. Both such constraints, moreover, were reported to have increased in severity between 1994 (when a comparable survey had been undertaken) and 1998. Both obstacles were more serious on the domestic level than on the foreign level, for smaller firms than for larger firms, and for firms in industry, construction, and trade than for those in oil or tourism. In the case of tax administration, the problem is not the tax rates per se, but rather their application and administration by the tax authorities.

TABLE 5. 2 COMPARISONS OF THE RESPONSES CONCERNING OBSTACLES
TO BUSINESS OPERATIONS BY PRIVATE FIRMS FROM THE MENA REGION
WITH THOSE FROM SSEA AND DEVELOPING COUNTRIES

Percentage of firms responding that:	MENA	SSEA	Developing countries
Government never, seldom, or only sometimes sticks to its policy pronouncements (lack of policy credibility).	30	11	30
Affected businesses are never, seldom, or only sometimes informed about the process of developing new rules or policies.	63	42	44
It is never, seldom, or only sometimes true that in the case of important changes in laws or policies affecting my business operation the government takes into account concerns voiced by either my business association or me.	73	48	63
We fear retroactive changes in regulations affecting our business operations.	56	37	23
Laws and policies have become more predictable (+) or less predictable (–) in the last 10 years.	–0.08	+0.27	–0.13
I fear unconstitutional government changes accompanied by far-reaching policy surprises with significant impact on my business.	62	37	19
All in all, I perceive the state as an opponent to my doing business.	12	0	9
It is always true that firms in my line of business have to pay some irregular payments to get things done.	12	7	1
Firms in my line of business seldom or never know in advance the amount of this additional payment.	52	42	58
Even if a firm has to make an additional payment, it always has to fear that another official will ask for more.	6	3	0
In the last 10 years difficulties in dealing with government officials have increased.	31	20	21
I have decided not to make a major investment because of problems related to complying with government regulations.	46	29	35
The share of senior management's time spent on negotiating with officials about the changes and interpretations of laws and regulations exceeds 25 percent.	19	12	2
I rate the overall perception of the efficiency of the customs services as good or very good.	12	10	38
I rate the overall conditions of roads that I use as good or very good.	21	21	48
Power outages occur more frequently than once every three months.	43	46	16
It takes less than three months to get a telephone line connected.	33	68	94
I would rate the efficiency of the government in delivering services as efficient or very efficient.	4	31	23
Unpredictability of the judiciary presents a major problem for my business operations.	70	52	41

Note: The MENA (Middle East and North Africa) sample is rather small (109 firms) compared with 254 for developing countries and 139 for SSEA (South and Southeast Asian countries) and was confined to three countries or economies (Jordan, Morocco, and the Palestinian territories of Gaza and the West Bank) believed to be among the best in the region with respect to the environment for private business.
Source: Brunetti, Kisunko, and Weder 1997.

Of particular concern are the arbitrariness in the determination of taxable profits by tax administrators and the inefficiency of dispute resolution. "The central problem . . . is that the criteria for tax assessment are ambiguous, and tax collectors enjoy unlimited discretionary powers" (Fawzy 1998).

Similarly, in the case of dispute resolution, Fawzy showed the frequency and severity of disputes to be in the following declining order: bankruptcy, broken agreements, problems with the tax authority, and the quality of supplies. Almost two-thirds of the firms' disputes were with other private firms, 22 percent had disputes with government agencies, and the rest had disputes with banks, labor, and public enterprises. "Apart from being time-consuming, investors also complain that litigation is expensive and that the judicial system is not well acquainted with commercial disputes related to market economies" (Fawzy 1998). She also reported their complaints about the lack of contract enforcement mechanisms and poor enforcement of laws. Such details on the problems related to dispute resolution are rare in the survey literature and thereby motivate further investigation of the costs of dispute resolution failures.

One of these costs, and one that is relatively well documented, is the long time it takes to resolve a dispute through the formal judicial system. Basing his argument on a World Bank survey that he applied to Egypt's commercial cases, Galal (1996) stated that the clearance rate of such cases taken to the formal court system was only 36 percent compared with 80 percent in Japan and 88 percent in Belgium. At the same time, the average time needed for the minority of cases that were settled had increased from two years in the 1970s to over six years in the early 1990s. Anderson and Martinez (1996) report times to completion of the average commercial case to be two to two-and-a-half years in Jordan and Lebanon—again, countries with among the best judicial systems and judges in the region. These time delays are not atypical of other developing countries, but are growing rapidly.[8] Naturally, the longer it takes to resolve cases and the lower the resolution rate, the higher are the firms' transaction costs.

Another important problem with the dispute resolution system is inconsistency in judicial outcomes. This is a general problem. For example, the World Bank's *World Development Report 1999* disseminated the results of a survey of 3,600 firms in 69 countries which stated that more than 70 percent of those in the sample reported that an "unpredictable judiciary was a major problem." As noted above, various surveys in the MENA region have come to the same conclusion.

Still another problem in MENA countries and elsewhere is the perceived inequity or lack of equal access to dispute resolution systems. Small firms often feel disadvantaged relative to larger ones, and poor households relative to rich ones. Such perceptions of inequity often show up in broader public opinion surveys of the effectiveness of the judiciary. Typically, these reveal even worse evaluations. For example, the results of a Gallup poll in Argentina in the 1990s showed that only 13 percent of the population considered the judiciary to be an effective institution (Buscaglia and Dakolias 1996). Where this is the case, naturally the respect for both law and legal institutions is likely to be weak.

Dispute Resolution Systems in the MENA Region and Transaction Costs

Given the high and increasing importance that businesspersons in the MENA region attach to dispute resolution problems as constraints on their business operations, we turn now to a brief survey of historical trends in the character of dispute resolution systems and their implications for transaction costs and firm competitiveness.

Evolution of the MENA Region's Diverse Dispute Resolution Systems

MENA countries have inherited an unusual mixture of traditional and modern approaches to dispute resolution. Generally speaking, informal and traditional dispute resolution systems were dominant until the mid-19th century. Most disputes were settled at the local level by village heads, religious leaders, or by councils of elders. In areas where economic activity was dominated by a particular commercial activity, these disputes were taken to an informal tribunal of peers. For example, in Bahrain where pearling (collecting pearls from oysters located on the Gulf's sea bottom by diving from ships) was the leading activity, there was a diving court that settled disputes with considerable efficiency.[9] Similarly, in the regional bazaars were "amins," who acted as intermediaries between the modern system of dispute resolution and the informal network of producers (guilds). These amins mediated disputes between individual producers and their customers, on the one hand, and among individual producers, on the other. Clearly, these were times in which the informal system of dispute resolution dominated. Remnants of these traditional institutions are still in evidence in some rural areas and even in the bazaars, although they have been eclipsed by government institutions, trademarks, and competition from outside the guilds.[10]

Because of the commercial success of producers in MENA countries in the period between the 8th and 12th centuries and the preference of foreign merchants to use the legal systems indigenous to MENA countries (largely Islamic) rather than their own, it would appear that at that time, the region's indigenous Islamic and other legal systems were perceived to offer advantages over foreign ones. Nevertheless, over the course of the following centuries, European legal systems gradually evolved to provide considerably greater flexibility for businesses than those prevailing in the MENA region. For example, corporations became legal entities and a body of law specific to them emerged in Europe that did not surface in the MENA region. By the mid-19th century, however, MENA elites became aware that their systems were comparatively unprogressive in these respects and began importing legal institutions from Europe.

This may have been one of the reasons why local leaders agreed to allow foreign merchants and citizens to be exempted from the domestic legal system in favor of foreign law (capitulations). The capitulations also greatly undermined the acceptance of Western law by much of the region's population. In particular, it was perceived as imposed on them by foreign colonial powers. By exempting citizens of the colonial powers (who were very numerous by end of the 19th century) from taxes as well as from prosecution in native or mixed national courts, the population indigenous to the MENA region perceived the justice system to have a dual standard, thereby undermining the legitimacy of both the modern formal system and international arbitration in the minds of most indigenous citizens of MENA countries.[11] While this did not occur in all parts of the region and was gradually eliminated in the 1920s and 1930s, the influence on both the respect for justice and the resentment of foreign intervention was widespread.

A fresh start on modern court law was made in Turkey after World War I, in Egypt after World War II, and in many other countries of the region after their independence. The Egyptian civil law code of 1948 was modeled closely on the French civil code and, thanks to Egyptian law professors who helped construct the codes of other countries of the region, so too were those of most other countries in the region. In recent years, Anglo-Saxon common law and the use of arbitration and other alternative dispute resolution (ADR) methods have increasingly influenced Egypt and other countries in the region. This has been more noticeable in those parts of the region formerly under British influence such as the southern part of the Republic of Yemen, Bahrain, the United Arab Emirates, and Kuwait. The statist tradition in much of the region has generally limited the extent to which these newer developments have had an impact relative to other parts of the world.

Another impediment to the development of commercial dispute resolution systems in the MENA region has been the region's heavy reliance on public enterprise and hence on government regulations in support of these enterprises. It is not only difficult and extremely costly for private firms to challenge public enterprises, but most of these disputes have to go through administrative procedures rather than legal ones.

In principle, having a multiplicity of legal systems that include the traditional and Islamic systems, modern European civil law codes, and perhaps even some modern ADRs, could be beneficial. This multiplicity of systems allows for greater flexibility and more choices. In some MENA countries, however, the multiplicity has created basic inconsistencies and lowered the predictability of outcomes. For example, in the Republic of Yemen where the North had imported the Ottoman civil law system and the South had English common law, reunification of North and South in the 1990s has led to some severe inconsistencies in legal systems. Other disputes have resulted in several MENA countries where the governments prescribed the use of Islamic law despite the opposition of some commercial firms.

There is also ample evidence from the MENA region—and virtually everywhere else—that the demand for dispute resolution is growing extremely rapidly. Many factors lie behind these trends: commercialization, privatization, globalization, increasing competition among large multinational enterprises around the globe, and perhaps also the changing character of high-level managers and corporate lawyers (Dezalay and Garth 1996). In MENA countries these rather universal trends are aided by growing frustration on the part of the private sector with ambiguous government regulations, the arbitrary way in which they are interpreted, and the absence of an effective judicial system for seeking redress.

Transaction Costs Resulting from Imperfect Dispute Resolution

Each of the various dispute resolution problems in the MENA region identified above raises the transaction costs of doing business in the region. For example, delays in resolving disputes raise the costs for all involved parties, in terms of both time and money. They also discourage the disputing parties from making other possible contractual relationships with each other and with other actual or potential contractual partners. Inconsistencies in the outcomes of resolution lower the incentive to reach out-of-court settlements to such disputes for at least one of the parties, reinforcing delays, and distorting managerial decisions. Inconsistent outcomes, moreover, can increase risk and uncertainty for investors and hence lower investment and growth. Perceived inequities in the outcomes of the dispute resolution systems undermine respect for the system in general, including law and order, quite possibly encouraging individuals and firms to act outside the law. They also contribute to underdevelopment of the law itself, leaving firms with fewer options for solving their problems. To the extent that loose law enforcement prevents contracts from being enforced, it also gives the contracted parties incentives to undersupply effort, lower product quality, and renege on payments.

To the extent that property rights are undermined by these shortcomings, a variety of additional transaction costs may be added. Where the property rights laws or their enforcement are vague and incomplete, the true owners of any product, service, or resource cannot easily be identified. If so, any potential buyer has less incentive to buy a particular product since, by doing so, he might not gain legal ownership or possession of the product. This may cause the seller to settle for a lower price than expected, or even to avoid trying to sell it. At the same time, when the veracity of a seller's right of ownership is in question, the potential buyer may have to incur higher information or transaction costs, or both, in order to determine the authenticity of ownership. Even if the seller is the true owner of the item, if such costs are sufficiently high the fear that he may not be the true owner may discourage the buyer's willingness to purchase. If the transaction is undertaken but the seller's claim of ownership should turn out to be false, there may be additional costs to the buyer, such as costs incurred in obliging the seller to return his payment or to protect him from the true owner or anyone else who may try to take the item away from him. Incomplete or ambiguous property rights can also reduce the incentive for investment and hence growth. Without clear property rights, any property possessed will be less useful as collateral, reducing credit availability, again discouraging investment and growth. Moreover, to the extent that these shortcomings in the system discourage new entrants and competition and reinforce existing inequality, they may worsen income distribution and, because of the likely positive relationship between equity and growth, can further retard growth and development. Each of these effects raises the costs of doing business both absolutely and relative to what these costs are elsewhere and what they could be under ideal circumstances. In the case of weak intellectual property rights, there will be insufficient incentive to innovate and hence the rate of technological change can be reduced.

The higher such costs, the more suppliers will attempt to pass these costs on to their customers by increasing their selling prices. Even worse, in many cases, this may raise the price to such an extent that transactions do not take place, causing producers to exit from the industry or discouraging or preventing firms from entering the industry. More commonly, the higher transaction costs derived from lengthy and ill-managed dispute resolution systems have the effect of increasing the degree of vertical integration, thereby undermining specialization and the technological benefits thereof and decreasing the competitiveness and flexibility of the economy. The high costs of dispute resolution, and other institutional failures, therefore, can constitute a plausible explanation for the paradox of how, if capital is so scarce in developing countries, the rate of investment (including foreign investment) can be so low.

Alternative Means of Reducing the Costs of Resolving Disputes

There are three general means of reducing the costs of dispute resolution. One is to clarify or streamline laws and regulations in order to reduce ambiguity and the potential for conflict. This involves *legal reform*. The second is by improving the process and functioning of the judicial system, that is, by *judicial reform*. The third is by strengthening *informal or ADR* systems.

As the following review of these three strategies indicates, there is no universal best way of reducing the transaction costs arising from such conflicts. Each general approach has several variants, and for each variant and approach, there are advantages and disadvantages. Since countries, regions, and sectors of economic activity vary in their culture, behavioral norms, environmental conditions, sources of conflict, and social and economic objectives, all such considerations have to be given careful consideration in choosing how best to reduce this important and development-retarding source of high transaction costs. Attempts at reform are bound to face strong resistance from those vested interests that see advantages in preserving the status quo. Moreover, since many reforms are complicated and have a long gestation period, careful assessments of the effectiveness of different dispute resolution reform strategies are difficult to accomplish, and for this reason are rare. Nevertheless, wherever possible, in identifying the main alternatives within each such approach in the following sections, attempts are made to identify examples of best practice.

Reforming the Formal System through Legal Reform

Given that laws and regulations frequently arise from compromises (often behind closed doors) among groups with different backgrounds, objectives, and points of views, and are crafted with considerable uncertainty about the likely effects, laws are often not clearly written. Many such laws, moreover, are likely to have originated from a much earlier time, making them difficult to understand and limiting their relevance and effectiveness in the contemporary period.

The degree of ambiguity and lack of knowledge concerning relevant laws are increased by both the frequency of issuance of new laws by the legislature and binding presidential decrees issued by the executive branch, or other binding decrees issued by the relevant department, and inconsistencies between some of these laws and the way they are enforced. Such problems are more severe when the process and debate leading to these laws are as nontransparent as in the MENA region and firms feel excluded from the process. Worse still, the new laws are often only published with a considerable time lag, or are sometimes never published at all. All these factors increase the likelihood that most citizens and firms will lack familiarity with existing laws and regulations. Even when the laws are known, the monitoring and enforcement of these laws may be done by several different agencies, each with different methods for and criteria in enforcement. As a result, there can easily be substantial differences between actual practice and the method prescribed by law, and individuals and firms may be uninformed about one or the other or both.

Whatever the source of such ambiguities in laws or regulations, they are likely to give rise to conflicts among private parties because each party will have an incentive to interpret the law in a way favorable to his own interests. As a result, many essentially avoidable conflicts will end up in formal courts, tying up scarce legal personnel and court time that could be more usefully devoted to other issues.

What can be done to reduce these ambiguities and thereby reduce the costs of dispute resolution?

PROPERTY RIGHTS LAWS

One way to reduce ambiguities is to define or clarify property rights by rewriting particular laws. Incompleteness or ambiguity in property rights can arise from many sources, such as the absence of a written document of ownership or lack of clarity in the location of the property, the character of the rights (use rights, sale rights, bequeathal rights, rental rights, and so on) and the manner of the enforcement of property rights. Hence, laws clearly defining the scope of property rights and how the rights are to be enforced can help to remove ambiguities and dispute resolution costs. Also needed is a clear demarcation rule concerning the amount of waiting time before a claim can be considered legitimate (with regard to the law of adverse possession). Without irrefutable proof of ownership in the form of clearly specified rights, there is always the chance that someone with a stronger claim of ownership will subsequently appear. If the waiting time allowed is too long, productive investments by the possessor may be discouraged in the meantime, or alternatively made but wasted. On the other hand, if the waiting time is too short, the true owner's right of ownership may be compromised and absentee owners may be discouraged from making investments on the property.

Other problems have to do with the vagueness of the rights conferred. One source of vagueness may derive from the regulatory powers of local or other governments. These need to be made as distinct and clearly limited as possible. Since one of the benefits of clearly defined private property rights is the usefulness of such property as collateral, there should be a simple, accessible means of registration of titles to property and qualifying property as collateral. Titling has often been associated with property grabbing by elites who have much better access to titled property than the poor. When this property grabbing occurs, respect for private property and the law is undermined. For this reason, titling legislation should make the means of doing so as transparent and accessible as possible to the poor and to the small entrepreneur.

Different forms of property may need special clarification, standardization of terminology, and regulation. For example, in the case of land the land needs to be surveyed and clear, generally recognized, and boundaries defined. Conflicts and inconsistencies among laws of different levels of government should be avoided, that is, by giving local governments exclusive rights. While many land titling programs have not been very successful and others are too new to evaluate, some especially well-documented cases should be noted. One such case is that of Costa Rica in the 1830s and 1940s. As described by Nugent and Robinson (1999), local governments that competed with each other to attract settlers characterized the Costa Rican success. Using the provision of land and titles as incentives, the government was able to develop a long-gestation crop (coffee) early on, and along with it, a credit system based upon titled land as collateral. This credit system, in turn, helped foster the development of banks, technological change, education, productivity growth, and perhaps even democracy. Another much-studied case is that of Thailand in the early 1980s. Although this program was more limited in its extent and may have been more biased toward more well-established and wealthier farmers, the titled plots were rather small in size (as in the Costa Rican case) and thus much more egalitarian than in other cases. Numerous studies have demonstrated the effectiveness of titles in increasing the access to credit, and hence the productivity and investment of farmers possessing such title relative to those without title.[12]

What were some of the ingredients of these successful cases? One factor was that they took place at times when land was becoming increasingly scarce. Another was the low costs and transparent processes used at the local level. Third, the processes were accomplished gradually over a decade or more in order to assure adequate administration and monitoring. Titles were also made mandatory for proving property rights.

The means of protecting industrial property rights are likely to be quite different. In the case of equity shares of enterprises, it is important that the rights of minority owners be clearly specified and given special protection through detailed provisions of the law. Otherwise, minority shareholders will have little incentive to buy shares in private firms and equity markets will remain absent or underdeveloped. How can this be done? Some ways include amending law provisions, making it easier for such stockholders to call and attend meetings of the board of directors, to exercise their votes (that is, by absentee ballots), and to require independent audits.[13]

As MENA countries move up the technology ladder and attempt to attract environmentally clean industries such as computer software development and information technology, the extension of property rights legislation to intellectual property rights may become increasingly necessary. One important way to do this is by signing on to the Treaty on Intellectual Property Rights (TRIPS) or by modifying patent laws in ways suitable for such industries and activities, or both. Especially where speed of action is essential to enforcement, claims of infringements of property rights (such as of trademarks and licenses) must be handled expeditiously.[14] In other words, legal reform should be tied to clear, well-functioning judicial enforcement.

BANKRUPTCY LAWS

Another area of legal reform with scope for reducing the costs of dispute resolution is bankruptcy law. In general, MENA countries are believed to be deficient in bankruptcy law, implying that there is considerable potential for reducing the costs of dispute resolution through appropriate changes in bankruptcy laws. In the absence of any legally established bankruptcy procedure, a creditor may not have the right to seize the assets that the debtor has put up as collateral. Similarly, in the absence of collateral he may not have the right to petition a court to sell some of the debtor's assets to cover the debt. If the creditor cannot obtain repayment of the loans provided, he will either refrain from lending in the future, or will pass on his losses in the form of higher interest rates to nondefaulters, or both. In either case, this raises the costs of credit to firms in general, thereby reducing their competitiveness.

Even if a country does have bankruptcy laws, those laws can give rise to disputes, delays, and inefficiencies if they are not clear. For example, it is important for the law to specify exactly how soon after an apparent default on a debt an action to claim assets of the bankrupt firm can be taken, what kinds of assets can be used as collateral, and when and how the motion to the court can be made and the response obtained. If there are multiple creditors, the order of priority among the creditors must be specified or recognized by the law to avoid unnecessary conflicts and delay. At a minimum, the law should establish an orderly bankruptcy procedure when none is specified in the contractual relationship.

Most bankruptcy procedures involve several steps. First, an individual, firm, or bank to which a debt is owed petitions a court or government agency to put a lien on the assets of the alleged defaulter. Second, the authenticity of the creditor's claim is investigated. Third, if the claim is verified, an investigation is made into the most appropriate means of resolving the problem. The options range from outright liquidation of the defaulter's assets (and using the proceeds to at least partially compensate the creditors in a designated order of priority) to leaving the defaulter's assets intact but restructuring the firm in order to return it to viability. Finally, the decision on liquidation or restructuring is implemented (in the case of liquidation, the liquidation of collateral may also be implemented), and the creditors receive at least partial compensation. Even under the best of circumstances these steps take time, more so if any of these steps is clouded by ambiguity in the law or in the law's enforcement.

What would make for an effective bankruptcy procedure? In particular, it should be designed in such a way as to satisfy certain desirable objectives. First, the decision of what to do with the firm should be based on maximization of the total value of the assets. Second, these assets should be divided among the debtor and the creditors (and possibly other parties such as workers or the government) in such a way as to penalize managers and shareholders of the bankrupt firm. Third, it should establish a rational order of priorities among the claimants.[15] In the last, it is important that shareholders not be entirely neglected. Such an action would give them and their managers an incentive to undertake highly risky actions that may minimize the probability of bankruptcy—but at the cost of lower expected returns and higher probability of large losses.

If capital markets were perfect, information were complete and rapidly communicated, and the firm were worth more as a functioning enterprise than as an inactive one, then it would be appropriate to resolve the situation through a competitive auction of the firm as a whole. However, if these conditions are not satisfied (as seems likely), the law should require a structured bargaining procedure. In establishing such a procedure, care should be taken to avoid mixing the decision of what to do with the firm with the process of identifying priorities among the creditors. Mixing these issues could complicate the bargaining and lead to substantial delays. Restructuring, however, should not give creditors and shareholders perverse incentives that could lead them to a wrong decision about the firm's future.

How might this be avoided? A modified version of a proposal by Hart (1999) might be considered. In particular, once bankruptcy is demonstrated, an automatic debt-equity swap (with the amount of equity going to each creditor predetermined) could be carried out, thereby removing that issue from bargaining and making shareholders of all the parties.[16] This would give all parties the incentive to make the best decision about what to do with the firm. The new stockholders could elect a new board of directors who then could decide by majority vote what to do and how to do it, thereby also minimizing reliance on the already overcrowded courts to solve the problem.[17] Clearly, such a procedure would provide more flexibility in the restructuring process than most existing schemes. Hence, a good bankruptcy procedure could be achieved with a much lower transaction cost and court time than in the Chapter 11–type of bankruptcy procedure used in the United States and elsewhere.

Other desirable features of a bankruptcy law might be dictating a means of mediating disputes if none exists in the contractual relationship, and providing a framework for restructuring if experience in such is limited. Such a framework would be especially important if the aforementioned automatic debt-equity swap procedure is unavailable and previous experience in restructuring is limited. But what is mandated should be confined to process since, in general, the parties themselves will be in a better position to select the best substantive solution. The smaller the extent of previous experience with restructuring, the more narrowly defined the procedure should be. As far as substance is concerned, experience has shown that it is better to keep the agreement voluntary rather than mandated, although it may generally be useful to supply the parties with a menu of best practice alternatives. Both Thailand's 1998 and Indonesia's 1998 bankruptcy law reforms come close to this prescription—with the exception that neither country provided the automatic debt-equity swap at the beginning. Something of an exception should be made for a country such as Korea, in which the government enjoys great credibility for making objective and efficient decisions about what to do with the bankrupt firm, and other matters.[18]

Because current bankruptcy law and practice in MENA countries are far from optimal, there may well be a tendency to suggest radical change. The larger the deviation of legal prescription from current practice, however, the greater the likelihood that the legal prescription will not be converted into actual practice unless the government brings strong sanctions to bear on the different parties involved. Since reliance on government to use such powers is likely to introduce numerous additional problems, there is a case to be made for avoiding radical change and instead codifying some of the best of existing practice in the country.

Using the Peruvian experience, de Soto (1989) suggested that dispute resolution and firm transaction costs could both be reduced through legal and administrative reform—in particular, by removing or at least reducing unnecessary regulations imposed by laws and decrees. Such an approach may be especially desirable in those circumstances where the cost burden of such regulations is high due to the proliferation of regulations and laws. In such cases, economic activity may be pushed underground into the informal sector, or altogether eliminated, in either case at great cost to the society.

The lesson of such an experience is that each country should carefully and periodically go through its existing regulations and remove all those that are irrelevant, that conflict with others, or are inefficient in terms of benefits and costs. Regulations should be pruned down to those that matter to the welfare of society; then these selected regulations should be made as clear and transparent as possible. By eliminating the inconsistent and irrelevant or redundant regulations, it can become considerably easier for those agents following the regulations or subject to them to identify the relevant regulations. Otherwise, the regulated are likely to be ignorant of the regulations. There are good reasons for some regulations. However, for many others the costs outweigh the benefits, which suggests they should be removed or modified. For example, Galal (1996), Bechri (1999), and Lahouel (1998) suggest that regulations over prices and labor markets should be candidates for removal or substantial reduction since they greatly reduce the ability of firms to adjust to changing circumstances and to remain viable in the face of bad times. They may also contribute to the high rates of unemployment that characterize many of these countries.

The regulations that would be retained, moreover, should be purged of ambiguities since they increase the vulnerability of such regulations to arbitrary and unequal treatment by administrative authorities. Such circumstances give rise to corruption. One example of this is tax regulation, which (as noted above in 1998) was regarded by Egyptian businesspersons as the most important constraint on their business activities. Since any tax authority may have an incentive to overcharge and may be subject to political pressures, the likelihood of both disputes and corruption arising from any given regulation can be reduced by making the rules as transparent as possible, limiting the responsibility for their enforcement to a single agency, and allowing for appeal to an easily accessible independent appeal agency.

Reforming the Formal System through Judicial Reform

As has been demonstrated by many failed attempts to improve the economy by simply rewriting laws, legal reform is unlikely to be sufficient in itself. Good laws are worthless unless they are properly enforced. Proper enforcement, in turn, requires legal procedures that are clear, efficient, and deemed fair in allowing equal access and outcomes to citizens and firms of different types, and qualified and properly motivated personnel to carry out these procedures. Hence, for each of the above types of legal reforms, procedural reforms or reforms to the judicial system may also be required.

In particular, even the best of property rights law will not really protect property rights if the procedures for their enforcement are too ambiguous, time-consuming, and uncertain in outcome. Indeed, insufficient enforcement can be another important source of market failure and lack of development. Since rental markets are an important means for the landless poor or small enterprises to gain access to land and equipment, the failure to enforce rental contracts can harm both equity and the allocative efficiency.

In choosing the best way to accomplish judicial reform, four important objectives should be considered. These are (a) to limit the arbitrary power of the legislative and executive branches of government, thereby making government operate within the rule of law; (b) to increase the speed and efficiency of the judicial system; (c) to increase the consistency (or predictability) of judicial decisions; and (d) to improve access to the system. Each of these objectives can be approached in different ways.

The first of these objectives would seem of special importance in the state sector–dominated MENA region and may be the most difficult to accomplish since it requires establishing judicial independence. Only with judicial independence can private entrepreneurs and their investments be protected from the changing and arbitrary whims of partisan politicians and government commitments to the private sector be deemed credible.[19] How can judicial independence be achieved?

One such means is to place the judiciary's budget out of the reach of other branches of government. Another is to sharply limit the powers of members of the legislative and executive branches over the appointment, evaluation, and punishment-reward system of members of the judiciary. Still another strategy is to increase the education and training requirements of members of the judiciary and to strengthen its internal esprit de corps. Since judicial independence may not protect citizens and firms from the judiciary itself, there still may be need for external monitoring of the judiciary. The legislative or executive branches of government, however, should certainly not act as the exclusive or even primary monitoring agencies.

The case of El Salvador since the mid-1980s constitutes an excellent example of how judicial independence can be accomplished. Prior to that period, before the peace accords brought the country's long civil war to an end, El Salvador's judiciary was extremely politicized. Thus, the supreme court changed with each change in government and every member of the judiciary was appointed by political criteria rather than judicial competence. The judiciary was almost universally seen as corrupt and unfair, and as carrying out the will of the political elites. What was done to change this?

First, the judiciary's budget was taken out of the general budget managed by the executive and legislative branches. Instead, its budget was set by law at 6 percent of total government receipts. Second, the power of the national assembly and executive over judicial appointments and monitoring was greatly reduced by introducing a national judicial council dominated by members elected by law faculties and law associations. The council, rather than the government, was given the responsibility to identify a ranked list of candidates to send to the assembly for selection. Third, the government's influence was further weakened by regularizing the terms of judges and that of any single political group or party by requiring a two-thirds vote of assembly members for some of the judges rather than only a simple majority. Fourth, the council became the monitoring agency in charge of training, evaluating, and applying incentives to members of the judiciary. Fifth, through major improvements in training and supervision, the quality and esprit de corps of the judiciary were improved. According to the Inter-American Development Bank (1999), there is already considerable consensus that judicial independence measures have greatly improved both the efficiency and equity of the judicial system.[20]

Similarly, the speed and efficiency objective can be accomplished in several ways: (a) streamlining judicial procedures; (b) improving the information-storing and retrieval capabilities of the judiciary; (c) providing the judiciary with management training; (d) lengthening the (often short) work week of the judiciary; (e) stripping judges of their nonjudicial functions (such as administration and bookkeeping); (f) discouraging frivolous suits that can clog up court calendars and "crowd out" more socially important cases;[21] (g) substituting simple, substantively and procedurally efficient "rules" that can be easily monitored for violations, for more multidimensional "standards" in laws;[22] and (h) increasing the degree of specialization in judicial responsibilities.[23]

The third objective of attaining consistency in decisions can also be achieved in a number of ways. One way is by creating specialized courts, such as courts for small claims, bankruptcy, family disputes, property theft, commercial contract violations, and so on. A complementary means is by training judges in specialized fields, and by having them reviewed and evaluated by peers in the same field of specialization. Still another means is to increase the use of precedent, either by use of the common law (as in Anglo-Saxon countries) in which precedent plays a large role[24] or by codification of existing commercial norms and social norms encouraging efficient forms of cooperation (Cooter 1996). By increasing consistency in decisions, uncertainties about judicial outcomes can be reduced and, along with them, the costs of litigation, corruption, and barriers to contractual relations. In the process, respect for the law can also be increased.

The last of the four objectives—that of improving access to the formal legal system—is perhaps the most essential. Even if a country has the best constitution, the most unambiguous laws, and the most effective system of specialized courts, all those conditions will be of little use if the costs of using them are prohibitively high. For the judicial system to be respected as "fair," access to it must not be limited to the privileged insiders, the rich, or the government. Having courts that specialize in small claims or in issues of special relevance to small firms can help in this regard, as can other measures that increase the efficiency and speed of the judicial system. If (as in Egypt) the revenues from commercial law courts are used to cross-subsidize criminal courts, access to commercial cases can be improved by simply removing the cross-subsidy component of the fees (Giugale and Mubarak, 1996). Consideration should also be given to subsidizing small firms' and the poor's access to the formal system.

While the costs of various means of achieving these reforms may be relatively easy to measure, the benefits are likely to prove more difficult to estimate. Notably, however, the World Bank has been trying to quantify judicial outputs more effectively, that is, by measuring the quality of judicial outcomes, weighting the quantity of judicial decisions by their quality, and adjusting for the complexity of the cases.[25] Another means of identifying benefits is to ask the entrepreneurs themselves how much their trade, investment, or other activities would increase if the formal judiciary were improved.[26] Still another is to construct a proxy measure of the efficiency of the judicial system at the aggregate (country) level, and relate the variation in such a measure across countries to the variation in income levels or alternatively to variations in income growth rates across countries.[27] Finally, another approach is to evaluate trends in the resulting hedonic pricing method. For example, in Brazil it is estimated that, after controlling for quality and other characteristics, apartment rental rates are some 20 percent higher in those cities and towns in which the courts are especially slow in processing evictions relative to those cities and towns where evictions can be obtained quickly.

While comparable benefit-cost calculations that gauge these various mechanisms' ability to improve the effectiveness of the formal judicial system are seldom available, several general conclusions can be drawn. First, throwing more money at the judiciary is not in itself a solution.[28] Second, as the complexity of the issues involved increases, so do the judicial costs, thereby decreasing most conventional measures of efficiency. Some factors lying behind such complexity are difficult to treat, such as the number of parties to the contracts, their heterogeneity, and technological issues. Other sources of complexity, however, are avoidable, such as by reducing the ambiguities or inconsistencies in existing laws, or by reducing the number of resolution-delaying legal maneuvers that are possible when the lawyers are paid by the court and compensated by time spent on the case. Since poverty of the plaintiff often contributes to delays by giving defendants an incentive to delay, a case can be made for providing legal assistance to poor plaintiffs.

While these conclusions may be excessively general, the potential for substantial cost savings through judicial reform can be detected by a judicial survey.[29]

Developing and Encouraging the Use of Alternative Dispute Resolutions

The last alternative means of lowering the costs of dispute resolution is through the strengthening of so-called ADR measures. ADRs are of two general types: traditional and modern. The former is often characterized by dispute avoidance (before the fact) as opposed to the second type, dispute resolution (after the fact). Under the right circumstances, however, both may be lower in cost than more formal means of dispute resolution, and, for this reason, should be encouraged.

TRADITIONAL INFORMAL MECHANISMS AND THEIR ADVANTAGES

There are two special features of traditional ADRs that tend to reduce costs—their greater reliance on reputation (by selecting parties to contracts who are more reliable and less prone to wind up with disputes) and mediation and arbitration procedures that may limit the scope of conflicts and resolve them more quickly and amicably.

The advantages of traditional ADRs are likely to be especially strong in relatively simple societies, well endowed with trust, social capital, and other social norms that encourage people and firms to fulfill their contractual and other obligations. In such contexts each has an incentive to establish a good reputation for being a reliable contractual partner or member of a mutual insurance society. Informal networks can also be used to support multiparty or collective enforcement mechanisms. For example, the penalty that may be exerted on a trader who defaults on payment to a producer without going to court may be considerably greater when many producers boycott that trader than when only the original producer does so (Greif 1996). Another characteristic of such societies is the existence of social norms underpinning the desire for reputation, cooperation, and collective enforcement. Sometimes these norms can be so well embedded in the society that they are internalized. In this case, because all parties may feel sufficiently badly if they were to violate this norm, they would simply never do so. Naturally, this can greatly reduce the need for legal penalties and hence also the need for a formal judicial system (Granovetter 1985).

The maintenance of informal systems, however, is not necessarily without cost. Indeed, the gift exchanges, the costs of hospitality, the provision of help when needed in such a setting, and the maintenance of informational networks in the face of modernizing influences can all be quite costly. Moreover, the usefulness of these mechanisms for dealing with contractual relations and dispute avoidance may be subject to rapidly diminishing returns as distance increases. Furthermore, while these norms and collective enforcement mechanisms may reduce transaction costs and increase exchanges among members within groups, they may actually discourage interactions between separate groups.

A device suitable for reducing the likelihood of disputes in more modern societies is the credit bureau. The credit bureau aims to mimic the role of the village network. It collects information on the reliability and reputation (that is, credit-worthiness) of potential contractual partners and then makes this information available to those parties looking for contractual partners (Klein 1992). A problem, however, is that the creation of the credit bureau is subject to free-riding.

MODERN FORMS OF ALTERNATIVE DISPUTE RESOLUTIONS

In urban areas of modern societies where such institutions are often no longer functional, there may exist professional mediators and arbitrators. Some services of these kinds are provided by governments, often by local governments; others are provided by NGOs, including professional associations and international arbitration centers; and others by private individuals or firms. These ADRs take an ever-increasing number of forms, such as dispute review boards, contract administrators, partnering, dispute resolution advisors, negotiation, mediation, expert determination, and a large variety of arbitration methods.

Despite the fact that in modern settings, these methods may not have the informational and stability-of-norm advantages of traditional settings, virtually all these forms of ADR are still likely to have several important advantages over the more formal methods. With fewer agents involved and with simpler procedures than are found in formal courts, they are likely to be faster. Being faster and having less complicated procedures, the informal mechanisms of dispute resolution are also likely to be considerably cheaper. Since the choice of mediator or arbitrator is that of the parties themselves, they can choose experts with considerable training and experience in the subject matter of the dispute, thereby avoiding the time required to educate the judge and possibly a jury on the relevant legal issues. Because these are private processes, mediation and arbitration can provide greater privacy concerning the nature of the conflict than if the parties went through public courts (which work best when they are open). Since these forms of ADR are more completely under the control of the disputing parties, these parties are less likely to complain that the process is out of control and on a path determined largely by lawyers and formal court procedures. As an essentially private process (in contrast to a judicial system), the private and social costs are likely to be much closer (if not identical) than in the case of litigation, where the social costs generally exceed the private costs and thereby suggest that litigation in the formal system is likely to be excessive.[30]

When one of the parties to the dispute is foreign, another advantage (for that party at least) is obtained when the procedure is taken out of the courts of the other party's country in which the domestic party may be seen to have an "unfair" advantage. Last but not least, because they are far less confrontational than the suits and countersuits of formal legal systems, such ADRs increase the likelihood that profitable contractual or other relationships between the disputing parties can be reinstated once the dispute is resolved.

Of course, there are also disadvantages of these more informal legal mechanisms relative to formal ones. In particular, since ADRs are done with the consent of the parties involved, there can be delays in getting one of the parties to agree to commence the process. For the same reason, each conflict resolution is extremely case- and party-specific, making consistency among similar kinds of cases less likely. Another disadvantage, especially in cases where the courts are not involved, is that the decisions may be nonbinding, especially when the ADR takes place outside the country. Hence, eventually, if one of the parties defaults on the agreement or decision, the other may have to resort to formal legal action even after having had a decision, reached by the ADR. If so, any cost advantage of having used the ADRs rather than the formal system may disappear. The comparative advantage and cost savings of ADRs also tend to decline sharply as the number of parties involved increases.[31] Since such procedures are much more common in industrial countries, skilled personnel to carry out ADRs may be in short supply in some developing countries. Finally, some forms of ADRs may be of little use in cases involving government.

These disadvantages, however, can be overcome in various ways. For example, their nonbinding character can be overcome by formal laws decreeing them to be legally binding and enforceable in court. Enforceability can also be enhanced when the judge himself serves as a mediator or makes a decision that the case must be taken to another mediator or arbitration court. Such procedures are allowed for under the civil codes of many countries.[32] Potential lack-of-consistency can be overcome by establishing a common framework for the particular form of ADR in a certain industry or country and encouraging the local development of a corps of professionals with similar training and experience. The lack of enforcement of an ADR conducted outside the country can be overcome if the host country signs the United Nations Convention on the Recognition and Enforcement of Foreign Arbitral Awards of 1958 (more popularly known as the "New York Convention"). This convention automatically makes foreign arbitral awards locally enforceable.[33] If a country's sense of sovereignty is threatened by using arbitration centers outside the country, the "foreignness" of international arbitration proceedings can be reduced if the country has a sufficiently satisfactory legal framework for arbitration and the quality and quantity of infrastructure to encourage the establishment of an International Arbitration Center in the country.

For each such means of compensating for the weaknesses of ADRs, however, there are also disadvantages. Hence, tradeoffs have to be evaluated. For example, whenever the formal system is to enforce or otherwise get involved with an ADR, it is likely to impose some more formal procedures on them. Such procedures might include the requirement that any agreements reached are put in writing, and that the agreement be preceded by another agreement to arbitrate (or mediate). Formal courts may also limit the types of disputes that can be settled through ADRs, set guidelines for the eligibility of persons to serve as arbitrators or mediators, and allow appeals of ADR agreements to the formal system. Frequently such interfaces with the formal system will slow down the resolution process. The lack of skilled personnel to manage ADRs domestically can be overcome through the use of incentives promoting their supply but may require either the use of foreigners or the underwriting of the costs of training nationals.

When seeking to arrive at the optimal tradeoffs, there are other choices to be made concerning the exact form of ADR to be used. These include whether the specific form of ADRs should be contract-mandated or strictly voluntary, whether or not the decisions arrived at should be considered legally binding, how early in the contractual relationship the ADR technique should be initiated, the method for choosing the person or persons to do the mediating, the schedule of when such choices should be made, and whether these individuals should be internal or external to the contractual relationship.[34] Surveys on these options are provided by Jones (1999) and USAID (1998).

Although comparable measures of the demand and productivity of ADRs across countries and over time are generally lacking, anecdotal evidence seems to make it clear that the use of ADRs has been growing relative to that of the formal court system, worldwide. While a major determinant of this is the growing backlog and delays of the formal system, another may be their relative efficiency and lower cost.[35]

Even under the best of circumstances, such as when there is a broad mandate for reform, the formal judicial system may be difficult to reform, as recent experience in Latin America and especially Eastern Europe has suggested. Legislators have to be convinced to change the laws to incorporate needed reforms and, when they do so, have to resist pressures to back away from the reforms. Then the procedures and qualified personnel have to be in place to implement, monitor, and enforce laws. If the formal system is the only legal means of resolving disputes, and members of the judiciary maintain the present system in their own interest, reform may be even more difficult. If for no other reason than to introduce competition among systems, measures to encourage the use of ADRs such as by increasing their legitimacy and effectiveness may be well justified. Once viable alternatives to the services of the formal system emerge, and those supplying them are faced with loss of business to these alternatives, even the most corrupt members of the judiciary may see it in their self-interest to accept reform of the formal system.

Another reason for promoting ADRs is their comparative advantage for small and medium-size enterprises (SMEs) and the poor. To the extent that ADRs will therefore allow SMEs to protect their legitimate interests vis-à-vis large firms, their encouragement may enhance the competitiveness of the economy, the dynamic efficiency and perceived legitimacy of institutions, and the respect for law, all of which could help accelerate development.

Actions that could be taken to encourage the development and use of ADRs in the MENA region are:

- To either allow or require certain kinds of cases to be taken out of the judiciary to specialized ADRs

- To recognize the decisions reached by ADRs as legitimate and enforceable by the formal system[36]

- To increase knowledge of the availability of domestic ADRs, based on their experience elsewhere

- To encourage professional associations of private individuals and groups to organize and provide standards for the supply of such services and peer review of their quality

- To overcome the vulnerability of the development of credit bureaus to free-riding by appropriate forms of encouragement

- To encourage the development of small business associations (independent of government) with means of practicing collective enforcement such as by blacklisting parties that default on contracts with association members.[37]

- Given the strong preference by foreign companies for extraterritorial arbitration procedures over national courts,[38] to sign on to both the United Nations (U.N.) Convention on the Recognition and Enforcement of Foreign Arbital Awards and the Model Law on International Commerce Arbitration put forward by the U.N. Commission on International Trade Law (UNCITRAL). The latter can help to attract an international arbitration center to the country, possession of which will naturally make any arbitration awards reached under its auspices seem less "foreign" and more acceptable. Having a center should also help the arbitration culture spread more fully through the society, increasing the supply of skilled practitioners, and increasing the accessibility of ADRs.

- For countries in which the host country's government or public enterprises may be involved in contracts with foreign investors, to sign on to

the 1965 Washington Convention for the Settlement of Investment Disputes between States and Nationals of Other States. This convention allows such cases (with the consent of both parties) to be submitted to
arbitration under the auspices of the International Center for Settlement
of Investment Disputes in Washington, D.C.

A comparison of the Islamic Republic of Iran and Indonesia provides dramatic
illustration of how far some MENA countries must go in terms of ADR development to be able to attract private foreign investment on any large scale. In Iran, for
a dispute involving the government or a public enterprise to go to an ADR—either
domestic or international—an act of parliament (the Majlis) is required (Entezari
1997). By contrast, in a best-practice country such as Indonesia that has been especially successful in attracting foreign investment, this can be written into contracts
and the process is automatic, requiring no further approvals (Hornick 1991). It
should be mentioned, moreover, that the strong preference of foreign firms for
international arbitration as a means of dispute resolution also encourages domestic
firms to agree to arbitration by virtue of a substantial price differential in contract
terms in favor of ADR.

Conclusions

From the above discussion it should be clear that there are several different ways
to reduce the costs of dispute resolution, while simultaneously encouraging private sector development. Since to some extent they are alternatives to one another,
each with advantages and disadvantages, each country should consider seriously
the relative benefits of each alternative relative to its own conditions before choosing its optimal reform strategy. Because of substantial differences among MENA
countries in (a) the character and strength of their existing formal and informal
judicial systems, (b) the degree of ambiguity in existing law, (c) the extent to
which complementary reforms have been or are being undertaken, and (d) the
extent to which privatization and private sector development are important social
objectives, no single approach is likely to fit all countries of the region.

Recent experience with legal and judicial reform in Latin America and in the
transition economies of Central and Eastern Europe, however, has demonstrated
that successfully accomplishing either of these reforms is quite difficult. Indeed,
the greatest success (that in El Salvador) has occurred only when both the legal and
judicial reforms were done simultaneously with massive external pressure, foreign
assistance, as well as with tremendous pressure from below, the latter backed up by
the threat of renewal of the civil war. In view of that, judicial reform should be
thought of as a complement to legal reform rather than a substitute. Similarly, a
healthy ADR system can offer alternatives to formal dispute resolution systems
that are likely to be more suitable to some firms, countries, and circumstances

than to others. When such alternatives are available, the competition they provide may make reform of formal systems easier. All three approaches may therefore be complementary in the broader sense, perhaps explaining why Singapore, a country in which all three approaches are well developed and well functioning (Chan 1998), scores so well on all institutional indicators in tables 5A.1–5A.3.

MENA countries would do well to consider some of the following, more general lessons:

1. There is no evidence that legal and other reforms should be undertaken far ahead of other reforms. At the same time, they must not lag too far behind other reforms if the conflict-resolution system is not to become a major constraint on efficient exchange and development.

2. Even though transplantation of constitutions and entire legal systems from one country to another is unlikely to be either successful or appropriate, with suitable adaptations to local circumstances, best practices elsewhere with respect to individual laws are more effectively and easily transplantable.[39]

3. Existing interest groups may impede even socially beneficial reforms to conflict-resolution systems if they see these reforms as threatening to their interests. Hence, if such reforms are to succeed, they must get around such potential opposition by incorporating them into the process.

4. Success in judicial reform may be quite unrelated to the amount of money spent on such reform, making it wise to aim at relatively low-cost, less ambitious reforms, especially in the early stages.

5. This experience has again illustrated the point that the types of reforms instituted need to be molded to the circumstances and historical and cultural endowments of the individual country—"One size and model does not fit all."

6. In view of the long time interval required for formal legal and judicial reforms and the likelihood of opposition by judges and lawyers to some reforms, it may be useful to emphasize more informal methods of dispute resolution.

7. Even though the judiciary needs to be independent from the legislative and executive branches of government, it too needs to be monitored by an independent agency, preferably by one dominated by professional peers but also including representatives of a broad range of political opinion.

Appendix 5A. Institutional Indicators

TABLE 5A.1 ALTERNATIVE AGGREGATE INDEXES OF ECONOMIC FREEDOM

Country	Economic freedom rating (maximum = 10)[a]					Index of economic freedom (maximum = 5)[b]	
	1975	1980	1985	1990	1995	1995	1998
MENA							
Algeria	2.6	1.5	1.5	2.1	1.9	1.85	1.75
Bahrain	7.2	6.4	7.0	7.1	6.7	3.30	3.40
Djibouti						2.00	1.80
Egypt, Arab Rep. of	2.1	2.7	3.2	4.2	4.0	1.50	1.65
Iran, Islamic Rep. of	4.7	2.5	2.7	3.2	2.9	0.30	0.30
Iraq						0.10	0.10
Jordan	4.4	5.3	5.6	4.7	5.4	2.10	2.25
Kuwait						2.60	2.60
Lebanon						2.05	1.75
Libya						0.30	0.30
Morocco	4.2	3.6	4.2	3.5	4.6	2.10	2.05
Oman	5.6	5.8	6.8	6.6	6.3	2.35	2.25
Saudi Arabia						2.10	2.20
Syrian Arab Rep.	3.7	3.2	2.8	3.4	2.7	0.80	1.00
Tunisia	3.1	3.0	2.7	4.3	4.7	2.15	2.25
Turkey	2.5	2.3	3.7	4.8	4.5	2.00	2.20
United Arab Emirates						2.90	2.90
Yemen, Rep. of						1.25	0.90
Non-MENA							
Singapore	6.4	6.8	7.7	8.3	8.2	3.75	3.70
Taiwan, China	4.8	5.3	5.4	6.2	6.8	3.05	3.05
Switzerland	7.0	7.2	7.4	7.3	7.4	3.20	3.10
United Kingdom	5.1	4.6	6.2	6.7	7.3	3.05	3.05
United States	7.0	7.2	7.4	7.3	7.4	3.10	3.10

Note: In the above table the original index (which was an inverse measure of economic freedom) was inverted by subtracting the score given from 5 (the highest possible score on the original index).
a. Gwartney, Lawson, and Block 1997.
b. Holmes, Johnson, and Kirkpatrick 1998.

TABLE 5A.2 COUNTRY SCORES ON THE COMPONENTS OF THE INDEX
OF RESTRICTIONS ON ECONOMIC FREEDOM, 1998

Country	Trade protec- tion	Tax rate	Govern- ment inter- vention	Mone- tary policy	Cap- ital flows	Restric- tions on banks	Wage and price con- trols	Prop- erty rights	Regula- tions	Black market
Algeria	5.0	3.5	3.0	3.0	3.0	3.0	3.0	3.0	3.0	3.0
Bahrain	2.0	1.0	3.0	1.0	2.0	2.0	2.0	1.0	2.0	1.0
Djibouti	4.0	2.0	5.0	1.0	3.0	3.0	3.0	3.0	4.0	4.0
Egypt	5.0	4.5	3.0	3.0	3.0	3.0	3.0	3.0	4.0	3.0
Iran	5.0	5.0	5.0	4.0	5.0	5.0	4.0	5.0	4.0	5.0
Iraq	5.0	5.0	5.0	5.0	5.0	5.0	5.0	5.0	4.0	5.0
Jordan	4.0	2.5	3.0	2.0	2.0	2.0	3.0	2.0	3.0	4.0
Kuwait	2.0	1.0	4.0	2.0	4.0	3.0	3.0	1.0	2.0	2.0
Lebanon	5.0	2.5	2.0	5.0	3.0	2.0	2.0	3.0	3.0	5.0
Libya	5.0	5.0	5.0	2.0	5.0	5.0	5.0	5.0	5.0	5.0
Morocco	5.0	3.5	3.0	1.0	2.0	3.0	3.0	3.0	3.0	3.0
Oman	2.0	3.5	4.0	1.0	3.0	4.0	3.0	2.0	2.0	2.0
Saudi Arabia	4.0	4.0	4.0	1.0	4.0	3.0	3.0	1.0	2.0	2.0
Syria	5.0	5.0	3.0	5.0	4.0	5.0	4.0	4.0	2.0	5.0
Tunisia	5.0	3.5	3.0	2.0	2.0	2.0	2.0	3.0	2.0	3.0
Turkey	2.0	4.0	2.0	5.0	2.0	2.0	3.0	2.0	3.0	3.0
United Arab Emirates	2.0	1.0	3.0	1.0	4.0	3.0	3.0	1.0	2.0	1.0
Yemen, Rep. of	5.0	3.0	4.0	5.0	2.0	4.0	3.0	4.0	4.0	5.0
Singapore	1.0	3.0	1.0	1.0	1.0	2.0	1.0	1.0	1.0	1.0
Taiwan, China	2.0	2.5	2.0	1.0	3.0	3.0	2.0	1.0	2.0	1.0
Switzerland	2.0	3.0	3.0	1.0	2.0	1.0	2.0	1.0	3.0	1.0
United Kingdom	2.0	4.5	2.0	1.0	2.0	2.0	2.0	1.0	2.0	1.0
United States	2.0	4.0	2.0	1.0	2.0	2.0	2.0	1.0	2.0	1.0

Source: Holmes, Johnson, and Kirkpatrick 1998.

TABLE 5A.3 COUNTRY SCORES ON THE COMPONENTS OF THE ECONOMIC
FREEDOM RATING FOR 1995

Country	1A	1B	1C	1D	2A	2B	2C	2D	2E	2F	3A	3B	4A	4B	4C	4D
Algeria	6	2	0	0	2	0	2	5	0	0	—	—	—	1	5	2
Bahrain	10	8	10	10	0	2	4	5	0	8	10	10	9	10	5	2
Egypt	8	4	10	10	8	0	2	2.5	0	10	4	3	5	6	5	0
Iran	1	2	0	0	6	2	2	2.5	0	0	8	4	6	1	3	0
Jordan	10	10	0	0	1	6	2	5	2.5	6	8	—	4	8	9	2
Morocco	10	10	0	0	4	2	4	5	0	8	8	3	1	8	5	5
Oman	10	4	10	10	0	4	4	2.5	2.5	10	8	10	9	10	5	2
Syria	3	6	10	0	6	2	0	2.5	0	0	—	—	6	0	6	0
Tunisia	10	10	0	0	4	2	6	5	0	8	5	—	1	8	8	5
Turkey	0	1	10	10	7	4	5	7.5	0	0	5	4	9	7	3	2
Singapore	10	10	10	10	6	8	8	7.5	0	10	9	9	10	10	10	10
Taiwan	10	10	10	10	4	6	6	7.5	5	10	5	5	8	10	5	5
Switzerland	10	9	10	10	5	8	6	10	10	10	2	8	8	10	4	10
United Kingdom	9	9	10	10	2	6	9	10	7.5	10	2	5	10	10	5	10
United States	10	10	10	10	5	8	9	10	7.5	10	3	7	9	10	3	10

No.	Definition of component	No.	Definition of component
1A	Inflation rate	3A	Transfers and subsidies as percent of GDP
1B	Standard deviation of inflation rate	3B	Top marginal tax rate and threshold
1C	Ability to own foreign currency		
1D	Ability to maintain a bank account abroad	4A	Taxes on trade as percent of exports plus imports
		4B	Black market premium
2A	Government consumption as percent of total consumption	4C	Measure of trade openness (actual relative to predicted trade share in GDP)
2B	Relative importance of government enterprise	4D	Freedom to make investment transactions with foreigners
2C	Extent of wage and price controls		
2D	Entry into business		
2E	Equality of citizens under the law		
2F	Extent to which government regulations distort real interest rates and disrupt credit markets		

Note: In each case the scores are assigned in such a way that a high score indicates economic freedom on the dimension measured, the index ranging from 0 to 10.
Source: Gwartney, Lawson, and Block 1997.

Notes

1. See Anderson and Martinez 1996; World Bank 1985, 1999a [p. 164], 1999b.

2. The open unemployment rate was estimated to average 15 percent in 1993 (World Bank 1995).

3. Krueger (1992) estimates that in the rapidly growing Republic of Korea 80 to 90 percent of GDP in the mid-1970s was accounted for by factors of production, which were employed in a very different activity in the early 1960s.

4. Wallis and North (1986) estimated that such costs for the United States were about 22.5 percent of GNP in 1870, and had risen to some 40.8 percent of GNP by 1970. Even though these costs may seem high, they do not include transport or transformation costs.

5. According to Kanaan (1998), Jordan was found to be a case in point with its recent reforms in tariff reduction, tax reduction, financial market liberalization, securities market reform, and privatization. Indeed, a well-known consultancy—Stanford Research Institute International— was asked to undertake a study that would resolve this paradox.

6. The author is extremely appreciative of comments received from Samiha Fawzy, Ahmed Galal, John Page, and other participants at the preliminary meeting in December 1999 as well as useful suggestions from Rick Messick, Lynn Hammergren, Margaret Popkin, and Andrew Stone.

7. Additional cross-country comparisons of institutional characteristics are available from foreign investors. One such widely cited source with good country coverage is the *Political Risk Yearbook*. Most MENA countries score just as badly (compared with the non-MENA countries) on the characteristics evaluated by foreign investors as on the above indicators developed from the responses of businesspersons in general.

8. For example, in 1993 it took 2.5 years to dispose of a case on average in Argentina, 1.9 years in Ecuador, and 2.4 years in Venezuela. In all three countries, both backlog and median delays were increasing over time at rates ranging from about 15 to 30 percent per year, and were more serious for commercial cases than for civil ones (Buscaglia and Dakolias 1996).

9. For details and references, see Datta and Nugent 1991.

10. For an interesting description of the historical role of the amins and their marginalization in contemporary Tunis, see Kuran 1989.

11. For evidence and discussion of the capitulations, see Issawi 1982 and El-Kosheri 1998. An analysis of the determinants of these capitulations and of the key elements of the relative decline of Islamic law and its consequences for industrial development is provided by Kuran 2000.

12. See Feder and Onchan 1987, 1989 and Feder and others 1988. The exclusive role of the local government and transparency of the titling system have generally not been adhered to in Brazil, which is perhaps responsible for the much weaker results (Alston, Libecap, and Schneider 1996).

13. La Porta, Lopez De Silanes, Schleifer, and Vishny (1998) use quantitative indicators of various aspects of creditor and investor rights and their enforcement from a sample of 49 countries of different legal traditions to show that these indicators are significantly lower for the civil-law countries that do not have such provisions than for the common-law countries that have them. Three MENA countries (Egypt, Jordan, and Turkey) were included in the sample of civil-law countries. They also showed that shareholdings were less dispersed and more highly concentrated in the countries of the French civil-law tradition than in the other countries. In a parallel study of bank sources of finance, Levine (1999) shows that financial intermediaries are also less developed in the countries of the civil-law tradition because of their weaker protection of creditors. He also shows that, once one controls for these individual legal provisions, there is no longer any significant difference in the concentration or dispersion of shareholders between civil-law and common-law countries. Hence, if MENA countries were to adopt creditor- and investor-friendly laws, and were to enforce them, MENA countries would be at no disadvantage relative to common-law countries.

14. See, for example, al Tamimi 1995.

15. For example, it could put secured lenders first, in the order in which they provided credit, then unsecured lenders (again, in order of their loans), and finally shareholders (perhaps again prioritized by type).

16. In a context where workers' rights as stakeholders are believed to be fundamental to any socially desirable solution, they, too, could be included in this process.

17. Rowat and Astigarraga (1999) provide examples from Latin America of excessive rigidity even in some of the procedures introduced under judicial reform.

18. Since the Korean government enjoys a much better reputation in this respect than Indonesia, this may explain why giving the government mandatory powers to arrive at a substantive solution might well be "best practice" for Korea, whereas prohibiting government from assuming such powers and thereby keeping the program strictly voluntary may be best practice for countries such as Indonesia (Gitlin and Watkins 2000).

19. See North 1990; Williamson 1995; Levy and Spiller 1993; Trebilcock 1997; Brunetti, Kisunko, and Weder 1997; and Henisz and Zelner 1999.

20. For example, cases that were taking two-and-a-half years to resolve prior to reform were taking an average of only four months after the reform. For a somewhat less positive evaluation of the Salvadoran experience, see Popkin 2000.

39. Cornell and Kalt (1995) show that the degree of success in transplanting a constitution drawn up by the Bureau of Indian Affairs in the United States for Indian reservations throughout the country varied with the extent to which pre-existing political systems were consonant with the imposed new constitution. Englebert (forthcoming) makes a similar point in the context of the legitimacy of the state in Africa.

Bibliography

The word *processed* describes informally reproduced works that may not be commonly available through libraries.

al Tamimi, Essam. 1995. "United Arab Emirates Trademarks Law." *International Lawyer* February: 76–80.

Alston, Lee J., Gary Libecap, and Robert Schneider. 1996. "Violence, and the Assignment of Property Rights on Two Brazilian Frontiers." In Michelle R. Garfinkel and Stergios Skaperdas, eds., *The Political Economy of Conflict and Appropriation*. New York: Cambridge University Press, 157–77.

Anderson, Robert E., and Albert Martinez. 1996. "Supporting Private Sector Development in the Middle East and North Africa." In Nemat Shafik, ed., *Prospects for Middle Eastern and North African Economies: From Boom to Bust and Back?* New York: St. Martin's Press, 178–93.

Barro, Robert J. 1997. *Determinants of Economic Growth: A Cross-Country Empirical Study*. Cambridge: MIT Press.

Bechri, Mohamed Z. 1999. "Institutional Obstacles, Reform Uncertainty and Tunisia's Integration with the European Union." Paper presented at the seminar "The Dynamics of New Regionalism in MENA: Integration, Euro-Med Partnership and After." February 6–7, Cairo.

Brunetti, Aymo, Gregory Kisunko, and Beatrice Weder. 1997a. "Institutional Obstacles to Doing Business: Region-by-Region Results from a Worldwide Survey of the Private Sector." World Bank Policy Research Working Paper No. 1759. World Bank, Washington, D.C.

————. 1997b. "Institutional Obstacles to Doing Business: Data Description and Methodology of a Worldwide Private Sector Survey." Background Paper for the 1997 *World Development Report*. World Bank, Washington, D.C.

Buscaglia, Edgardo, and Maria Dakolias. 1996. "Judicial Reform in Latin American Courts: The Experience of Argentina and Ecuador." World Bank Technical Paper No. 350, World Bank, Washington, D.C.

Buscaglia, Edgardo, Maria Dakolias, and William Ratliff. 1995. *Judicial Reform in Latin America: A Framework for National Development.* Stanford, Calif.: Hoover Institution.

Castelar Pinheiro, Armando. 1998. "Economic Costs of Judicial Inefficiency in Brazil." Final Report to the Tinker Foundation. Instituto de Estudios Economicos, Sociais e Politicos de São Paulo, Brazil.

Chan, Philip. 1998. "Resolving Construction Disputes in Singapore—Litigation, Arbitration and ADR." *The International Construction Law Review* 259–85.

Cooter, Robert D. 1996. "The Rule of Law Versus the Rule of the State: Economic Analysis of the Legal Foundations of Development." *Annual World Bank Conference on Development Economics 1996.* Washington, D.C.

Cornell, Stephen, and Joseph P. Kalt. 1995. "Where Does Economic Development Really Come From? Constitutional Rule Among the Contemporary Sioux and Apache." *Economic Inquiry* July 33 (3): 402–26.

Dakolias, Maria. 2000. "Initiatives in Legal and Judicial Reform." Legal and Judicial Reform Unit, Legal Department, World Bank, Washington, D.C.

Datta, Samar K., and Jeffrey B. Nugent. 1986. "Adversary Activities and Per Capita Income Growth." *World Development* 14 (11/November).

———. 1991. "Bahrain's Pearling Industry: How It Was, Why It Was That Way and Its Implications." In Jeffrey B. Nugent and Theodore H. Thomas, eds., *Bahrain and the Gulf: Past Perspectives and Alternative Futures.* London: Croom Helm, 25–41.

de Soto. Hernando 1989. *The Other Path.* New York: Harper and Row.

Dezalay, Yves, and Bryant G. Garth. 1996. *Dealing in Virtue: International Commercial Arbitration and the Construction of a Transnational Legal Order.* Chicago: University of Chicago Press.

El-Kosheri, Ahmed Sadek. 1998. "Is There a Growing International Arbitration Culture in the Arab-Islamic Juridical Culture?" In Albert Jan Van Den Berg, ed., *International Dispute Resolution: Toward an International Arbitration Culture.* The Hague: Kluwer Law International, 47–48.

Englebert, Pierre. Forthcoming. *State Legitimacy and Development: Moving Beyond Social Capital and Ethnic Theories of African Stagnation.* Boulder, Colo.: Lynn Rienner.

Entezari, Shririn O. 1997. "Iranian Arbitration Proceedings." *Journal of International Arbitration* 14 (December): 53–58.

Fawzy, Samiha. 1998. "The Business Environment in Egypt." Paper presented to the Mediterranean Development Forum II in Marrakech, Morocco, September 1998.

Feder, Gershon, and Tongroj Onchan. 1987. "Land Ownership Security and Farm Investment in Thailand." *American Journal of Agricultural Economics* 69(2): 311–20.

———. 1989. "Land Ownership and Farm Investment: Reply." *American Journal of Agricultural Economics* 71 (1): 215–16.

Feder, Gershon, Tongroj Onchan, Yongyuth Chalamwong, and Chira Hongladarom. 1988. *Land Policies and Farm Productivity in Thailand*. Baltimore, Md.: Johns Hopkins University Press.

Foley, C. Fritz. 1999. "Going Bust in Bangkok: Lessons from Bankruptcy Law Reform in Thailand." Cambridge, Mass.: Harvard University. Processed.

Galal, Ahmed. 1996. "Can Egypt Grow without Institutional Reforms? If Not, Which Institutions Matter Most?" In *Industrial Strategies and Policies, Management and Entrepreneurial Skills*. United Nations Economic and Social Commission for Western Asia.

Gitlin, Richard A., and Brian N. Watkins. 2000. Institutional Alternatives to Insolvency for Developing Countries. Paper presented at the conference on "Building Effective Insolvency Systems Insolvency Alternatives," Washington, D.C., September 14–15, 1999.

Giugale, Marcelo, and Hamed Mubarak. 1996. "Introduction: The Rationale for Private Sector Development in Egypt." In M. M. Giugale and Hamed Mubarak, eds., *Private Sector Development in Egypt*. Cairo: American University in Cairo Press, 1–11.

Granovetter, M. 1985. "Economic Action and Social Structure: The Problem of Embeddedness." *American Journal of Sociology 91(3):* 481–510.

Greif, Avner. 1996. "Contracting, Enforcement and Efficiency: Economics beyond the Law." *Annual World Bank Conference on Development Economics 1996*, 239–65.

Gwartney, James, Robert Lawson, and Walter Block. 1997. *Economic Freedom in the World 1975–95*. Vancouver: Fraser Institute.

Hart, Oliver. 1999. "Different Approaches to Bankruptcy." World Bank Conference on Governance, Equity, and Global Markets, Paris, June 21, 1999.

Henisz, Witold J., and Bennet A. Zelner. 1999. "The Institutional Environment for Telecommunications Investment." *Journal of Economics and Management Strategy 10(1):* 123–147.

Holmes, Kim R., Bryan T. Johnson, and Melanie Kirkpatrick. 1998. *1998 Index of Economic Freedom.* Washington, D.C. and New York: Heritage Foundation and *The Wall Street Journal.*

Hornick, Robert N. 1991. "Indonesian Arbitration in Theory and Practice.*" American Journal of Comparative Law* 39 (Summer): 559–97.

Inter-American Development Bank. 1999. "Legal Reform." *IDB America* November/December.

Issawi, Charles. 1982. *An Economic History of the Middle East and North Africa.* New York: Columbia University Press.

Jones, Douglas. 1999. "The Dispute Resolution Process in Asia." *The International Construction Law Review* 359–419.

Kanaan, Taher H. 1998. "Business Environment in Jordan." In S. Fawzy and A. Galal, eds., *Partners for Development: New Roles for Government and Private Sector in the Middle East & North Africa.* Washington, D.C.: The World Bank.

Kaplow, Louis. 1986. "Private versus Social Costs in Bringing Suit." *Journal of Legal Studies* 15 (June): 371–85.

Klein, Daniel B. 1992. "Promise Keeping in the Great Society: A Model of Credit Informational Sharing." *Economics and Politics* 4 (2): 117–36.

Knack, Stephen, and Philip Keefer. 1995. "Institutions and Economic Performance: Cross-Country Tests Using Alternative Institutional Measures." *Economics and Politics* 7: 207–27.

Krueger, Anne O. 1992. "Institutions for the New Private Sector." In Christopher Clague and Gordon Rausser, eds., *The Emergence of Market Economies in Eastern Europe.* Cambridge: Blackwell.

Kuran, Timur. 1989. "The Craft Guilds of Tunis and Their Amins: A Study in Institutional Atrophy." In Mustapha K. Nabli and Jeffrey B. Nugent, eds., *The*

New Institutional Economics and Development: Theory and Applications to Tunisia. Amsterdam: North-Holland, 236–64.

―――. 2000. "The Commercial Retreat of Islam." Paper presented to the Middle East Economic Association in Boston, Mass., January 7, 2000.

Lahouel El Hedi, Mohammed. 1998. "The Business Environment in Tunisia." Paper presented to the Mediterranean Development Forum, September 3–6, Marrakech, Morocco.

La Porta, Rafael, Florencio Lopez De Silanes, Andrei Schleifer, and Robert W. Vishny. 1998. "Law and Finance." *Journal of Political Economy* 106(6): 1113–55.

Levine, Ross. 1999. "Law, Finance, and Economic Growth." *Journal of Financial Intermediation* 8: 8–35.

Levy, Brian, and Pablo Spiller. 1993. "Regulation, Institutions and Commitment in Telecommunications: A Comparative Analysis of Five Countries." In *Proceedings of the World Bank Annual Conference on Development Economics.* Washington, D.C.: World Bank.

Mahoney, P. G. 1999. "The Common Law and Economic Growth: Hayek Might Be Right." Paper presented at the Corporate Governance Conference at the Davidson Institute, University of Michigan, September 24–25, 1999.

Mauro, Paolo. 1995. "Corruption and Growth." *Quarterly Journal of Economics* 110(3): 681–712.

North, Douglass C. 1990. *Institutions, Institutional Change and Economic Performance.* New York: Cambridge University Press.

Nugent, Jeffrey B. 1989. "Collective Action in Tunisia's Producer Organizations: Some Variations on the Olsonian Theme." In Mustapha K. Nabli and Jeffrey B. Nugent, eds., *The New Institutional Economics and Development: Theory and Applications to Tunisia.* Amsterdam: North-Holland, 289–322.

Nugent, Jeffrey B., and James Robinson. 1999. "Are Endowments Fate? On the Political Economy of Comparative Institutional Development." Department of Economics Working Paper. University of Southern California, Los Angeles. Processed.

Page, John, Joseph Saba, and Nemat Shafik. 1997. "From Player to Referee: The Changing Role of Competition Policies and Regulation in the Middle East and

North Africa." Paper presented to the seminar on "The Role of the State in a Changing Arab Economic Environment," Kuwait, March 1997.

Popkin, Margaret. 2000. *Peace without Justice: Obstacles to the Rule of Law in El Salvador.* State College: Pennsylvania State University Press.

Posner, Richard A. 1998. "Creating a Legal Framework for Economic Development." *World Bank Research Observer* 13(1): 1–12.

Rowat, Malcolm, and Jose Astigarraga. 1999. "Latin American Insolvency Systems: A Comparative Assessment." World Bank Technical Paper No. 433. World Bank, Washington, D.C.

Shavell, Steven. 1982. "Suit, Settlement, and Trial: A Theoretical Analysis under Alternative Methods for the Allocation of Legal Costs." *Journal of Legal Studies* 11(January): 55–73.

Sherwood, Robert M., Geoffrey Shepherd, and Celso Marcos de Souza. 1994. "Judicial Systems and Economic Performance." *The Quarterly Review of Economics and Finance* 34 (Summer): 101–16.

Stone, Andrew, Kristin Hurley, and R. Shyam Khemani. 1998. "The Business Environment and Corporate Governance: Strengthening Incentives for Private Sector Performance." Business Environment Group, Private Sector Development Department, World Bank, Washington, D.C.

Trebilcock, Michael J. 1997. "What Makes Poor Countries Poor? The Role of Institutional Capital in Economic Development." In Edgardo Buscaglia, William Ratliff, and Robert Cooter, eds., *Law and Economics of Development.* Greenwich: JAI Press, 15–58.

USAID (United States Agency for International Development). 1998. *Alternative Dispute Resolution Practitioners Guide.* Center for Democracy and Governance, Technical Publication Series. Washington, D.C.: USAID.

Wallis, John Joseph, and Douglass C. North. 1986. "Measuring the Transaction Sector in the American Economy." In S. L. Engerman and R. E. Gallman, eds., *Long-Term Factors in American Economic Growth.* Chicago: University of Chicago Press, 95–161.

Williamson, Oliver E. 1995. *The Institutions and Governance of Economic Development and Reform.* Proceedings of the World Bank Annual Conference on Development Economics, 1994.

centives (which define the relationship among the key players in the corporation) and external forces (notably policy, legal, regulatory, and market forces) that together govern the behavior and performance of the firm.

The Internal Architecture Defines the Relationships among Key Players in the Corporation

In its narrowest sense, corporate governance can be viewed as a set of arrangements internal to the corporation that define the relationships between managers and stakeholders. The shareholders may be public or private, concentrated or dispersed. These arrangements may be embedded in the company law, securities law, listing requirements, and so on, or they may be negotiated among the key players in governing documents of the corporation, such as the corporate charter, by-laws, and shareholder agreements.

At the center of this system is the board of directors. The board's overriding responsibility is to ensure the long-term viability of the firm and to provide oversight of the firm's management. In many countries the board is responsible for approving the company's strategy and major decisions, and for hiring, monitoring, and replacing management, if and when necessary. In some countries the board has fiduciary responsibility for ensuring compliance with laws and regulations, including accounting and financial reporting requirements. For a going concern the board is answerable to shareholders, and in some systems it is also answerable to employees and creditors. Its task is to protect the interests of the company. When the company runs into financial difficulty, the duty of the board shifts to the company's creditors; this is why the primary duty of the director is to the company rather than to shareholders.

The governance problems that need to be addressed vary according to the ownership structure in the corporate sector. At one end of the spectrum is the publicly traded company with widely dispersed share holdings. There, the challenge is for outside shareholders to control the performance of managers. Since managers dominate, the key governance mechanism is the rules for selecting directors, who need to have enough independence to ensure that they will properly monitor managers' performance. At the other end of the spectrum is the closely held company with a controlling shareholder and a minority of outside shareholders, where the managers act at the dictates of the controlling shareholder. There, the primary governance issue is how outside shareholders can prevent the controlling shareholder from extracting excess benefits through self-dealing or disregard of minority shareholders' economic rights. Common protection include limits on insiders' dealings, antidilution provisions, and appraisal or withdrawal rights for minority shareholders. Where a controlling shareholder dominates a publicly traded corporation, additional governance mechanisms may include voting rights, allowing outsiders representation on the board, and takeover rules limiting the "control premium" that insiders can appropriate.

External Rules Provide a Level Playing Field and Keep Players in Line

These internal mechanisms for corporate governance are strengthened by external laws, rules, and institutions that provide a level, competitive playing field and discipline the behavior of insiders, whether managers or shareholders. In developed market economies these policies and institutions minimize the divergence between social and private returns and reduce costly agency problems, primarily through greater transparency, monitoring by regulatory and self-regulatory bodies, and compliance mechanisms. Notable among the institutions that discipline corporations are the legal frameworks for competition policy, the legal machinery for enforcing shareholders' rights, systems for accounting and auditing, a well-regulated financial system, and the bankruptcy system.

FIRMS ARE DISCIPLINED BY CONTESTABLE MARKETS

The broader business environment creates compelling incentives for insiders to enhance the value of the enterprise. Competition and trade policies that ensure contestable markets reduce rent-seeking behavior. Together with policies that encourage foreign direct investment, competitive markets force insiders to improve corporate performance or risk bankruptcy or turnover. The discipline from competition is likely to be felt earlier and more sharply if there is an effective market for corporate control. Underperforming enterprises become targets for acquisition by firms or investors who believe that they can create more value by running the enterprise themselves. Insiders have a powerful motive to improve the company's performance in order to retain control. A control market may also redress some of the imbalance of power between insiders and outsiders. If the market is orderly and transparent, a contest for control often produces greater economic benefits for outside investors and creditors (at least in the short run) than if insiders had continued to operate an underperforming enterprise without challenge.

A WELL-REGULATED BANKING SYSTEM THAT OPERATES AT ARM'S LENGTH FROM THE CORPORATE SECTOR

Competition for credit can produce better insider behavior as banks demand greater and more accurate information and better compliance with contracts. This ability to discipline insider behavior is greatly restricted, however, if the business environment has few creditor protections, weak contract enforcement, or unworkable bankruptcy laws. If the banking system and the corporate sector are closely interlinked, corporate insiders may fail to share value with their creditors (and governments). If they are, in addition, insiders of the banks, they may appropriate bank resources for their purposes. It has become increasingly clear in recent years that for corporate governance to be effective the banking system also needs good governance. This is especially important in many developing countries, where banks provide most of the corporate financing. This means that an effective governance system must include consideration of the role and responsibility of capital providers.

TRANSPARENT, EFFICIENT, AND LIQUID EQUITY AND BOND MARKETS

Efficient securities markets send price signals rapidly, rewarding or penalizing insiders through changes in the value of their interests in the company, or in the company's access to capital. The system of rewards and penalties is severely diluted, however, if markets are not transparent, investments are costly to exit, or, in the case of institutional investors, if the investors themselves are poorly governed.

THEIR PERFORMANCE IS MONITORED AND SPURRED BY REPUTATIONAL
AGENTS AND ACTIVIST SHAREHOLDERS

Developed markets increasingly feature a dense network of reputational agents[3] who significantly reduce monitoring costs. They include accounting and auditing professionals, lawyers, investment bankers and analysts, credit rating agencies, consumer activists, environmentalists, and the media. Keeping an eye on corporate performance and insider behavior, these reputational agencies can exert pressure on companies to disclose relevant information, improve human capital, recognize the interests of outsiders, and otherwise behave as good corporate citizens. They can also put pressure on government through their influence on public opinion.

INVESTORS AND ACTIVIST SHAREHOLDERS HAVE ALSO CHAMPIONED
GOVERNANCE REFORMS

Particularly in the United States, but increasingly in other developed market economies, investors and activist shareholders have worked actively to ensure that managers and boards of directors act in the interest of shareholders. Although these active institutional investors do not typically take a controlling ownership stake, their visibility and influence in capital markets give them a leverage that few corporations can afford to disregard. Venture capital firms play a monitoring role in the governance of startup firms, particularly in knowledge-based industries. They have the expertise, resources, and responsibility to undertake intensive monitoring and overcome the information disadvantage that other investors may.

THERE IS NO SINGLE MODEL OF CORPORATE GOVERNANCE

These internal and external features have come together in different ways to create a range of corporate governance systems that reflect specific market structures, legal systems, traditions, regulations, and cultural and societal values. The systems may vary by country and sector and even for the same corporation over time, but they affect the agility, efficiency, and profitability of all corporations—private, publicly held, and state-owned. Among the most prominent systems of corporate governance in industrial countries are the U.S. and U.K. models, which focus on dispersed controls, and the German and Japanese models, which reflect a more concentrated ownership structure. Recently, many countries and firms have updated their systems of corporate governance to reflect a broader and more inclusive concept of responsibility that includes stakeholders, as reflected in the King Report for South Africa,[4] the Commonwealth principles of business practice (that is, the Commonwealth principles of best practice in corporate governance), and others.

BUT GLOBALIZATION IS BRINGING HARMONIZATION

Despite the diversity of corporate governance systems, the globalization of markets is producing a degree of convergence in actual operations and governance practices. Countries and firms compete on the price and the quality of their goods and services (which has led to a convergence of cost structures and firm organization that in turn has spilled over into firm behavior and decisionmaking). They compete for financial resources in global capital markets. Increasingly, countries and firms also compete on their regimes for corporate governance systems. These global market pressures are providing the impetus for private investors to harmonize corporate governance practice—to reduce risk to investors, and to hold down the cost of capital to corporations.

UNIFORM STANDARDS ARE GAINING CURRENCY

Governments—which retain priority in protecting savers, investors, suppliers, and the broader interest of the economy—are increasingly requiring that corporations operate in a fair, transparent, and accountable manner. Numerous public and private bodies have responded by establishing standards and norms related to important aspects of corporate governance. Among them are the International Accounting Standards Committee (IASC), the Bank for International Settlements (BIS, for banking supervision and prudential regulation), the International Organization of Securities Commissions (IOSCO), the World Trade Organization (WTO), and the International Labour Organization (ILO).

AGREEMENT ON BASIC PRINCIPLES FOR CORPORATE GOVERNANCE IS SPREADING

Through a consultative process involving Organisation for Economic Co-operation and Development (OECD)–members and observers, the private sector, international organizations, and various stakeholders, the OECD has distilled from diverse national practices a set of principles of corporate governance. These Principles deal mainly with internal mechanisms for directing relationships of managers, directors, shareholders, and other stakeholders. They are also intended primarily for listed companies that function within an effective legal and regulatory environment with adequate competition.

The preamble to the Principles states:

> The Principles are non-binding and do not aim at detailed prescriptions for national legislation. They can be used by policy makers, as they examine and develop their legal and regulatory frameworks for corporate governance that reflect their own economic, social, legal and cultural circumstances and by market participants as they develop their own practices.

The OECD recognizes these broad Principles as a starting point for debate and consideration by governments seeking to raise standards of corporate governance. In brief, the Principles cover:

- *The rights of shareholders and others* to receive relevant information about a company in a timely manner; and the rights of shareholders to have the opportunity to participate in decisions concerning fundamental corporate changes, and to share in the profits of the corporation, among others. Markets for corporate control should be efficient and transparent, and shareholders should consider, before voting, the costs and benefits of exercising their voting rights.

- *Equitable treatment of shareholders,* especially minority and foreign shareholders, with full disclosure of material information and prohibition of abusive self-dealing and insider trading;[5] all shareholders of the same category should be treated equally. Members of the board of directors and managers should be required to disclose any material interest they have in transactions.

- *Recognition of the role of stakeholders in corporate governance* as having been established by law, and the corporate governance framework as encouraging active cooperation between corporations and stakeholders in creating wealth, jobs, and financially sound enterprises.

- *Timely and accurate disclosure and transparency* on all matters material to company performance, ownership, and governance and relating to other issues such as employees and stakeholders; financial information should be independently audited and prepared to high standards of quality.

- *The responsibilities of the board:* the corporate governance framework should ensure the strategic guidance of the company, the effective monitoring of management by the board, and the board's accountability to the company and shareholders.

What It Takes to Succeed: A Mix of Regulatory and Private Voluntary Actions

The OECD Principles draw on a report prepared by the Business Sector Advisory Group that emphasizes that good corporate governance can best be achieved through a combination of regulatory and voluntary private actions. On the regulatory side the report noted that government interventions on corporate governance are most effective when consistently and expeditiously enforced and when focused on ensuring fairness, transparency, accountability, and responsibility. It stresses that regulatory measures, although necessary, are not sufficient to raise standards. Indeed, many corporate leaders who recognize that prospering in the long term requires balancing business objectives with society's concerns have supported the strengthening of corporate governance standards.

These companies have gone far beyond the strictures of law by adopting voluntary measures that improve the quality of disclosure, ensure that directors discharge their fiduciary responsibilities, and increase the commitment of managers to running companies transparently, in order to maximize value but with due regard to stakeholders' interests. The evidence increasingly suggests that such behavior enhances the reputation and the value of companies. That recognition has spurred the voluntary adoption of good governance practices by firms that now find it necessary to abide by global rules set by global markets.

The Challenge of Corporate Governance in Emerging Markets Is Daunting

The rich and complex mosaic that makes up the governance system—policy laws, regulations, public institutions, self-regulated professional bodies, and managerial ethos—has evolved over centuries in developed market economies. In emerging markets, however, many elements of this mosaic are absent or countries are ill equipped to address the corporate governance challenges they face. These challenges are all the more daunting because of the complexity of the ownership structure of the corporate sector, interlocking relationships with government and the financial sector, weak legal and judicial systems, absent or underdeveloped intuitions, and scarce human resource capabilities.

The Range of Corporate Structures Makes the Problems More Complex

The ownership patterns across *developed, developing, and transition economies* are extremely varied. In successful developed economies, both dispersed and concentrated shareholdings have provided an efficient base for growth and capital accumulation as long as there has been a well-functioning legal and regulatory framework, active oversight by reputational agents, and adequate institutional and professional infrastructure.

The environment is different in many *emerging market economies*. The widely held publicly traded firms that constitute a significant part of the corporate sector in many industrial countries are rare in emerging market economies. A more common pattern in developing countries is one of dominance by public sector companies or closely held family-owned and family-managed conglomerates with complex shareholdings. This concentrated pattern of ownership allows insiders to have tight control on the firm, but it also opens up opportunities for expropriation by outside shareholders.

Transition economies face a different problem. Much of their corporate sector consists of "instant corporations," created through mass privatization programs implemented without the legal and institutional structures necessary to operate in a competitive economy. With diffuse ownership this has sometimes allowed insiders to strip assets and leave little value for minority shareholders. In both systems there is a need to build institutions and professional capacity.

These corporate structures complicate the problems associated with asymmetries of information, imperfect monitoring, and opportunistic behavior and make corporate governance reform more complex.

Less Competitive Markets and Weaker Institutions Make the Solutions More Difficult

There are significant differences in legal and regulatory systems and traditions across developing and transition economies, but disclosure requirements and legal protection for shareholders are seldom up to international standards. Outdated contract and bankruptcy laws impede efficient operation and orderly exit, and judicial systems are poorly equipped to offer the speed and predictability required in today's global market. Even where legal and regulatory frameworks have been updated, enforcement remains uneven and sometimes selective, reflecting a critical shortage of skills and sometimes a misuse of official power.

In emerging market economies, the business environment lacks many of the elements needed for a competitive market and a culture of enforcement and compliance. Inadequate competition policies entrench large dominant firms, prevent new entry, and discourage entrepreneurship. Change in corporate control is often subject to ambiguous laws with uncertain implementation, giving management considerable latitude to delay or derail any takeover attempt.

Often the state has a heavy presence in both the real and financial sectors. It may direct credit to privileged firms on subsidized terms through a poorly regulated banking system that conducts little credit analysis, or it may inadequately monitor or discipline large borrowers. In many countries private conglomerates are formed around banks, which then dominate both the real (production) and the financial sectors. These alliances, and the absence of "arm's length" transactions within them, have led to excessive concentration of ownership, overreliance on debt financing, high leveraging, and in many cases, investments in marginal or speculative projects.

These practices have also undermined the development of securities markets. Typically, trading volumes and liquidity are low, and a few large firms dominate securities markets. There are almost no long-term debt instruments. Institutional investors are few and not yet strong enough to insist on fairness, efficiency, and transparency. Their investments in emerging markets generally represent only a small part of a diversified portfolio, and even the bigger institutional investors generally lack the confidence or incentives to assert their influence as shareholders because of opaque rules. They often "vote with their feet" (and leave the firm as a way of showing objection), instead of voting their proxies, contributing to the volatility in global capital flows that has hurt many developing and transition economies.

These conditions have also impeded the development of local pensions and mutual funds. This environment offers little incentive for sound corporate governance in either the real or the financial sector.

Some Countries Have Made Major Strides by Focusing on the "Basics"

Although reform is difficult, many countries have taken some of the steps that are necessary to improve their institutions and human resources, and a few have taken most of the steps. Those that have stayed the course have seen impressive gains in corporate governance and economic performance, but even in this group reform has been a long, uneven, and sometimes fragile process of ups and downs, successes, and reversals. Some institutions, such as reputational agents and active shareholders, are just beginning to emerge.

Reforms have proved most effective when they have focused on the fundamentals; combined complementary laws that are consistently enforced; and focused on incentives to encourage the firms to take voluntary actions. They have emphasized a comprehensive strengthening of external sources of discipline and internal incentives to improve corporate governance, especially by making corporate boards more effective and competent to exercise their duties of oversight and control over management. Reforms have typically involved one or more of these elements:

- *Establishing competitive markets* by removing barriers to entry, enacting competition laws, establishing fair trade priorities, and removing restrictions on foreign direct investments, particularly in low-income transition economies where foreign investors can take on the role of strategic investors.

- *Requiring transparency*, notably through the timely disclosure of material information about the financial and nonfinancial operations of the corporation.

- *Enforcing financial discipline* by severing the links between government, banks, and corporations; restricting directed and connected lending; restructuring banks and allowing private ownership of banks by reputable local and foreign strategic partners (to bring much-needed financial, managerial, and technical capabilities to restructure the corporate sector); strengthening prudential regulation and supervision; and improving enforcement of contracts to suppliers and creditors. These measures should lead to less reliance on banking systems for corporate financing and provide greater incentives for raising capital on equity and corporate debt markets.

- *Fostering the growth of well-regulated and liquid securities markets* by developing the infrastructure required for efficient capital markets, protecting minority shareholders, allowing open-ended mutual funds, enlarging the volume of equity through privatization of state-owned enterprises in financial and real sectors (particularly infrastructure firms), reforming the social security system, and allowing private firms to manage properly regulated pension funds.

- *Updating and strengthening the legal, judicial, and tax systems* to ensure clarity and effective enforcement.

- *Building capacity* in major areas (such as accountants, regulators, bankers, or company directors), and by upgrading existing capabilities and preparing the next generation of professionals.

Internally, the focus of the reforms is to make corporate boards more effective and competent to exercise their duties of oversight and control over management.

For these measures to work effectively, countries need to develop the necessary institutions and build human capacity. This takes years. While institution and capacity building are essential tasks, countries no longer have the luxury of waiting until these measures come to fruition. In the short term, countries have "borrowed" or drawn on the discipline imposed by global markets, such as global investors, regulations, and reputational agents.

Many countries have allowed privatized infrastructure firms and utilities (often accounting for 50 to 75 percent of market capitalization) to issue American Depository Receipts and Global Depository Receipts, or to list themselves on large foreign stock exchanges, where financial disclosure requirements are generally higher than on local exchanges. This has raised the capacity of firms in an important segment of the local market to meet higher disclosure and reporting standards. Although some corporations still offer lower standards of reporting to domestic investors, they are gradually raising the benchmark for locally listed companies. Listing on external exchanges has also subjected firms to the scrutiny of foreign institutional investors, investment banks, credit rating agencies, and other reputational agents that follow the performance of listed firms. Drawing on foreign sources of discipline may initially raise local resistance, but it can help the economy integrate with world markets, prepare firms for global competition, and serve the interests of both domestic and foreign investors. These benefits can more than compensate for any short-term loss of liquidity in local markets.

They Face Resistance from Powerful Interest Groups

Reform of corporate governance systems is politically difficult. Vested interests within firms generally oppose greater transparency and disclosure of both financial and nonfinancial information, arguing that the requirements are costly to comply with and put them at a disadvantage relative to local or foreign competitors. These immediate drawbacks, they claim, outweigh the potential longer-term benefits of higher share-values and lower financing costs that can come with greater transparency. Because they are worried about diluting their privileged position in the company's decisionmaking, insiders often oppose substantive corporate governance requirements such as one-share one-vote, cumulative voting, public tender offers, and independent directors. Giving greater power to minority shareholders is often opposed on the grounds that it could lead to foreign control of local firms, ignoring the benefits that greater power to minority shareholders could bring. Large firms tend to have considerable political influence and access to the public media, opening the door for bribery and corruption. In developing countries and transition economies, regulators or supervisors rarely have the political, human, and financial resources to prevail against the determined opposition of these vested interests.

Members of exchanges (brokers, dealers, banks), who fear a loss of revenue if the measures discourage firms from listing, sometimes oppose tough disclosure requirements and substantive changes in corporate governance. The threatened loss of privileged access to information can also provoke resistance to reform, particularly in smaller economies where ownership and control of industrial companies may overlap.

With such opposition it is not surprising that corporate governance reforms (in industrial countries as well as in developing and transition economies) have often been driven by major economic crises or serious corporate failures. The recent financial crisis in East Asia prompted countries to take major steps to strengthen governance—closing insolvent banks, strengthening prudential regulation, opening the banking sector to foreign investors, revamping bankruptcy and takeover rules, tightening listing rules, requiring companies to appoint external directors, introducing international accounting and auditing standards, requiring conglomerates to prepare consolidated accounts, and enacting fair trade laws.

The Solution: Ownership with Due Diligence

The challenge for developing countries is to take the next steps toward sound corporate governance before another crisis erupts. The important initial steps already taken will not become fully effective until the supporting institutions and implementation capacity evolve and adjust to new monitoring and regulatory needs. Large conglomerates used to a culture of state intervention and policy influence will have to adapt to a global environment that puts a high premium on a culture of compliance and enforcement.

Changing this culture will require a combination of regulatory reform and voluntary private action in a sustained process of consensus and capacity building that involves all the players. Each country will have to find its own formula by assessing its strengths and weaknesses, setting priorities and sequencing reforms, creating strong institutions, and developing the necessary human capital. The winning formula has to be adapted to the corporate structure and the implementation capacity in the private and public sectors. It has to provide both the incentive and the discipline for the private sector to adopt and consistently practice sound principles of corporate governance. It also needs to encourage a broadening and deepening of local ownership that will enable firms to compete more effectively in world markets—often by adhering to best practices and rules set by global markets.

For countries where companies obtain financing mainly through the banking system, reforms center on restructuring and privatizing banks and strengthening prudential and regulatory systems. For countries with a large number of listed companies, the most effective tools have been tightening listing requirements, improving protection of minority shareholders, attracting reputational agents, and encouraging companies with large financing requirements to list overseas. In all countries these steps have to be complemented by measures that minimize rent seeking, promote transparency and disclosure, and strengthen the enforcement capacity of the legal system. Given the limited institutional and human resource base, these policy and regulatory changes have to minimize the role of government in the day-to-day operation of business and focus on the core agenda of reducing economic regulation, strengthening prudential rules, and enforcing those rules consistently and relentlessly.

Corporate governance is not merely about enacting legislation. It is about establishing a climate of trust and confidence through oversight. Ethical business behavior and fairness cannot simply be legislated into being. Strengthening corporate governance is fundamentally a political process in which the government and the private sector have to join hands. There will never be sustained and meaningful public sector reform of governance laws and regulations until the private sector understands that support of reform creates a level playing field, which is in its best interest. Ultimately, for governance to be fully implemented, the private sector needs to build on the base of law and regulation with voluntary actions of its own.

World Bank Group Strategy for Helping Countries Develop and Implement a Comprehensive Reform Program

The Bank has long been active in supporting client countries in undertaking difficult structural changes requiring reforms of legal and regulatory structures, the financial sector, and enterprises, including privatization of state-owned enterprises. The following programs have addressed many issues that are central to corporate governance: (a) creating competitive markets, (b) establishing regulatory and supervisory capability in banking and capital markets, (c) introducing greater transparency, (d) adopting international accounting and auditing standards, and (e) strengthening the competence and independence of boards of directors. Because a scarcity of qualified professionals often poses the most daunting challenge to effective reform, the Bank has also financed technical assistance operations in support of institutional development and capacity building in many areas affecting corporate governance, including auditing and accounting standards, legal and judicial systems, financial sectors, and capital markets.

The International Finance Corporation (IFC) too has promoted better corporate governance by requiring that the firms in which it invests practice sound corporate governance, and by insisting on proper internal controls and reporting. The IFC has been instrumental in developing equity and corporate bond markets, including listing and securities regulations. It has provided hands-on technical assistance to transition economies to establish sound systems of corporate governance. Similarly, the Multilateral Investment Guarantee Agency has ensured that its guarantee operations have a high standard of corporate governance.

Marshaling Support for Corporate Governance Reform

The Bank Group is scaling up its work on structural reform in developing countries, and corporate governance is a key element in that agenda. The Bank Group's and others' objective is to work with partners (multilateral agencies, international organizations, the private sector) to broaden the debate on corporate governance beyond OECD countries, to include developing and transition economies. While the Bank Group will respond to the growing need of client countries to adapt international best practices to their own circumstances and to implement legal and regulatory reforms, it will not be in the business of setting standards or creating codes. Rather, it intends to marshal support nationally, regionally, and globally for countries' own initiatives. This work will be supported by a more concerted emphasis on governance by the Bank Group in its ongoing policy, lending, technical assistance, and private sector activities.

At the national level the Bank and its partners have supported a series of country self-assessments that identify strengths and weaknesses in corporate governance, and help countries establish priorities. Complementing these assessments are investor surveys that identify market perceptions about the same issues. Together, the two assessments paint a clearer picture of corporate governance practices in individual countries, identify priority areas and pressure points, and set the stage for a comprehensive reform agenda. The twin objectives are to strengthen regulatory reform and enforcement while fostering private voluntary actions. This is consistent with the approach of the Bank's Comprehensive Development Framework, which emphasizes good corporate governance as a key factor in the development process. It calls for a participatory process that involves all the major stakeholders in the design and implementation of a comprehensive reform strategy.

At the regional level the Bank has cosponsored with other multinational agencies (particularly the OECD, Asia Pacific Economic Cooperation, the Asian Development Bank, the European Bank for Reconstruction and Development, and others that have also been active in this area) a series of roundtables for Commonwealth, government officials, legislators, regulators, local and foreign firms, investors, and rating agencies to help craft a consensus for reform.

On the global front the World Bank Group has worked closely with the OECD to broaden the dialogue on corporate governance beyond OECD countries. The OECD Principles would be a starting point—but not a reference point. The Bank Group has also worked closely with the BIS on banking systems, with the IOSCO on harmonizing listing requirements, and with the IASC and the International Forum for Accounting Development on transparency issues. It has supported the WTO and the ILO on competition policy and labor issues. In the private sector, it has engaged the major accounting and auditing firms to ensure that their affiliates, which carry their name and reputation, adhere to the same international standards and guidelines.

Catalyzing Reform through the Global Corporate Governance Forum

A good part of the knowledge and expertise needed to support corporate governance and related reforms already exists in the public and private sectors. A wide range of organizations have begun focusing on corporate governance. Although many of these efforts are still small and dispersed, together they account for substantial and diversified international reform efforts. If the corporate governance agenda is to be scaled up properly, a major effort is needed to distill this expertise and marshal it in a coordinated and timely way to support countries' efforts on both regulatory and voluntary fronts.

In a major step in this direction, the World Bank Group and the OECD signed a Memorandum of Understanding on June 21, 1999, to sponsor the Global Corporate Governance Forum. The Forum will bring together other multilateral development banks, bilateral and international organizations, the International Monetary Fund (IMF), the Commonwealth, APEC, IASC, IOSCO, and the private sector. It will provide a rapid-response mechanism for coordinating and channeling practical technical assistance to specific constituents, on a national, regional, and global basis, to help design and implement reforms. Above all, the Forum will mobilize local and international public and private sector expertise and resources to champion and advance corporate governance on a fast track, emphasizing dialogue and consensus building.

The Forum will build on what has already been achieved to help countries develop their own programs and institutions. To this end, the Forum's activities will include:

- Broadening the dialogue to include perspectives from developing and transition economies

- Supporting countries in carrying out self-assessments and investor surveys on the status and practice of corporate governance

- Building consensus for policy, regulatory, and institutional reforms at global, regional, and local levels

- Framing corporate governance strategies to take full advantage of the potential for private sector involvement

- Developing the capacity of governments to design and implement reforms and the capacity of self-regulatory bodies to develop and execute their own regulations

- Strengthening reputational agents

- Sharing knowledge and best practices

- Developing human capacity and building institutions to sustain and expand corporate governance practices

- Addressing corporate governance issues that go beyond a specific country.

In implementing this ambitious agenda, the Forum will be advised and supported by a high-level Private Sector Advisory Group. Leaders and captains of industry with established track records in corporate governance will lend their names and reputations to efforts to bring key stakeholders to the table to build a coalition for reform. The forum will also provide a channel for extensive consultation with important stakeholders (labor, organizations active in corporate governance, environmental agencies, nongovernmental organizations, and others), and to build on initial efforts already begun through roundtables and consultative groups.

Time is short. Crises highlight challenges and offer opportunities for governments and the private sector to change behavior and the rules of the game. While reforms are most often initiated in the wake of a crisis, they should not be viewed in the context of a short-term anticrisis package. Corporate governance change will take a concerted effort in building consensus and sharing experience, expertise, and resources among all players. Above all, the private sector must see that implementing reform is in its own best interest. Likewise, reform of the public sector is central to an active partnership. Because reforms are likely to yield results only over the medium to long run, sustainability and comprehensiveness in design, and staying power during implementation, are critical.

Notes

1. The South Sea Company was proposed in 1710 by George Caswall, London merchant, financier, and stock broker, and John Blunt, London scrivener turned stock broker. They proposed to the government of Robert Harley to convert the outstanding short-term war debts into equity in a new joint-stock company. This South Sea Company would enjoy future profits anticipated from a monopoly on English trade with the Spanish colonies of South America. At the beginning, the company was successful. When the first installment payments of the first and second money subscriptions on new issues of South Seas stock were due, a liquidity squeeze was created and generated pressures to sell shares. Furthermore, the rush for liquidity appeared international as "bubbles" and the price of South Sea shares started to decline. The South Sea Company was susceptible to the Bubble Act (prohibiting any chartered joint-stock company from engaging in activities outside those authorized in its original charter). The financial crisis was resolved by writing down assets and liabilities. All remaining shares held by the company were distributed to

existing shareholders. (For further information, check: http://www.few.eur.nl/few/people/smant/m-economics/southsea.htm.)

2. This overview is based on a longer report, *Corporate Governance: A Framework for Implementation*, published by the World Bank. The report was prepared under the direction of Magdi R. Iskander, Director of the Private Sector Development Department. The main report was written by Nadereh Chamlou, with input from Malcom Rowat and with the assistance of Uzma Ahmad and Z. Selin Hur. The authors extend special appreciation to Anne Simpson. Valuable contributions to the preparation of the report were received from Noritaka Akamatsu, Randolph Anderson, Robert E. Anderson, David Cook, Olivier Fremond, Omkar Goswami (India), Holly Gregory, Kris Hurley, Michael Lubrano, Sue Rutledge, Manuel Schiffler, Andrew Stone, and Douglas Webb. Helpful comments were received from Joseph E. Stigliz, Shyam Khemani, Stijin Claessens, Chad Leechor, Christopher Juan Costain, John Williamson, Simeon Djankov, and Milan Brambhatt. Informal comments were also received from the following experts: Ira Millstein, Holly Gregory (Weil, Gotshal, and Manges), Sir Adrian Cadbury, Jonathan Charkham (United Kingdom), Stilpon Nestor (Organisation for Economic Co-operation and Development), Michael Gillibrand, Phil Armstrong (Commonwealth), and Herbert Morais (International Monetary Fund). Meta de Coquereaumont and Bruce Ross Larson edited the report. Vannee Dalla and Nenuca Robles provided organizational and production support. Additional reference materials on corporate governance are available through the World Bank's help desk and the corporate governance Web site: www.worldbank,org/html/fpd/privatesector/eg.

3. *Reputational agents* refer to the private sector agents, self-regulating bodies, the media, investment and corporate governance analysts, and civic society that reduce information asymmetry, improve the monitoring of firms, and shed light on opportunistic behavior. Their actions influence both companies and governments.

4. Anticorruption Unit, International Cricket Council, "Report on Corruption in International Cricket," April 2001.

5. Directors can extract excess benefits through self-dealing or disregard of minority shareholders' economic rights.

CHAPTER 7

Transparency between Government and Business

John D. Sullivan

There are few topics more central to the international business and development agendas than corporate governance. A series of events over the last two decades have made corporate governance issues a top concern for both the international business community and international financial institutions. Spectacular business failures such as the infamous Bank of Credit and Commerce International (BCCI) scandal, the United States's savings and loan crisis, and the gap between executive compensation and corporate performance have driven the demand for change in industrial countries since the 1980s. More recently, several high-profile scandals in the Russian Federation (1998) and the recent East Asia crisis (1997) have brought corporate governance issues to the fore in developing countries and transitional economies. Furthermore, national business communities are learning and relearning the lesson that there is no substitute for getting the basic business and management systems in place in order to be competitive internationally and to attract investment.

As a result, the World Bank, the Organisation for Economic Co-operation and Development (OECD), most of the regional development banks, and the various national development agencies have either launched or expanded programs in this area in the last several years. Similarly, business-related organizations such as the Center for International Private Enterprise (CIPE), an affiliate of the U.S. Chamber of Commerce, have placed corporate governance at the top of their lists of concerns. Think tanks and business associations throughout the developing world and in the transitional economies are also focusing resources on these key issues.

In developing countries the roots of what is now recognized as corporate governance–type issues can be found in the drive for privatization that grew in the late 1970s and throughout the 1980s. Clearly, creating a sound corporate structure should have been central to the success of privatization in order to ensure success, both from the point of view of the government seeking to sell the firm and from the point of view of the potential investors. In fact, some of the most telling failures in the early privatization experiences can be traced back to a lack of sound regulatory structures that allowed unwise business practices. Chile comes to mind in this respect. In the mid-1970s Chilean business groups were able to purchase banks, often with only 20 percent initial payments. In 1982 Chile experienced an economic crisis generated by a combination of external shocks and an overvalued exchange rate. The business groups responded by using their banks to shore up the firms, which led both into even more serious trouble. Finally, the government responded by renationalizing a host of firms and banks.[1]

It was the fall of the Berlin Wall, however, and the subsequent drive to rapidly privatize the entire business structure of the transforming or post communist economies that really increased interest in corporate governance as a development topic. In the first instance, state-owned firms had to be "corporatized," that is, converted from a governmental to a corporate structure. Second, the overarching body of commercial law had to be put into place: bankruptcy regulations, laws on property, accounting systems, and a host of other fundamental "rules of the game." Most dauntingly, talent had to be nurtured. Few individuals had any experience as members of a board of directors, for instance. It is perhaps not surprising that the countries that rushed into large-scale privatization, especially the Czech Republic and Russia, have experienced large-scale corporate governance failures. Hungary, which chose to sell its firms to Westerners, and Poland, which chose not to delay privatization of large companies, have had better results. Today, think tanks and business organizations throughout Central and Eastern Europe, including much of the former Soviet Union, are working hard to press for adoption of key institutional reforms and corporate governance practices.[2]

As noted above, the East Asia financial crisis has now driven the process even further. One of the lessons learned from that crisis is that weak or ineffective corporate governance procedures can potentially create huge liabilities for both individual firms and, collectively, for society. In this sense corporate governance failures can be as devastating as any other large economic shock. As M. R. Chatu Mongol Sonakul, the governor of the Bank of Thailand, has observed:

> There is no doubt in my mind that for the Asian economic crisis to be solved in a sustainable and long-lasting fashion, the government and the corporate sector have to work together better. By this, I don't mean that not working together was the cause of the recent economic crisis. Probably it was the other way around, working far too well together and in collusion with each other. . . . The Asian financial crisis showed that even strong economies lacking transparent control, responsible corporate

boards, and shareholder rights can collapse quite quickly as investor's confidence erodes.[3]

As can be seen from Dr. Sonakul's observations, corporate governance is at the very heart of the development of both a market economy and a democratic society. That view may be a bit of a surprise to those who think of corporate governance as the issues of shareholder protection, management control, and the famous principal-agent problems—problems that concern management and economic theorists.

The focus of this chapter is the concept of corporate governance as a key feature of the market system of competitive enterprise. In addition, the chapter shows why corporate governance should also be of direct concern to those focusing on democratic development, especially in terms of "rule of law" issues. Corporate governance ultimately depends on public sector–private sector cooperation to both create a competitive market system and develop a law-based democratic society.

These concerns are not limited to developing countries. Even in the advanced industrial societies there is a global trend toward strengthening corporate governance. For example, in recent years, the Cadbury Commission in the United Kingdom (October 1999) (http://www.worldbank.org/html/fpd/privatesector/cg/codes.htm), the Vienot Commission in France (July 1995) (http://www.ecgi.org/codes/country_pages/codes_france.htm#1), and the OECD have all issued new guidelines (May 1999) (http://www1.oecd.org/daf/governance/principles.htm). In the United States there is mounting concern over the actual independence of "independent" audits, as witnessed in the recent publicity surrounding violations of rules prohibiting auditors to invest in companies that they audit (for example, see: http://money.cnn.com/2000/01/06/companies/pricewaterhouse/). In all of these cases, the underlying concerns center around ways to accomplish the core values of corporate governance, including transparency, accountability, and building value.

This chapter starts by introducing the notion of corporate governance, then looks at the OECD Principles adopted by the governments of OECD member countries. Then we will assess the benefits of adopting a strong corporate governance on societies.

Definitions

Corporate governance is typically perceived by academic literature as dealing with "problems that result from the separation of ownership and control."[4] From this perspective corporate governance would focus on the internal structure and rules of the boards of directors, audit committees, shareholder reporting, and control of management. In fact, a recent academic survey began with the following quote: "Corporate governance deals with the ways in which suppliers of finance to corporations assure themselves of getting a return on their investment. How do the suppliers of finance get managers to return some of the profits to them? How do they make sure that managers do not steal the capital they supply or invest it in bad projects? How do suppliers of finance control managers?"[5]

From this point of view, corporate governance tends to focus on a simple model:

- Shareholders elect directors who represent them.

- Directors vote on key matters and adopt the majority decision.

- Decisions are made in a transparent manner so that shareholders and others can hold directors accountable.

- The company adopts accounting standards to generate the information necessary for directors, investors, and other stakeholders to make decisions.

- The company's policies and practices adhere to applicable national, state, and local laws.[6]

Focusing on these types of internal control processes is quite natural when the subject is corporate governance within the advanced market economies. Point number five, for instance, assumes that an external legal system is in place. Although there are considerable differences among the Anglo-American, German, French, and other national systems, they all share the common luxury of defining the subject of corporate governance within the context of functioning market systems and highly developed legal institutions.

As noted earlier, when the subject of corporate governance is discussed in the context of transitional or developing countries, it tends to involve looking at a much wider range of issues. The combination of the recent East Asia crisis, the continuing turmoil in Russia, and the recent experience of the Czech economy pushed the issue of corporate governance from the sidelines to center stage. In Asia what began as a financial crisis is now viewed to be a crisis of corporate transparency involving relationships between government and business, between holders of debt and holders of equity, and the legal remedies for bankruptcy and cronyism. Further, as seen in the daily papers, the lack of adequate institutions in Russia has resulted in several highly publicized cases involving allegations of asset stripping, stock register manipulation, and fraud.[7] The Czech Republic's Privatization Program, on the other hand, has demonstrated the weakness of the voucher method in the absence of sound corporate governance mechanisms; it has resulted in a lack of corporate restructuring and a consequent decline in competitiveness.[8]

What these examples have in common is that they all involve the basic rules of the economy and the relationship between these rules and the way companies are governed. These issues touch upon some very familiar topics, including:

- Corporate transparency—or full disclosure of financial information

- Conflicts of interest involving boards of directors and managers

- Procedures for bankruptcy

- Property rights

- Contract enforcement

- Corruption and theft.

Each of these issues poses grave challenges for both the functioning of a market economy and a democratic society. Solving corporate governance problems such as those listed above involves going beyond a narrow view of how owners and managers of capital interrelate. In this sense, a broader definition should be adopted:

> Corporate governance results from a set of institutions (laws, regulations, contracts, and norms) that create self-governing firms as the central element of a competitive market economy.

The key point in this definition is that the public and private sectors have to work together to develop a set of rules that are binding on all, and which establish the ways in which companies must govern themselves.

One interesting illustration of how transitional economies have been forced to come to grips with this issue stems from the first law on private enterprise passed in Poland in 1988. The Law on Economic Activity stated, "Within the scope of their economic activity, economic subjects may perform operations and actions which are not forbidden by law." Some might find that wording slightly odd. The clear expectation in the market-oriented society (that is, the nonstatist society) is that all actions not forbidden by law are allowed. Indeed, that expectation is at the heart of private, individual initiative. The converse rule—that of only allowing those actions specifically authorized by law, regulation, or written permission—has traditionally been applied only in command economies and in economies with a statist tradition.

Building a market economy requires a complete overhaul of legal norms to allow for innovation and initiative, rather than a system of predefining areas of allowable activity. That is why corporate governance should be thought of as a mechanism for creating self-governing organizations. However, it is equally important to emphasize that a market economy is not simply the absence of governmental intervention.

How often has it been said, "the government should get out of the way and let the market function"? Of course, the idea that the absence of government will lead to a strong market is a myth. Government is essential for setting up the framework of a market economy. Without binding rules and structures there would be anarchy. Under such conditions business becomes nothing but "casino capitalism," where investments are simply bets: bets that people will keep their word, bets that the firms are telling the truth, bets that employees will be paid, and bets that debts will be honored. What corporate governance is all about in larger terms is how a structure can be set up that allows for a considerable amount of freedom within the rule of law. Ultimately, these arrangements provide the basis for the establishment of trust—which is one of the most important ingredients in business.

OECD Principles

A useful first step in creating or reforming the corporate governance system is to look at the OECD Principles referred to above that were adopted by the governments of OECD-member countries.[9] In summary, they include the following elements:

Rights of the Shareholders
These include a set of rights, including secure ownership of shares; the right to full disclosure of information; voting rights; and the right to participate in decisions on sale or modification of corporate assets, including mergers and new share issues. The guidelines go on to specify a host of other issues connected to the basic concern of protecting the value of the corporation.

The Equitable Treatment of Shareholders
The OECD is concerned with protecting minority-shareholders' rights by setting up systems that keep insiders, including managers and directors, from taking advantage of their roles. Insider trading, for example, is explicitly prohibited.

The Role of Stakeholders in Corporate Governance
The OECD recognizes that there are other stakeholders in companies in addition to shareholders. Workers, for example, are important stakeholders in the way in which companies perform and make decisions. The OECD guidelines lay out several general provisions for stakeholder interests.

Disclosure and Transparency
The OECD also lays out a number of provisions for the disclosure and communication of key facts about the company, ranging from financial details to governance structures, including the board of directors and their remuneration. The guidelines also specify that independent auditors should perform annual audits in accordance with high-quality standards.

The Responsibilities of the Board of Directors
The guidelines outline in some detail the functions of the board in protecting the company, its shareholders, and its stakeholders. These include concerns about corporate strategy, risk, executive compensation and performance, as well as accounting and reporting systems.

It should be noted that the OECD guidelines are somewhat general and that both the Anglo-American system and the Continental European (or German) systems would be quite consistent with them. However, there is growing pressure to put more enforcement mechanisms in those guidelines. The challenge will be to do this in a way consistent with market-oriented procedures by creating self-enforcing procedures that impose large new costs on firms. The following are some ways to introduce more explicit standards:

- Countries should be required to establish independent share registries. All too often newly privatized or partially privatized firms dilute stock or simply fail to register shares purchased through foreign direct investment.

- Standards for transparency and reporting of the sales of underlying assets need to be spelled out, along with enforcement mechanisms and procedures by which investors can seek to recover damages.

- The discussion of stakeholder participation in the OECD guidelines needs to be balanced by discussion of conflict-of-interest and insider-trading issues. Standards or guidelines are needed in both areas.

- Internationally accepted accounting standards should be explicitly recommended.

- Internal company audit functions and the inclusion of outside directors on audit committees both need to be made explicit.

A good example of model corporate governance procedures that builds on many of these points is the General Motors guidelines, which are frequently used as a code of corporate governance by others.[10] Interestingly, the pension funds have also become a major source of improved corporate governance along the same lines. Specifically, the California Public Employees' Retirement System (CalPers) has developed a very active program to promote good corporate governance and they, along with other pension funds, are using their investment clout to force change. CalPers has taken this approach in order to increase the return on their investments by ensuring that the firms are well run and that corporate strategies are well-thought-out. As more and more pension fund investments flow into developing countries, these funds can be expected to make similar demands in such countries.[11]

Some may think that these are exclusively American standards and are not necessary in most countries. However, as a recent study by the Center for European Policy Studies noted (CEPS 1995), the wider the distribution of shareholding, the greater is the role of the market in the exercise of corporate control. Hence there is more need for corporate governance procedures in this type of economy than in one where shareholding is relatively concentrated. The report went on to note, however, that financial market liberalization, increased privatization, and the growing use of funded systems to support pensions are driving European countries toward more explicit and more comprehensive rules on corporate governance.[12]

The reason why it is important to take note of this trend is that, traditionally, many in developing countries have cited the European experience as proof that corporate governance issues apply only to countries that follow an Anglo-American tradition, such as India. Recent history would seem to show that, without sound corporate governance procedures, including the larger institutional features mentioned earlier, economic crises in developing countries are likely to become more frequent. Many developing countries face stark choices: either create the type of governance procedures needed to participate in and take advantage of globalization (and thus run the risk of severe and possibly frequent economic crises), or seek to build defensive walls around the economy. It should be noted that the last option usually entails the risk of keeping out investors and new technologies, and lowers growth rates dramatically.

Another consideration in the debate over corporate governance systems is the risk that individual firms face. Unless a company is able to build the kinds of governance mechanisms that attract capital and technology, they run the risk of simply becoming suppliers and vendors to the global multinationals. In this respect, the 1999 Asian conference on corporate governance, dubbed the "Bangkok Conference," holds a number of lessons for countries in the Middle East. During this conference the participants debated quite extensively the need for outside directors and independent audit committees, in particular. Several of those present—including representatives from Indonesia and the Republic of Korea—noted that there was some reluctance to adopt rules requiring audit committees to be made up of outside directors and requirements that audits should be public. In the end, however, there was general agreement that such reforms are essential to prevent a repeat of the East Asia crisis.[13]

Benefits to Society

A strong system of corporate governance can be a major benefit to society. Even in countries where most firms are not actively traded on stock markets, adopting standards for transparency in dealing with investors and creditors is a major benefit to all in that it helps to prevent systemic banking crises. Taking the next step and adopting bankruptcy procedures also helps to ensure that there are methods for dealing with business failures that are fair to all stakeholders, including workers as well as owners and creditors. Without adequate bankruptcy procedural regulations, especially enforcement systems, there is little to prevent insiders from stripping the remaining value out of an insolvent firm to their own benefit.

Recent research has also shown that countries with stronger corporate governance protections for minority shareholders also have much larger and more liquid capital markets. Comparisons of countries that base their laws on different legal traditions show that those countries with weak systems tend to result in the majority of domestic companies being controlled by dominant investors rather than by a widely dispersed ownership structure. Hence, for countries that are trying to attract small investors—whether domestic or foreign—corporate governance matters a great deal in getting the hard currency out of potential investors' mattresses and floorboards.[14]

Many economists and management experts make the point that competition in product markets and competition for capital act as constraints on corporate behavior, in effect forcing good corporate governance. The fact that pension funds such as CalPers have had to take a very active role in improving corporate governance would seem to contradict this point. However, whether or not this is really the case in developed market economies, competition is surely a much smaller factor in transitional and developing countries. In many developing countries competition in product or goods markets is quite limited, especially where significant regulatory barriers exist. These realities further underscore the importance of adopting the best possible corporate governance systems in countries where the market system is underdeveloped.[15]

Corporate governance is also directly related to another topic that has emerged to a position of great prominence worldwide—combating corruption. This subject is not easy to deal with, in many societies, both because of political sensitivities and because of fear of potential legal action. Yet corruption has to be dealt with in order to secure a position in the global economy and to secure the benefits of economic growth. The signing of the OECD Antibribery Convention in 1997 is the beginning, not the end, of a concerted global anticorruption campaign. Actions to improve corporate governance, especially in the provision of transparency in corporate transactions, in accounting and auditing procedures, in purchasing, and in all of the myriad individual business transactions, require a large-scale effort. Nevertheless, strengthening the corporate governance standards along the lines suggested above would be one place to start.

The point has already been made that improving corporate governance procedures can also improve the management of the firm, especially in areas such as setting company strategy, ensuring that mergers and acquisitions are undertaken for sound business reasons, and ensuring that compensation systems reflect performance. However, it is also important to note that good corporate governance systems have to include improvements in management systems. In many developing countries there has been a tradition of very centralized management usually involving the owners of the firms directly. Throughout Latin America, for example, the family business groups have tended to dominate the business landscape. This is now changing rapidly, due to financial globalization, adherence to the World Trade Organization's (WTO's) liberalization rules, and the increasing integration of Latin America's regional markets.[16] As a result, Latin America's firms are increasingly adopting modern management techniques, financial accounting systems, and business strategies. All of this requires the delegation of authority, paying increased attention to developing highly trained staff, and use of management information systems in lieu of the older centralized decisionmaking structures. It is highly probable that these trends will force similar changes throughout the Middle East.

Conclusions

One way to sum up the concept of corporate governance is to look at it from the perspective of the corporate director. Increasingly, directors are being held liable for their actions or inaction, at least in the industrial countries. What, then, does a director need to be able to function and have a balanced view of the firm? According to one seasoned corporate director, the following is the minimum essential information:

- Operating systems, balance sheets, and cash flow statements that compare current period and year-to-date performance to target performance and previous year performance

- Management comments about current performance that focus on explaining the deviations from the target performance and revise performance targets for the remainder of the year

- Information on the company's market share

- Minutes of management committee meetings

- Financial analysts' reports for the company and its major competitors

- Employee attitude surveys

- Customer preference surveys

- Key media articles on the company, its major competitors, and industry trends.[17]

The list not only sums up the key responsibilities of a board but also reinforces the argument that corporate governance reflects the underlying systems of law and regulation. Most important, without sound and accurate accounting systems, how could the director function? As seen in OECD (1999), maintaining these accounting standards that all firms have to meet is a considerable challenge (http://www.oecd.org/EN/document/0,,EN-document-76-3-no-15-8293-0,FF.html). The list also points out that good corporate governance will bring with it modern management systems. For example, reviewing the minutes of the management committee meetings implies that a functioning management committee system is in place with delegation of authority and accountability.

Creating sound systems of corporate governance is a high priority for both the public and private sectors. However, there may be a temptation for the private sector to just say, "Well, we'll let the government work this out and then we'll follow the results." In some cases there may also be a temptation—especially for the countries with protected markets and a large state sector—to put off corporate governance reform until after the privatization process and other types of reforms are fully completed. Experience indicates that this would be a very unfortunate decision. Both the private and public sectors have much to gain by setting up clear and simple rules for all to follow. A sound corporate governance structure will be a great inducement to international trade and investment. In addition, sound corporate governance systems are a major advantage to those countries seeking to fight corruption. In this sense, good corporate governance is a way for the private sector to protect itself from outside demands and for the public sector to prevent undue influence in governmental decisionmaking.

It is vital to avoid simply copying other countries' systems or asking foreign experts to write model laws. Although the foreign donor community often pushes this type of approach, it should be resisted. Throughout the Middle East a network of extremely capable policy research institutes and think tanks have been formed and others will surely follow. Many of these centers have been formed with the backing of business leadership and are in a position to devise, adapt, and advocate systems that will be appropriate to the status of each country. In the process, not only will the resulting policy reforms advance better systems of corporate governance, they will point to the need for other reforms. The need for adoption of modern management systems, including areas such as knowledge management and strategic planning, will become more apparent in the process. As more and more countries in the region enter the WTO process and further their participation in the global market, the demand for corporate governance will surely grow. It's up to the policy research centers, the national business associations, and others in civil society to work with governments to craft the best national systems.

Appendix 7A. Business Leaders Call for Incorporating Corporate Governance into International Standards Organization Standards

An unprecedented gathering of senior business executives from six Asian countries convened on September 12–14, 1999, in Bangkok, Thailand. Some 40 corporate, business association, and private think tank executives from India, Indonesia, the Republic of Korea, Malaysia, the Philippines, Singapore, and Thailand participated in the conference and offered their ideas on how businesspeople can encourage positive changes in the way in which corporations are structured and managed. They agreed that business can and must play a leading role in promoting more transparent interchanges between the public and private sectors, and recommended possible structural and democratic reforms to help prevent a recurrence of the East Asia economic crisis and to help restore international investor confidence in the region.

Corporate governance is the body of "rules of the game" by which companies are managed internally and by which they are supervised by boards of directors, in order to protect the interests and financial stake of shareholders and stakeholders, who may be located thousands of miles away and far removed from the management of the firm. Just as good government requires transparency so that the people can effectively judge whether their interests are being served, corporations must also act in a democratic and transparent manner so that their owners can make educated decisions about their investments.

The Asian executives in Bangkok said they would contact the International Standards Organization (ISO) in Geneva and propose the incorporation of standards for corporate governance into the ISO system. They said Asian business organizations would be willing to work with the ISO in developing corporate governance standards that would promote adoption of best management practices in corporations worldwide.

The business leaders also called for regional and country-specific awards that recognize companies that adhere to sound corporate governance practices. They said the new awards would help promote public understanding of the importance of corporate governance not only to firms, but also to consumers, employees, and other public stakeholders.

The Bangkok meeting was sponsored by the Thai Federation of Industries, the Thai Chamber of Commerce, the Institute for Management Education for Thailand Foundation (IMET), and CIPE of the United States. The recommendations drew on the Confederation of Indian Industries' guidelines.

Recommendations for Action

The business participants explored corporate governance reforms by examining the impact on four sets of constituencies: the general public, the media, the business community, and government and policymakers. The business participant executives developed the following list of specific initiatives that businesses and business organizations can undertake with each constituency:

GENERAL PUBLIC

- Educate the general public that good corporate governance is beneficial for all. This education of the public will help elevate the status of corporate governance in the national business agenda.

- Initiate education and training programs with target groups (chambers of commerce, federations of industry, and other business associations) that promote good corporate governance.

- Encourage companies to promote positive interaction between suppliers and consumers, formulate transparent guidelines for transactions, offer recourse for consumer complaints, and establish mechanisms to receive complaints and feedback.

- Establish third-party monitoring and evaluation systems on corporate governance, and foster collaboration among firms, business associations, and consumer groups.

- Promote good corporate citizenship and social responsibility among firms, and standards of fairness in interaction with the public.

- Organize periodic reviews and information exchanges with businesspeople both nationally and internationally to ensure continued relevance of standards and possible adoption of new ideas.

- Establish new awards by November 2000 in Association of Southeast Asian Nations (ASEAN) Chambers of Commerce and Industry to be conferred on firms in the region that practice sound principles of corporate governance.

- Create a regional database on good corporate governance, including information on corporate success stories and dissemination to the public.

BUSINESS COMMUNITY

- Increase the percentage of independent directors on corporate boards initially to 33 percent, and eventually increase it to 50 percent.

- Disclose information on directors, including remuneration, family relationships, and business relationships that may constitute conflict of interest.

- Propose legislation to hold directors legally responsible for failure to discharge fiduciary responsibility, taking into account differences in liabilities between executive and nonexecutive directors consistent with national legislation.

- Place the responsibility for company management in the hands of professional and experienced executives, establish clear management policies, and make them known to employees and shareholders.

- Establish an audit committee consisting of at least three independent directors; the committee should report directly to the board. Internal auditors should also report directly to the board.

- Publish annual reports containing extensive information on a firm's financial condition, ownership structure, and corporate governance standards.

- Encourage business associations to serve as resources for training and information on corporate governance practices for small- and medium-size firms.

MEDIA

- Organize press events immediately after the conference in other participating countries led by participants to publicize the conference findings.

- Promote development of a strong financial press by disclosing information, and by preparing short objective articles and editorials defining the concept of good corporate governance for publication in the business media.

- Encourage the media to publicize corporate governance reforms by providing success stories from regional and national business associations and others in the business network to identify companies that practice good corporate governance.

- Incorporate the principles of good governance into the agenda of the media seminars or workshops held regularly by institutes and associations.

LEGISLATIVE AND GOVERNMENT

- Incorporate corporate governance into the ISO system.

- Adopt a grading system utilizing corporate governance principles to help business evaluate the efficiency of government agencies.

- Encourage the evaluation and review of current laws, rules, and regulations to improve the quality of existing legislation and simplify administration.

- Encourage governments to sign on to the anticorruption convention of the OECD.

- Recommend that governments adopt simplified, clearly defined, transparent, and time-limited systems for any government process.

- Recommend adoption by the accountancy profession of international generally accepted accounting principles.

- Propose that governments adopt full disclosure of information on economic conditions as recommended by the International Monetary Fund.

- Develop corporate governance workshops for government officials.

Notes

1. Galal and Shirley (1995).

2. A number of programs can be reviewed at CIPE's Web site, www.cipe.org, under the corporate governance tab. The World Bank's Web site contains a number of corporate governance links, as well: www.worldbank.org.

3. Sonakul and Mongol (1999).

4. OECD (1999).

5. Shleifer and Vishny (1997).

6. This list is drawn from a course for new directors developed by the Central European University and CIPE. See CIPE's Web site for more information: www.cipe.org.

7. For example, see Jack (1999).

8. Stiglitz (1999).

9. These Principles can be found on the OECD Web site: www.oecd.gov.

10. These guidelines can be found in the corporate governance section of CIPE's Web site: www.cipe.org.

11. CalPers also has an excellent Web site which hosts their recommendations for improvements in corporate governance: www.calpers-governance.org

12. See Bosh (1995): www.ceps.be. See also the European Corporate Governance Network: www.ecgn.ulb.ac.be.

13. See annex 7.1 for the full list of recommendations from the Bangkok Conference.

14. La Porta and others (1997).

15. For a review of the available literature with special reference to Russia, see Berglof and von Thadden (1999).

16. For a concise summary of these trends in Latin America and the response of Latin America's leading firms, see the interview with Cesar Souza (Souza 1999). Souza is Senior Vice President of Odebrecht of America, a heavy construction firm operating in 14 countries.

17. Salmon 1993.

Bibliography

Bergolf, Erik, and Ernst-Ludwig von Thadden. 1999. "The Changing Corporate Governance Paradigm: Implications for Transitional and Developing Countries." Presented at the "Annual World Bank Conference on Development Economics." Available on the World Bank Web site: www.worldbank.org.

Corporate Governance in Europe: Report of CEPS Working Party. 1995. Center for European Policy Studies (CEPS), Chairman Dr. Ulrich Bosh (Senior Vice President, Deutsch Bank), Rapporteur, Karel Lannoo (CEPS), June.

Galal, Ahmed, and Mary Shirley. 1995. *Bureaucrats and Business*, Oxford, U.K.: Oxford University Press.

Jack, Andrew. 1999. "Oil Giant Bogged Down in Siberian Intrigue: BP Amoco's Stake in Sidance Has Become a Litmus Test for Foreign Investment in Russia." *Financial Times*, October 20.

La Porta, Rafael, Florencio Lopez De Silanes, Andrei Schleifer, and Robert Vishny. 1997. "Legal Determinants of External Finance." *Journal of Finance* 52 July.

OECD (Organisation for Economic Co-operation and Development). 1999. "OECD Principles of Corporate Governance." Paris. www.oecd.gov.

Salmon, Walter. 1993. "Crisis Prevention: How to Gear Up Your Board." *Harvard Business Review* 7(1). Quoted in Marek Hessel (ed.), *In Search of Good Directors: Corporate Boards in Market and Transition Economies*. (2nd ed., 1998) Washington, D.C.: Center for International Private Enterprise.

Schleifer, Andrei, and Robert Vishny. 1997. "A Survey of Corporate Governance." *Journal of Finance* 52 (2/June).

Sonakul, M. R., and Chatu Mongol. 1999. "Corporate Governance and Globalization." Opening address at the "Asian Economic Crisis and Corporate Governance Reform" conference held September 12–14, Bangkok. Full text at www.cipe.org.

Souza, Cesar. 1999. "Latin America's Rapidly Changing Corporations." *Economic Reform Today* 1.

Stiglitz, Joseph E. 1999 "Quis Cutoiet Ipsos Custodes? (Who Is to Guard the Guards Themselves?)." Presented at the "Annual World Bank Conference on Development Economics"—Europe. Available on the World Bank Web site: www. worldbank.org.

www.calpers-governance.org.

www.cipe.org.

http://www.worldbank.org/html/fpd/privatesector/cg/codes.htm.

http://www.ecgi.org/codes/country_pages/codes_france.htm#1.

http://www.oecd.org/EN/document/0,,EN-document-76-3-no-15-8293-0,FF.html.

http://money.cnn.com/2000/01/06/companies/pricewaterhouse/.

PART IV

Sectoral Applications

CHAPTER 8

Strengthening Small and Medium Enterprises for International Competitiveness

Sanjay Lall

This chapter deals with the competitive problems facing small and medium-size enterprises (SMEs) in developing countries. It concentrates on the manufacturing sector, where the competitive threat is felt most directly at this time, and where there is enormous export potential.[1] It draws on the experience of the advanced and newly industrializing countries, and on an on-going study of SMEs in Europe and East Asia.[2] Following an introductory discussion of the importance of increasing the competitiveness of SMEs, the chapter will identify the types of problems SMEs are currently facing, and then will go on to evaluate how various countries are addressing these problems. After evaluating the relative successes and failures of these support schemes, the study concludes by offering a set of policy implications.

SMEs form, by number, the majority of manufacturing enterprises at all levels of development. In many economies they provide the bulk of employment. In some they are also substantial contributors to exports and innovative activity. In developed economies SMEs tend to be in "modern" manufacturing and services, often in cutting-edge technology-based activities. It is generally the case, in all economies but particularly in the more industrialized ones, that SMEs learn most from each other and from larger enterprises (Levy 1994). These market-based learning mechanisms are often not enough to support technology development, however, particularly when competition intensifies and technical change becomes very rapid.

Governments are trying to enhance the benefits offered by SMEs, even in mature industrial countries where market-based information and support systems are well developed. Governments are investing considerable effort and resources in supporting SME growth and SME upgrading.[3] The recognition of the competitive significance of SMEs is relatively recent, however, even in the industrial world. As Albu (1998, p.1) puts it:

> The revival of interest in small manufacturing enterprises as important agents in the industrial economy is a relatively recent phenomenon in Europe. In the U.K., and other early industrializing countries, small firms' share of manufacturing output was in decline for most of this century. This decline was regarded by many as inevitable: the reflection of large companies' inherent potential to realize economies of scale and technological proficiency, as well as to exploit their market power. . . . The end of the 1960s also marked a turning point: evidence suggests that a resurgence in small manufacturing firms' economic importance began at this time. For example, small firms' share of manufacturing, which had fallen to 19 percent in the 1960's, rose to 32 percent by 1990. The number of manufacturing establishments with 10 or fewer employees, which had fallen to only 35,000 during the 1960's, subsequently rose to over 100,000 by 1985. Although these striking patterns were not visible in all European countries, it is clear that a shift in the structure of manufacturing industry was (and still is) taking place. In Germany, the United States, and Italy a similar, but weaker or delayed pattern is discernible.

Smaller enterprises have been active in manufacturing since before the Industrial Revolution began in the 18th century. Even with the advent of large-scale production, smaller enterprises have flourished in "niches" in which achieving economies of scale is not important for the success of SMEs—or where flexibility, customization, locational advantages, subcontracting to larger firms can offset their importance. They have also been able to reap scale economies in functions such as marketing, information, training, design, and so on by cooperating with each other or "clustering" together. The revival of interest in SMEs may reflect a growing recognition of their basic advantages; it also reflects new trends. The ability of SMEs to grow, compete, export, and innovate has been enhanced by several factors:

- The declining competitiveness of industrial countries in mass production activities, forcing them into activities with a greater skill and technological edge, sometimes in smaller facilities, that respond better to what Best (1990) calls "the new competition"

- The turbulence caused by rapid and continuous technological progress, favoring small enterprises that have an advantage in the early stages of innovation before technologies "settle down" and become scale economies in production, marketing, or research and development (R&D) become important

- The growing availability of risk capital for small technology-based firms in the form of venture capital, special government financing, or specialized financial services

- The increasing demand for specialized, custom-made products, combined with information-based technologies that reduce SME handicaps in accessing and processing information

- The availability of computerized technologies that allow smaller, more flexible production units to compete directly on cost with larger, more specialized ones

- Competitive pressures on larger firms to cut costs by subcontracting traditional "in-house" activities to SMEs, or to spinning off smaller affiliates

- Technological changes in transport and communication, enabling subcontracting to be more efficient, with closer linkages (one result being just-in-time production)

- Policy changes favoring smaller enterprises such as a strong competition policy within industrial countries, stronger SME support, incubator schemes, and so on

- The liberalization of trade and investment flows, opening up new opportunities for overseas investment by small firms[4]

- The growth of dynamic clusters of SMEs, in both industrial and developing countries, with active cooperation by clusters of SMEs to achieve international competitiveness.

In developing countries there are also significant numbers of SMEs flourishing in modern activities, often exporting significant amounts. However, the proportion of "modern" SMEs differs considerably between countries; most are found in the newly industrializing countries with strong entrepreneurial bases, vibrant export sectors, and a large base of educated and technical manpower. Table 8.1 illustrates the situation in some East Asian and industrial countries.

In many developing countries, particularly the less industrial ones, there is a sharp divide between modern and traditional SMEs. A significant section of SMEs in developing countries remains in traditional activities with low levels of productivity and poor quality products, serving small, localized markets. There is little or

TABLE 8.1 ROLE OF SMALL AND MEDIUM ENTERPRISES IN SELECTED COUNTRIES

Country/economy	Share in employment (percent)	Share in number of enterprises (percent)	Share in exports (percent)
East Asian countries and economies			
China	84		50
Hong Kong, China	63	97	>70
Korea, Rep. of	78	99	43
Taiwan, China	68	96	56
Philippines	50	98	—
Thailand	74	98	—
Indonesia	—	97	—
Industrial countries			
Japan	79	99	13
Germany	66	99	—
Italy	49[a]	99	—
Greece	91	99	—
France	57	99	—
United Kingdom	58	—	—
United States	53	99	29

— Not available.
a. Manufacturing only.
Source: Van Houtte 1997.

no technological dynamism in this group, and few SMEs "graduate" into large size or modern technologies. In many poor countries there is also a large underclass of microenterprises that ekes out a bare survival. Some of these small and micro-enterprises (formal and informal) may be economically viable over the long term, but the majority are not. With import liberalization, changing technology, and growing demand for higher quality modern products, many traditional SMEs face closure or very difficult upgrading.

Even "modern" SMEs face very difficult competitive challenges in many countries in the new world with import liberalization, changes in technology, growing and higher demand for higher-quality modern products, and so on. The threat of facing competition challenges is one aspect of the larger competitive challenges posed by accelerating technical change, globalization, and liberalization. The pace of change is so rapid, and its scope so wide, that some analysts see the emergence of a new technological "paradigm" (Freeman and Perez 1990). Others, such as

Best (1990), point to the changing competitive context. Traditional modes of competition, based on low costs and prices, are being replaced by the "new competition," driven by quality, flexibility, design, reliability, and networking.

This change is not just in advanced manufactures but also in mundane consumer goods such as clothing, footwear, and food products. Firms are specializing increasingly in different segments of the production chain, and are outsourcing segments and services to other firms to reap economies of scale and specialization. At the same time, most leading firms are broadening their field of technological competence to manage effectively the complexities of supply chain management and innovation. Information flows, interaction, and networking are the new weapons in the competitive armory; in technology-intensive activities these often include strategic partnerships with rivals and close collaboration with vertically linked enterprises.

The new technological paradigm defines the world in which SMEs increasingly must grow and compete. The paradigm is leading to large shifts in the location of productive and innovative activity and patterns of comparative advantage. The world is increasingly driven by technological competence within given activities, and by a structural shift from low- to high-technology (high-tech) activities (those with rapidly changing technologies and high rates of R&D spending). Technology-based activities are growing more rapidly in production and trade in all major industrial and developing economies (figure 8.1).

Recent analysis of patterns of export growth shows that trade dynamism is increasingly correlated with technology intensity (Lall 1998). Primary products are the slowest growing category of world exports. Within manufactures, resource-based products lag behind others, while the leading group is high-tech products. This pattern is even more noticeable for developing countries than industrial ones, although technological dynamism in the developing world is highly concentrated in a few countries, largely in East Asia (see appendix 8A).

Competitive Problems Facing Small and Medium Enterprises

SMEs in general tend to face *three sets* of competitive problems. Some are inherent in being small, some reflect distortions in markets and institutions, and some are caused by policy intervention. The "remedies" to these problems clearly differ according to their nature and source.

1. The Disadvantages of Small Size
The first set of disadvantages relates to disadvantages of small size per se. Where manufacturing, marketing, technological, or other functions have inherent scale economies, small size imposes cost and innovative penalties on SMEs. These are structural features of the industrial scene, however—they simply indicate that SMEs have to specialize in different activities or processes from large firms. By so specializing they can flourish and exploit their own advantages of flexibility and

FIGURE 8.1 GROWTH RATES OF TOTAL AND HIGH-TECH PRODUCTION
AND EXPORTS, 1980–95

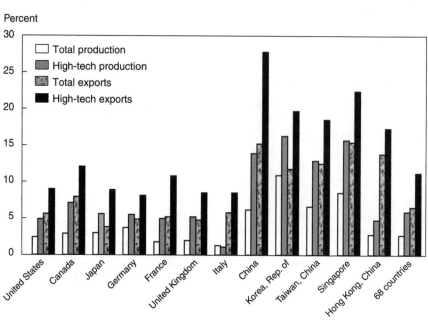

internal coordination. The relative advantage of SMEs is where scale economies
are less marked, or where they can offset such economies by choosing technologies
that allow them to offset their cost handicap by responding rapidly to changing
conditions, finding niche markets or customizing their products. In the early stages
of technological innovation, before the industrial structure has "settled down," small
firms can be more innovative than large firms. Many electronics and software technologies illustrate this clearly. The spread of computer-controlled equipment helps
SMEs, since large investments in specialized machinery become less important in
certain activities.

Where SMEs cannot individually establish a competitive advantage, they can
realize scale advantages by cooperating with other small enterprises and subcontracting from larger enterprises. As noted at the start, SMEs learn collectively—
from each other, from large firms, and from support services and institutions. The
growing literature on clusters[5] suggests that firms in close proximity (or able to
establish information and other linkages across geographical distance) reap various agglomeration economies. Some of these are enjoyed by a simple act of being
in the right place—the availability of particular skills, materials, or markets, sav-

ing transaction costs for buyers, and the development of ancillary activities and institutions. Others need active collaboration. Enterprises can jointly undertake functions where scale economies arise: for instance, training workers, designing new products, conducting quality control or research activity, storing and transporting goods, and so on. This generally involves setting up institutions, but it may involve others forms of collective action to influence existing institutions or policymakers.

Subcontracting to large firms, with or without a cluster, is also an effective way for SMEs to build on their advantages. As noted, the growing trend on the part of large firms to specialize, "downsize," and network has increased their reliance on small suppliers and contractors. In many industries it has also made them more willing to integrate SMEs into their technological activities. The falling costs of information technology (IT) and communication enhance this tendency, and it makes extensive networking by SMEs themselves less dependent on geographical proximity.

However, small size does impose certain disadvantages despite potential clustering and subcontracting. SMEs are at a disadvantage in activities where the risks involved are large, technology is exceptionally fast-moving and based on massive R&D, or investments have to aim at global markets from the start. As noted, their advantages of flexibility and innovativeness diminish as technologies stabilize and large-scale production and marketing become more important. Clustering also has its limitations. Some activities may be too difficult to manage on a cooperative basis, such as where valuable proprietary knowledge, market-branded products, the tapping of particular markets, or creation of specific skills is involved. Many agglomerations do not develop into genuine clusters, but remain a group of traditional SMEs: technologically stagnant and with low productivity. This may be because of the larger environment in which they operate (say, with policy constraints of growth or low levels of general skill and technology development) or because they are unable to undertake cooperative activity to enhance competitiveness. This may, in turn, reflect a lack of trust between SMEs, cultural traditions of noncooperation, or the absence of an internal or external catalyst to collective action. Clustering can also have costs—such as congestion, excessive duplication, free-rider problems, or domination by a few members—that lead to inefficiency, lack of innovation, or inflexibility. Clusters may breed inward-looking attitudes and deter members from seeking external alliances.

2. Distortions in Markets and Institutions

The second set of disadvantages is that SMEs may face segmented factor markets. In other words, large firms may have greater or more privileged access to input, credit, labor, infrastructure, information, and technology markets. There are economic reasons for this: providers of productive factors find it easier, safer, and cheaper to deal with a few large customers than a range of small and dispersed customers. It is difficult to collect detailed information on the latter. They are more difficult to monitor, and the cost of enforcing contracts may be disproportionately large in relation to the size of the transaction.

The best-known case of this is in credit and capital markets, where the literature on information economics analyzes how SMEs face problems created by missing markets and asymmetry. However, there are similar tendencies in all other factor markets where transactions are discrete and involve direct relations between buyer and seller. In the present context an important asymmetry is in the ability of SMEs to find, evaluate, purchase, and master new foreign technologies. International technology markets are notoriously imperfect, and finding the right technology at the right price can be a costly and lengthy task. More important, learning to master a new technology, particularly one involving new skills, materials, and methods, can be an uncertain and costly process. The problems of technological mastery are far greater when, as in most developing countries, factor markets and institutions are themselves underdeveloped and unresponsive.

Empirical research in less developed countries shows that SMEs are poorly placed to deal with technical change and upgrading (Lall 1999b). Not only do they lack the information and resources to access new technologies and skills, they often do not know how weak they are. They may be unaware of competing technologies in other countries. They may not realize the nature of the new skills and techniques needed to keep up. They may lack the entrepreneurial knowledge and education to seek the technology or assistance needed. The problem is clearly much greater for SMEs in the traditional and rural sectors of developing countries, but information and skill problems affect SMEs everywhere. Even in highly industrialized countries such as the United States and Japan, SMEs find it difficult to keep abreast of international technological and market trends (OTA 1990).

3. Biases in Government Policies

The third set of disadvantages is that policies and institutions relevant to manufacturing can be biased against SMEs. This is particularly the case in developing countries, where the widespread use of investment and import licenses and controls, directed credit, location incentives, infrastructure provision, and so on may favor firms with better resources and connections. Corruption and rent seeking by bureaucrats and politicians generally enhance the ability of large firms and groups to exploit the system.

Interestingly, some policies intended to favor SMEs also have undesirable effects on their dynamism and competitiveness. For instance, tax privileges given to smaller firms—and the effective exemption of microenterprises and informal enterprises from the tax system—provide strong incentives to stay small rather than grow large. It can lead to a proliferation of units below the taxable size, some of which may be technically efficient (although many are not). In countries such as India, where certain industrial products are reserved for SMEs, it has led to the stifling of competition and retardation of technological upgrading. In areas of export strength such as textiles, the protection policies adopted by India to protect the textile industry from competition have eroded an established area of national competitiveness.

Most developing countries tend to provide much weaker support systems for SMEs compared with industrial or newly industrializing ones. Elements of SME support systems in some of these countries are described below.

Support Policies for Small and Medium Enterprises in Selected Countries

Most governments are aware of the costs and market failures facing SMEs. The promotion of clusters has recently become a popular means of promoting competitiveness. The policy responses fall under three broad headings:

1. *Lowering transaction costs:* Removal of policies that discriminate against SMEs; raise entry, exit, and operational costs; and reduce access to support services and institutions.

2. *Remedying market failures:* Proactive measures to overcome market deficiencies by institutional support, incentives and subsidies, special access to finance, targeted training, and consultancy. Some of the most important stem from inadequate technological development. As Bessant puts it in his analysis of U.K. policies, "The reality is that many SMEs lack the capability to understand and articulate their needs, and rarely scan for sources of new technological opportunity. Even those that have an awareness of their needs may lack the information or capability to find and access sources of technology" (Bessant 1999, p. 3).

3. *Promoting clusters:* Encouragement of existing or potential agglomerations by provision of suitable infrastructure, promotion of linkages among SMEs and with large firms, and encouragement of local support institutions.

Some of the strongest, best-organized efforts to support SMEs are found in the mature industrial economies such as the United Kingdom, and in some developing East Asian countries.

U.K. Policies

The United Kingdom offers interesting lessons in support for SMEs; it is the most mature industrialized country in the world, and is traditionally very open to trade and investment. Under the long period of Conservative rule, from 1980 to 1997, the government's approach embodied the free-market beliefs of the government. Despite these beliefs, there was the clear need to help SMEs cope with intensifying competition and accelerating technical progress. The following description, taken from Albu 1998, provides a brief map.

The U.K. government considers favorable tax treatment for SMEs as a distortion of the free market. Instead, it seeks to influence the enterprise environment, which entails capital markets, advisory services, and the science, engineering, and technology base. Where SMEs have been featured in U.K. public policy, it has been principally within the context of promoting "competitiveness." Some general support for SMEs is found in recent attempts to modify and simplify various statutory and financial systems (Albu 1998). Business rates, income tax, national insurance systems, and value added tax systems have been adjusted, as have regulations governing audits and accounts. The government has also sought to reduce the obligations of SMEs in respect of labor rights (that is, labor laws). In general, however, the delivery of significant fiscal concessions or subsidies to SMEs in the United Kingdom has been felt to conflict with wider economic policy objectives. As a result, public support to SMEs aimed at reducing barriers in areas such as access to capital markets, business advisory services, and technological developments.

Policy measures thus fall into two spheres: (a) removing regulatory obstacles and reducing statutory costs faced disproportionately by SMEs and (b) information, advisory, and counseling initiatives aimed at improving performance in relation to exports, design, innovation, and technology. Responsibility for developing and managing these policies lies with the Department of Trade and Industry's (DTI's) Small Firms and Regional Development section.

BUSINESS LINK

One of the most tangible outputs of public policy and investment in SMEs since 1992 has been the Business Link (BL) program. This is intended to provide single points of easy access for SMEs to an integrated range of business support services. Government support to BL is worth £120 million a year. The national BL network currently has over 200 outlets and achieves significant coverage. In any quarter, around 35 percent of firms with between 50 to 200 employees are using BL services, although the proportion is less for the more numerous smaller firms. Client firms get personal business advisors; access to counselors specializing in export development; design, innovation, and technology; and other services such as loan guarantees. In around 40 percent of cases examined, the assistance enabled firms to achieve results and improvements in performance that would not otherwise have been possible.

U.K. BENCHMARKING INDEX

One of the services being promoted through BL is designed to encourage greater use of performance benchmarking by SMEs. A central database of information with over 60 indicators of financial, operational, and managerial performance has been collected nationally. The object of the exercise is to benchmark around 10,000 SMEs per year, comparing company performance to national, regional, or sectoral standards. The comparison is used to offer subsidized consultancy services to firms to help them improve their performance. Large firms conduct intensive benchmarking exercises on their own, or with the support of the Confederation of British Industry (the Probe software they use contains benchmarks based on thousands of leading European Union [EU] firms). In addition, the government conducts productivity comparisons of major industries to assess if and why there are gaps with regard to major competitors. The importance of benchmarking as a practical policy tool must be stressed: Not only is it a skill- and information-intensive tool, but it is also able to provide essential microdata to feed into policy support.

SMALL FIRMS LOAN GUARANTEE SCHEME

Loan guarantee schemes (LGSs) provide DTI-secured loans to SMEs through the commercial banks, worth about £250 million per year. These loans are for all types of firms; only about 6 percent go to technology-based firms.

SMALL FIRMS' TRAINING INITIATIVES

Three initiatives have been designed exclusively for small firms since 1994. Skills for Small Businesses provided £63 million to train 24,000 key workers; Small Firms' Training Loans offered deferred repayment loans of up to £125,000 for skill upgrading; and the Small Firms' Training Challenge provided awards for joint training by groups of 10 or more firms: £3.5 million was awarded in the first year.

REGIONAL SELECTIVE ASSISTANCE

This is a discretionary scheme to attract investment and create or safeguard jobs in assisted regions. Grants of up to 15 percent of project costs are made for a company to carry out an investment project. Qualifying projects include purchase of fixed assets, including purchasing new plants, or modernizing or adding on new facilities to existing plants.

LINK SCHEME

This is quite distinct from the BL mentioned above. LINK is the principal mechanism for supporting collaborative research partnerships between U.K. industry and the research base (also see Bessant 1998). LINK aims to enhance the competitiveness of U.K. industry through support (including 50 percent finance) for "managed programs of precompetitive Science & Technology in market or technology sectors, and by encouraging industry to invest in further work leading to commercially successful products, processes, systems, and services" (LINK mission statement—http://www.nerc.ac.uk/funding/thematics/eolink/WhatIsLink.shtml). LINK currently has programs in electronics, communications, and IT; food and agriculture; biosciences and medicine; materials and chemicals; and energy and engineering. Public sponsorship comes from a variety of government departments and research councils, totaling £40 million a year.

WORKING PARTY

DTI is sponsoring the Confederation of British Industry's Tech-Stars group, which aims to identify ways of removing barriers to growth of small, technology-based firms, in particular by effective management teams and corporate alliances. All DTI-supported SME services are now supplied through the BL network of outlets.

Services for technology-based small and medium enterprises include the following:

The Smart Scheme—Reintroduced in April 1997, this provides grants to SMEs for precompetitive feasibility studies into innovative technology and for development up to the preproduction prototype stage of new products and processes. It combines previous SMART: Small Firm Merit Award for Research and Technology, SPUR: Support for Products Under Research schemes, and the innovation element of regional enterprise grants. Awards are made on a competitive basis in two forms:

1. Feasibility Studies. Small businesses with fewer than 50 employees may submit proposals for support with feasibility studies. Assistance will be 75 percent of eligible project costs up to a maximum of £45,000.

2. Development Projects. All SMEs may compete for support with development projects. The awards are 30 percent of eligible project costs up to a maximum grant of European currency unit (ECU) 200,000. A very small number of exceptional development projects may receive a higher grant (up to ECU 600,000).

Innovation & Technology Counselors (ITCs)—As part of the BL's service, networks of local advisors coordinate the use of local sources of innovation support by BL's clients. Approximately 70 ITCs were in place in 1997 at a cost of about £2.5 million a year. The impact is difficult to assess from the information available, but will depend largely on the quality of the innovation support available from local research and technology organizations (RTOs) or other services to which they refer their clients.

Focus Technical—A £6 million program launched in 1995, initially intended to last three years, is an attempt to address this last problem. The program aims to assist RTOs to extend their technological products and services to better meet the needs of SMEs, and to improve RTOs' networking capabilities with other business support organizations, including BL, so as to direct innovation and technology services to SMEs.

Business Incubators—Business incubators are special estates to create a nurturing, instructive, and supportive environment for "fast track" small companies, providing access to a range of business skills, training, and finance. Incubator directors are directly involved in selecting companies, and in assessing these companies' success in growing and graduating from the incubator. The Enterprise Panel, a Treasury-established working party, reported a positive potential for developing more incubators as a means of promoting development of high-tech and innovative SMEs. At least 50 incubator-type projects exist in the United Kingdom.

Asian Newly Industrialized Economies

In terms of developing countries, Asian Newly Industrialized Economies (NIEs) offer several outstanding and successful examples of SME support policies. Let us now consider the following: Taiwan (China), the Republic of Korea, Singapore, and Hong Kong (China).

TAIWAN (CHINA)

Taiwan has perhaps the best-developed system of any developing country.[6] It has around 700,000 SMEs, accounting for 70 percent of employment, 55 percent of gross national product (GNP), and 62 percent of manufactured exports, and an impressive set of programs to support them. In 1981 the government set up the Medium and Small Business Administration to support SME development and coordinate the several agencies that provide assistance to them. As a result the range of services currently available for SMEs in Taiwan includes financial assistance from several banks, funds, and centers; government-subsidized management and technology assistance; and R&D support.

The government also offers a variety of highly specialized programs that target such industries as handicraft and automation, and topics of special concern to SMEs such as the promotion of technology, and production efficiency. In terms of research the government strongly encourages SMEs to contract research to universities, dedicating half of the National Science Council's research grants (about $200 million per year[7]) to matching funds to industry for such contracts. It has also set up a science town in Hsinchu where 13,000 researchers in two universities, six national laboratories (including ITRI), and a huge technology institute, as well as some 150 companies specializing in electronics operate, integrate, and promote SMEs.

In addition, the government orchestrates technological activity in a number of what it considers strategic activities, where free markets by themselves will produce insufficient innovation. As Poon and Mathews (1997) explain:

> IBM unveiled its first PC based on the new PowerPC microprocessor, a product made by the alliance of IBM, Motorola and Apple, in New York in June 1995. It was followed one day later by the unveiling in Taipei of PowerPC based products by a group of 30 firms from Taiwan (China). Taiwan was the first country [sic] outside the US to have developed a range of state-of-art products based on the new technology. The Taiwanese firms had not done this on their own: they were part of an innovation alliance, the Taiwan New PC Consortium formed by a government research institution, the Computing and Communications Laboratory (CCL). The Consortium was set up in 1993 to bring together firms from all parts of the information technology industry in Taiwan. The firms involved were relatively small by international standards, and CCL brought them together and negotiated on their behalf with IBM and Motorola.

This was not the only instance of strategic alliance formation by the Taiwanese government to stimulate innovation and take industry to technological frontiers. The Industrial Technology Research Institute (ITRI) had led in the formation of some 30 consortia in the IT industry over the 1990s. In each case ITRI identified the products, tapped channels of technology transfer, mobilized the firms, handled the complex negotiations with industrial country firms, and covered intellectual property issues. The individual firms developed their own versions of the jointly developed core products and competed in final markets at home and abroad. Their size limited their ability to have done this on their own.[8]

REPUBLIC OF KOREA

Korea deliberately promoted large private conglomerates, the *chaebols*, to spearhead its strategic drive into heavy and high-tech industry at world-class technological levels, under national ownership (Lall 1996). However, it has also sponsored a range of SME support programs, including the promotion of R&D by these enterprises. The results have been impressive. The number of SME R&D units has grown from 24 in 1985 to 2,278 in 1997, and by 1996 their R&D expenditures accounted for 13 percent of total manufacturing R&D (Chung and Park 1998). SMEs have also set up several collaborative centers and contracted universities and research institutes to conduct R&D on their behalf. The Korean government promoted the import of technology by tax incentives. Transfer costs of patent rights and technology import fees were tax deductible. Income from technology consulting was tax-exempt, and foreign engineers were exempt from income tax. In addition, the government gave grants and long-term low-interest loans to participants in "National Projects," which gave tax privileges and official funds to private and government R&D institutes to carry out these projects.

Since the early 1980s a number of laws were passed to promote SMEs, leading to a perceptible rise in their share of economic activity (over 1975–86 the share of SMEs in employment, sales, and value added rose by at least 25 percent). This policy support, which covered SME start-up, productivity improvement, technology development, and export promotion, was crucial to the reversal in their performance. A host of tax incentives was provided to firms participating in these programs, as well as finance at subsidized rates for using support services, credit guarantees, government procurement, and the setting up of a specialized bank to finance SMEs. A number of other institutions were set up to help SMEs (such as the Small and Medium Industry Promotion Corporation to provide financial, technical, and training assistance; and the Industrial Development Bank to provide finance). The government greatly increased its own budget contribution to the program, although SMEs had to pay a part of the costs of most services provided to them.

SINGAPORE

Singapore is justly renowned for the excellence of its infrastructure, in technology as well as in other fields. While relying heavily on giant multinational corporations (MNCs) to lead its industrial drive, the government has also attempted to boost indigenous SMEs. In 1962 the Economic Development Board (EDB) launched a program to help SMEs modernize their equipment with funds provided by the United Nations Development Programme (UNDP). In the mid-1970s several other schemes for financial assistance were added; of these, the most significant was the Small Industries Finance Scheme to encourage technological upgrading. The 1985 recession induced the government to launch stronger measures, and the Venture Capital Fund was set up to help SMEs acquire capital through low interest loans and equity. A Small Enterprises Bureau was established in 1986 to act as a one-stop consultancy agency; this helped SMEs with management and training, finance and grants, and coordinating assistance from other agencies. In 1987 a $519 million scheme was launched to cover eight programs to help SMEs, including product development assistance, technical assistance to import foreign consultancy, venture capital to help technology start-ups, robot leasing, training, and technology tie-ups with foreign companies.

In addition, the Singapore Institute of Standards and Industrial Research (SISIR) disseminated technology to SMEs, and helped their exports by providing information on foreign technical requirements and how to meet them. The National Productivity Board provided management advice and consultancy to SMEs. The Technology Development Center (TDC) helped local firms to identify their technology requirements and purchase technologies; it also designed technology-upgrading strategies. Since its founding in 1989, the TDC provided over 130 firms with various forms of technical assistance. It also administered the Small Industry Technical Assistance Scheme (SITAS) and Product Development Assistance Scheme to help firms develop their design and development capabilities. In fact, it gave grants of over $1 million for 29 SITASs in the past five years, mainly to local enterprises. Its earnings have risen to a level where its cost-recoverable activities are self-financing.

The EDB encouraged subcontracting to local firms through its Local Industries Upgrading Program, under which MNCs were encouraged to source components locally by "adopting" particular SMEs as subcontractors. In return for a commitment by the MNCs to provide on-the-job training and technical assistance to subcontractors, the government provided a package of assistance to the latter, including cost-sharing grants and loans for the purchase of equipment, or consultancy and the provision of training. By end-1990, 27 MNCs and 116 SMEs had joined this program. Over 1976–88 the total value of financial assistance by the Singapore government to SMEs amounted to $1.5 billion, of which 88 percent was in the Small Industries Financing Scheme. Grants of various kinds amounted to $23.4 million; the Skills Development Fund was for $48.6 million.

HONG KONG (CHINA)

Despite its *laissez-faire* approach to industry, this former colony provides strong technical support to its SMEs through the Hong Kong Productivity Council (HKPC). HKPC was the first support institution of its kind in the region, started in 1967 to help the myriad small firms that constitute the bulk of the industrial sector. The focus of HKPC has been to help firms upgrade from declining intensive–intensive manufacturing to more advanced, high-value-added activities. It provides information on international standards and quality, and gives training, consultancy, and demonstration services on productivity and quality to small firms at subsidized rates, serving over 4,000 firms each year. Its on-line information retrieval system has access to over 600 international databases on a comprehensive range of disciplines. Its library takes over 700 journals and has over 16,000 reference books.

The HKPC acts as a major agent for technology import, diffusion, and development for all the main industrial activities in the economy. It first identifies relevant new technologies in the international market, then builds up its own expertise in those technologies, and finally introduces them to local firms. Successful examples of this approach include surface-mount technology and three dimensional laser stereo-lithography. HKPC has also developed a number of computer-aided drafting and design (CAD), computer-aided manufacturing (CAM), computer-aided engineering (CAE), and computer-aided systems for the plastics and moulds industry, of which over 300 have been installed already. HKPC provides a range of management and technology-related courses, reaching some 15,000 participants a year. For firms unable to release staff to come to training, it organizes in-house training programs tailored to individual needs. To help the dissemination of IT, the council has strategic alliances with major computer vendors, and provides specially designed software for local industry, consultancy, and project management in computerization. HKPC provides consultancy services in International Standards Organization (ISO) 9000 systems, and has helped several firms in Hong Kong (China) to obtain certification. It assists firms in automation by designing and developing special-purpose equipment and advanced machines to improve process efficiency.

HKPC is a large organization with over 600 consultants and staff, a laboratory, and a demonstration center that can show the application of new technologies (in CAD/CAM), advanced manufacturing technology, surface mount technology, microprocessor technology, rapid prototyping, and so on). In 1993–94, it undertook 1,354 consultancy and technology assistance projects, trained over 15,000 people, and undertook 2,400 cases of manufacturing support services. Because small firms have trouble getting information on, and adopting, new technologies and are exceptionally averse to the risk and cost involved, the HKPC has always had to subsidize the cost of its services. Despite the growth in its share of revenue-earning work and its withdrawal from activities in which private consultants have appeared, the government still contributes about half its budget. It is important to note that technological information market failures, and the need for subsidized services, occur even in economies such as Hong Kong, China, with highly market-oriented economies and highly developed financial services.

The Hong Kong government also supported local design capabilities by joining the private sector in starting a school of design. It financed the Hong Kong Design Innovation Company (HKDIC) because private sector design services were lacking and local firms were not aware of their value. Over the four years of its existence (mainly on government financing), this value has been recognized, but the HKDIC (now under the HKPC) is still not financially self-supporting. Nevertheless, the growth of garment design capabilities in Hong Kong has helped its exporters to upgrade their products and to start to establish their own brands in international markets.

Conclusions

The above descriptions illustrate clearly the need for governments to support their SMEs. The most mature or dynamic industrial countries in the world, with well-functioning markets and institutions, feel the need to mount comprehensive measures to support SMEs; the need is even greater in countries at lower levels of development. The competitive challenges for countries at lower levels of development, related to competitiveness, are just as great, and the response capacity of SMEs is far more limited.

To start with, the business environment must be conducive to private sector development, with minimal transaction costs for smaller enterprises, with clear and transparent rules, and with a stable macroeconomic environment. As Levy puts it, "The leading source of support [for SMEs] comes from private channels—from buyers and traders, similar firms, suppliers and subcontracting principals, from banks and from the determined efforts of SMEs themselves. . . The first order of business . . . is to ensure that the private marketplace can work, that liberal rules govern the international flow of technical and marketing resources, and that private banks can go about their business of making and collecting loans and earning profits in the process" (Levy 1994, p. 55).

However, private support mechanisms, while necessary, are not sufficient. Proactive policy is needed to promote SME competitiveness. While some of it can be self-financing, a large component may need to be subsidized. In a globalizing context, perhaps the first need is to make firms fully aware of the competitive challenges they must face. Once the firms are aware of the challenges, the next need is to help them prepare to meet the challenge, by understanding their strengths and weaknesses (through benchmarking, technology audits, or skills audits), and by receiving the inputs they need to help them upgrade. The main inputs they need are finance, market information, management tools, technology, skills, and links with support institutions. The experience of Taiwan suggests that the best way to provide these inputs is by combining them in an attractive *package* rather than delivering them piecemeal. SMEs tend to avoid going to support institutions where a lot of time must be spent, and many formalities are involved before the SME is able to receive assistance. SMEs often cannot identify and define their own needs clearly enough to seek the best remedies, so the first step may be difficult for them to take. Thus, a service that can reach out, help firms to define their problems, and then help them devise a package of measures to deal with these problems has the best chance of success.

Too many specific policies can be undertaken to support SMEs for us to be able to discuss them all fully here. What is perhaps more useful is to present some general principles of support, taking support policies for SMEs per se separately from clusters.

Support Policies for SMEs

Romijn (1998) provides a useful catalogue of policy recommendations, which she terms the "Nine-fold C" approach, building upon the "Triple C" approach proposed by Humphrey and Schmitz (1996). Romijn's recommendations for supporting SMEs are the following:

1. *Customer orientation:* An approach in which support institutions' project efforts are driven by meeting customer needs and demands, rather than by "supply push."[9]

2. *Collectivity*: Support is likely to be more effective when it is provided to groups of SMEs rather than to individual producers. Group-based assistance is not only more cost-effective and practical than individual support, it can also lead to the establishment of linkages between SMEs that can lead to increased efficiency and on-going interactive learning.

3. *Cumulativeness:* One-off improvements are of limited use. Being competitive is not a state of being, or a result, but rather is a process that requires continuous improvements. This in turn requires that firms (or clusters of firms) build up a capacity to continuously upgrade their products, processes, and production organization and become more self-reliant in this respect. A similar criterion of self-reliance is now also applied to some support programs themselves, in that they must evolve institutional forms (usually collective) of self-help that will, over time, start to function independently from any external aid agency.

4. *Capability focus:* Although the nonavailability of appropriate "hardware" (such as machinery or equipment) can sometimes be a crucial constraint on the competitiveness of an SME, the development of the capabilities is as important as the acquisition of hardware. Usually SMEs need to acquire enhanced knowledge and skills about how to choose, use, and improve technology before they would be able to use it efficiently.

5. *Context and complementarity:* A supportive macroeconomic environment is of the utmost importance to the success of SMEs. In the current context, "supportive" is primarily defined in terms of the presence of growing and technologically dynamic markets that constantly provide new opportunities for technological upgrading of the SMEs. The content of the assistance has to be tailored to fit the general level of economic and technological development of the economy in question. This may appear obvious, but older projects did suffer from the lack of this support. For example, many low-income countries tried to promote subcontracting schemes prema-

turely. Now, however, it is only in the relatively advanced economies of Southeast and East Asia (such as the Republic of Korea) where the weaknesses in local subcontracting are emerging as a bottleneck. This is the sort of "demand-pull" environment where there is much scope to build technological support programs for SMEs around backward linkage development in the economy in general.

6. *Concentration:* Earlier programs often lacked effectiveness because the institutions delivering them were "spreading their efforts too thinly" in terms of the number and variety of economic activities. Thus, it was very difficult to build up in-depth expertise about the technological and market characteristics of specific industries and the main actors in these industries, how SMEs are positioned in these industries, and what their main industry-specific problems might be. Research and assistance should concentrate on commodity-specific subsectors. By giving considerable weight to the study of interactions between firms of different sizes and at different stages in the supply chain, this approach can provide a more thorough insight into the competitive context in which the target enterprises operate.

7. *Competence and credibility:* The "thin spread" of technical assistance projects and programs was not the only factor responsible for the inadequate expertise of agencies. The quality of many projects also suffered due to the inadequate professional and educational background of the assistance personnel. In recent assistance interventions a trend toward professionalization of assistance is noticeable, especially in the more industrial developing countries in Asia. This has also improved the assistance personnel's credibility with beneficiaries and other actors whom they need to involve in their projects and programs.

8. *Coordination:* Early assistance efforts also suffered from lack of coordination between different service providers and support activities. This is most evident in the East and Southeast Asian countries where governments have tended to establish very elaborate and wide-ranging support structures for SME, encompassing many different financing, training, and consulting projects and programs. The responsibility for these programs would be distributed widely over different governmental institutions and departments. Inefficiencies in assistance delivery were common because of duplication of effort. To make matters worse, programs would frequently be revamped, merged with other initiatives, or replaced with new ones. Such an obvious lack of transparency must have been a nightmare for many potential beneficiaries. It must have been a considerable effort simply for

the SMEs to find out how the support structure worked and where to turn for which type of assistance. In recent years we see that governments in these countries have begun to improve matters by introducing "one window" assistance delivery (Meyanathan 1994).

9. *"Carrot-and-stick" approach:* We have seen that the flawed incentive structure for both the assistance providers and the beneficiaries was perhaps the single most important cause of failure in the early SME technology (and other types of) support projects. A more effective approach is a combination of "carrots," potential rewards that will motivate the participants to take action, and "sticks," a set of sanctions that come into operation when the participants fail to do their best. The design of a balanced combination of carrots and sticks is a difficult task. It generally requires attention to economic aspects as well as to the institutional and sociopolitical context within which projects are to be implemented.

Cluster Development

In the context of clusters, it is useful to look at the recommendations by Albaladejo (1999) based on his study of a toy-manufacturing cluster and the assistance provided by La asociación de investigación de la industria del Juguete (the Spanish Toy Research Institute, or AIJU), which is the toy institute in Spain. His practical advice for support centers focuses on the principles of networking and coordination. He offers advice for support centers on such important matters as (a) how to select an accessible location; (b) what the best way might be to provide the service; and (c) how to set reasonable fees to attract the targeted companies. He also addresses other important responsibilities, such as how to encourage active SME participation in policy reform, foster the capabilities of local firms, act as an intermediary in technological diffusion, and encourage the development of well-researched and innovative products (see appendix 8C).

Other measures to promote SMEs involve the encouragement of subcontracting, both domestically and internationally. Some of the most dynamic SMEs in East Asia are in export activities, with foreign buyers or subcontractors providing the "missing elements" needed for the SMEs to be fully competitive. These elements generally include technical and quality assistance, help with purchasing the right equipment and inputs, product design, and, of course, marketing. Apart from providing suitable infrastructure (such as export processing zones), conducive trade and foreign direct investment policy environment, and flexible, trainable labor, the government can assist subcontracting linkages by various means (see Singapore's example above under the discussion on Asian newly industrialized economies).

Appendix 8A. Changing Technology Composition of World Exports and Developing Countries

The share in world trade of technologically complex products has risen steadily in recent years (Lall 1998). In fact, the higher the level of technological sophistication, the higher the growth rate—and the differences in technological dynamism increase over time. World exports of primary products grew at a modest 2.3 percent a year during 1980–90 and at only 1.4 percent over 1990–96 (figure 8A.1). At the other end of the spectrum, high-tech products (fine chemicals, sophisticated electronics, aircraft, and precision instruments) grew at around 12 percent a year compound in both periods. Medium-technology (medium-tech) products (machinery, simple electronics, chemicals, and transport equipment other than aircraft) grew at 8.4 percent and 6.9 percent during the same time periods, respectively. Low-technology (low-tech) products (textiles, clothing, toys, simple metal and plastic products, and footwear) grew at 7.7 percent and 5.6 percent, respectively, and resource-based manufactures at 6 percent and 5.3 percent, respectively. When export growth rates generally declined after the 1980s, complex products maintained their growth better than simpler products.

FIGURE 8A.1 GROWTH IN SHARE OF WORLD TRADE, 1980–96

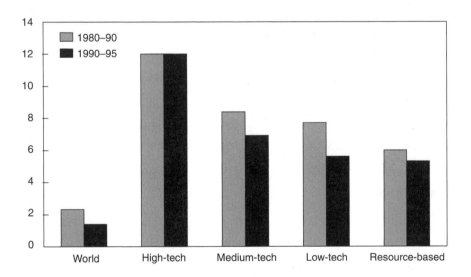

Of the value of the 50 most dynamic exports in the world over 1980–96, medium- and high-tech products accounted for a full 75 percent. Within these "ultra-dynamic" exports, high-tech products again grew the fastest, followed by medium-tech products. Low-tech products were the slowest growing category. Technological sophistication is thus increasingly important for trade growth.

Export success in the developing world, however, was highly concentrated by region and country. Asian developing countries accounted for 78 percent of the developing world's total manufactured exports and 89 percent of high-tech exports. Latin American developing countries accounted for 17 percent of total manufactured exports, 28 percent of resource-based, 12 percent of low-tech, 28 percent of medium-tech, and 11 percent of high-tech manufactures. Mexico dominated Latin American export activity after 1990, primarily because of the North American Free Trade Agreement: In 1996, Mexico alone accounted for 90 percent of the region's high-tech, 62 percent of medium-tech, and 50 percent of low-tech exports. Sub-Saharan Africa contributed 1.4 percent of the developing world's manufactured exports in 1996; if South Africa and Mauritius are excluded, the share drops to 0.1 percent in high-tech products.

Just 12 economies accounted for 92 percent of total manufactured exports by developing countries in 1996. These are composed of nine countries in Asia (the four mature newly industrialized economies [NIEs], the three new NIEs, India, and China) and three countries in Latin America (Argentina, Brazil, and Mexico). The level of concentration has increased over time, from 78 percent in 1985. In 1997, the level of concentration rose by technological sophistication, being lowest in resource-based developing-country exports, and were: high-tech 98 percent; medium-tech 87 percent; low-tech 84 percent; and resource-based 72 percent. The concentration level for total manufactured exports was 85 percent.

Appendix 8B. Small- and Medium-Enterprise Support in Taiwan (China)

Taiwan, China, has around 700,000 SMEs, accounting for 70 percent of employment, 55 percent of GNP, and 62 percent of manufactured exports, and an impressive set of programs to support them.

The following provides a thumbnail sketch (Dahlman and Sananikone 1990; Hobday 1995; Lall 1996; Mathews and Cho 2000).

In 1981, the government set up the Medium and Small Business Administration to support SME development and coordinate the several agencies that provided assistance to them. The Taiwan Medium Business Bank, the Bank of Taiwan, the Small and Medium Business Credit Guarantee Fund, and the Small Business Integrated Assistance Center provided financial assistance.

Management and technology assistance was provided by the China Productivity Center, the Industrial Technology Research Institute (ITRI), and a number of industrial technology centers (including centers for the metal industry, textiles, biotechnology, food, and information). The government of Taiwan covered up to 50 to 70 percent of consultation fees for management and technical consultancy services for SMEs. The Medium and Small Business Administration established a fund for SME promotion of (new Taiwan dollars—NT$) 10 billion. The "Center-Satellite Factory Promotion Program" of the Ministry of Economic Affairs integrated smaller factories around a principal one, supported by vendor assistance and productivity-raising efforts. By 1989 there were 60 networks with 1,186 satellite factories in operation, mainly in the electronics industry.

Several technology research institutes support R&D in the private sector, primarily in SMEs. The China Textile Research Center, set up in 1959 to inspect exports, was expanded to include training, quality systems, technology development, and the direct acquisition of foreign technology. The Metal Industries Development Center was set up in 1963 to work on practical development, testing, and quality control work in metalworking industries. It later established a CAD/CAM center to provide training and software to firms in this industry. The Precision Instrument Development Center fabricates instruments and promoted the instrument manufacturing industry, and has moved into advanced areas such as vacuum and electro-optics technology.

The most important center is ITRI, which conducts R&D on projects considered too risky for the private sector. It has seven laboratories, dealing with chemicals, mechanical industries, electronics, energy and mining, materials research, measurement standards, and electro-optics, but electronics is the principal focus, with its ERSO division accounting for two-thirds of its $450 million budget.

ERSO has spun off laboratories as private companies, including UMC in 1979 and TSMC in 1986, Taiwan's most successful integrated circuit makers. TSMC was a joint venture between the government and Philips of Holland: an illustration of the strategy of the government's willingness to play a lead role in orchestrating technology import, absorption, and development. TSMC's growth has supported design and manufacturing capabilities in many small electronics firms in Taiwan, leading to further entry of private manufacturers of semiconductors, microprocessors, and related electronics products. TSMC has grown into the world's largest dedicated chip manufacturing foundry, with a 24 percent global market share, followed by UMC with 20 percent. These foundries are increasingly used, not just by local chip design houses without in-house manufacturing capabilities, but also by U.S. giants such as Intel and Motorola, which out-source chips because of business cycles in the industry and the rising cost of new wafer-fabrication plants.

The government also strongly encourages SMEs to contract research to universities, and half of the National Science Council's research grants (about $200 million per year) provide matching funds to industry for such contracts.

The Taiwan Handicraft Promotion Center supports handicraft industries, particularly those handicrafts with export potential. Its main clients are small entrepreneurs, most with fewer than 20 employees. In addition, the Program for the

Promotion of Technology Transfer maintains close contact with foreign firms with leading-edge technologies in order to facilitate the transfer of those technologies to Taiwan.

The China Productivity Center (CPC) promotes automation in industry to cope with rising wages and increasing needs for precision and quality. It sends out teams of engineers to visit plants throughout the country, demonstrate the best means of automation, and solve relevant technical problems. CPC also carries out research projects on improving production efficiency, and has linked enterprises to research centers in order to solve more complex technical problems.

The government has set up a science town in Hsinchu, with 13,000 researchers in two universities, six national laboratories (including ITRI), and a huge technology institute, as well as some 150 companies specializing in electronics. The science town makes a special effort to attract start-ups and provides them with prefabricated factory space, five-year tax holidays, and generous grants. In the 1980s the government invested $500 million in Hsinchu.

The Program for the Promotion of Technology Transfer maintains close contact with foreign corporations that have developed leading-edge technologies in order to facilitate the transfer of those technologies to Taiwan (China).

Appendix 8C. Advice on Supporting Clusters:
The Experience of Toy Manufacturing in Spain

- Service centers should be located close to the industry they serve (Albaladejo 1999). Toy firms acknowledge that the provision of some technical services such as training and laboratory testing requires weekly or even daily contact, and that many SMEs would not benefit from technical assistance if the service center was not located in the cluster itself. Close location to the SMEs means a reduction of transaction costs and a quicker response to technical problems. In terms of innovation, technological upgrading and innovation processes gain from local institutions. Developing countries should ensure that centralized administrations and bureaucratic barriers do not impede the location of these institutions.

- Service centers should benefit SMEs more than large firms, especially in developing economies where the difference between large and small tends to be more acute. Membership entrance fees and prices for services should be fixed according to profits and size. Such prices should also be lower than market prices for the same or similar services. For instance, the AIJU membership fee system is oriented to benefit the weakest, with a minimum membership fee of £176 for firms with fewer than 50 employees. Toy-related firms point out that this extraordinarily low entrance fee is an incentive for SMEs to become members and actively participate in AIJU's services. Policymakers should ensure that service centers located in SME clusters adopt a policy oriented to benefit groups of small firms rather than large individual firms. This collective approach strengthens interfirm cooperative links.

- Although horizontal institutions are of great importance, sectoral institutes can be crucial for the welfare of particular industrial sectors because they reflect the specific needs of the SMEs they serve. A participatory approach to the planning and design of policy interventions offers the advantage of a more precise understanding of the SME needs. In order to achieve this, SME representatives should sit on the Supervisory Board of every support institution; this is the case with AIJU. Policymakers should be aware of the great benefits of sectoral institutes and the importance of SME involvement and participation in their policy design and intervention.

- Service centers should be run on business lines, with a demand base to ensure their sustainability. The ability to earn a substantial portion of the budget is a good indicator of an institution's credibility and relevance. The higher the SME control and ownership, the higher the institution's capacity for sustainability and success. A good indicator of AIJU's sustainability is that 85 percent of its revenues come from the private sector. Support policies designed and implemented with the help of SME representatives tend to result in more practical, cost-effective, and realistic technical services.

- Being aware of the technological limitation of clusters, service centers should foster the capabilities of local firms through teaching them to make good use of external technological resources. Innovation processes are uncertain, costly, and very risky, especially in the case of SMEs, since they have to struggle to find the appropriate equipment as well as to develop the necessary skills and capabilities to use the machinery efficiently. From the AIJU experience, service centers in developing countries should learn to reduce these "limitations on innovation" that SMEs face by doing the following:

    - Designing support services on the basis of the indigenous capacities and the spread of technologies through interenterprise learning. Service centers should act as intermediaries in technological diffusion and upgrading in the cluster rather than triggering change and growth.

    - Focusing on R&D-intensive services to encourage SMEs to move toward more innovative products.

- Putting science on the shop floor by having technological commissions where scientists and entrepreneurs work together. The AIJU
  experience shows that this is one of the most practical and efficient
  ways to increase innovation within firms.

- Focusing on the final stage of the production process (such as marketing and commercialization). Innovation means nothing if there is
  no market niche for the new product. SMEs should be encouraged to
  conduct marketing research so that they can discover the viability
  and prospects of innovations.

- Finally, the effectiveness of support centers also depends on the wider
  institutional framework. Governments should design policies to create an
  appropriate consensual and regulatory environment for SME development.
  Financial support schemes by commercial banks, private organizations,
  and so forth can help SMEs in technology upgrading. Other local institutions such as employers' organizations and trade unions can act as vehicles for decentralizing initiatives in favor of local producers. However,
  an effective support system does not rely as much on the number of institutions actively functioning as on their *networking* and *coordination*.

Notes

1. The service sector, where SMEs are most prominent, is also of great competitive significance. The liberalization of investment flows and the international spread of service providers
from advanced countries mean that developing-country service SMEs are facing increasing
pressures. This chapter does not deal with this sector, however.

2. The EU project is on "Small and Medium Enterprises in Europe and East Asia: Competition,
Collaboration and Lessons for Policy Support," and involves several groups in Europe, Israel,
Japan, the Republic of Korea, and Taiwan (China). The author is grateful to the following
members of the Queen Elizabeth House team: Manuel Albaladejo, Mike Albu (now with the
Intermediate Technology Development Group), and Henny Romijn (also lecturing at Eindhoven
University, Holland).

3. See the references to SME-related activities in the United Kingdom and the European Union
in the bibliography.

4. On the growth of small transnational enterprises, see UNCTAD 1999.

5. See Advani 1997; Bianchi 1993; Luthria 1998; Nadvi 1999; Nadvi and Schmitz 1994; Pyke,
Becattini, and Sengenberger 1990; Rabellotti 1997; Schmitz 1992, 1995; UNCTAD 1994; Van
Dijk and Rabellotti 1997.

6. Based on findings from Dahlman and Sananikone 1990; Hobday 1995; Lall 1996; Mathews and Cho 2000. For more information, see appendix 8B.

7. All dollar amounts are U.S. dollars.

8. Poon and Mathews 1997.

9. Romijn 1998.

Bibliography

Advani, A. 1997. "Industrial Clusters: A Support System for Small and Medium Sized Enterprises." PSD Occasional Paper No. 32, Private Sector Development Department, World Bank, Washington, D.C.

Albaladejo, M. 1999. "A Service Center Approach to Local Innovative SMEs: The Case of the Spanish 'Toy Valley' Cluster." Queen Elizabeth House, Oxford. Draft.

Albu, M. 1998. "Public Policy toward Small and Medium-Sized Manufacturing Enterprises in the U.K. and EU." Queen Elizabeth House, Oxford. Draft.

Bessant, J. 1998. "Developing Continuous Improvement Capability." *International Journal of Innovation Management,* 2(4): 409–29.

———. 1999. "The Rise and Fall of 'Supernet': A Case Study of Technology Transfer Policy for Smaller Firms." Center for Research in Innovation Management, University of Brighton. Draft.

Best, M. 1990. *The New Competition.* Cambridge, Mass.: Harvard University Press.

Bianchi, P. 1993. "The Promotion of Small-Firm Clusters and Industrial Districts: European Policy Perspectives." *Journal of Industry Studies* 1(1): 16–29.

Chung, S., and D. H. Park. 1998. "Technological Capabilities of Korean SMEs: A Preliminary Analysis." Science and Technology Policy Institute, Seoul. Draft.

Cosh, A., A. Hughes, and E. Wood. 1998. "Innovation in U.K. SMEs: Causes and Consequences for Firm Failure and Acquisition." In Z. Acs and B. Carlsson, eds., *Entrepreneurship, SMEs and the Macro Economy.* Cambridge: Cambridge University Press.

Dahlman, C. J., and O. Sananikone. 1990. "Technology Strategy in Taiwan: Exploiting Foreign Linkages and Investing in Local Capability." Working Paper, World Bank, Washington, D.C.

DTI (Department of Trade and Industry). 1996. "Small Firms in Britain." Her Majesty's Stationery Office, Annual Report.

————. 1997a. "SME Statistics for the U.K. 1996." *Statistical Bulletin,* July.

————. 1997b. "Differences in Companies' Performance: British Industries Under-performing Tail." Discussion document, November. http://www.dti.gov.uk/comp/differen.pdf.

————. 1997c. "Competitiveness U.K.: A Benchmark for Business." November. http://www.dti.gov.uk/comp/bench.htm.

European Commission. 1995. "Small and Medium-Sized Enterprises: A Dynamic Source of Employment, Growth and Competitiveness in the European Union." DG XXIII, CSE (95) 2087, Brussels.

Freeman, C., and C. Perez. 1990. "Structural Crises of Adjustment, Business Cycles, and Investment Behavior." In G. Dosi, C. Freeman, R. Nelson, G. Silverberg, and L. Soete, eds., *Technical Change and Economic Theory.* Printer Publisher Ltd.

Hobday, M. G. 1995. *Innovation in East Asia: The Challenge to Japan.* Cheltenham: Edward Elgar.

Humphrey, J., and H. Schmitz. 1996. "The Triple C Approach to Local Industrial Policy." *World Development* 24(12): 1859–77.

Lall, S. 1992. "Technological Capabilities and Industrialization." *World Development* 20(2): 165–86.

————. 1996. *Learning from the Asian Tigers.* London: Macmillan.

————. 1998. "Exports of Manufactures by Developing Countries: Emerging Patterns of Trade and Location." *Oxford Review of Economic Policy* 14(2): 54–73.

————. 1999a. *Promoting Competitiveness in Developing Countries: Lessons from East Asia.* London: Commonwealth Secretariat Economic Paper.

————, ed. 1999b. *The Technological Response to Import Liberalization in Sub-Saharan Africa.* London: Macmillan.

Lee, C. J. 1995. "The Industrial Networks of Taiwan's Small and Medium Sized Enterprises." *Journal of Industry Studies* 2(2): 75–88.

Levy, B. 1993. "Obstacles to Developing Indigenous Small and Medium Enterprises: An Empirical Assessment." *World Bank Economic Review* 7(1).

————. 1994. "Successful Small and Medium Enterprises and Their Support Systems: A Comparative Analysis of Four Country Studies." World Bank Conference on "Can Intervention Work? The Role of Government in SME Success." Washington, D.C. Draft.

Little, I. M. D., D. Mazumdar, and J. M. Page. 1987. *Small Manufacturing Enterprises*. Oxford: Oxford University Press (for the World Bank).

Luthria, M. 1998. "Cluster Development: Frequently Asked Questions." World Bank, Private Sector Development Department, Washington, D.C. Draft.

Mathews, J. A., and D. S. Cho. 2000. *Tiger Technology: The Creation of a Semiconductor Industry in East Asia*. Cambridge: Cambridge University Press.

Meyanathan, S., ed. 1994. *Industrial Structures and the Development of Small and Medium Enterprise Linkages: Examples from East Asia*. Washington, D.C.: World Bank.

Nadvi, K. 1999. "The Cutting Edge: Collective Efficiency and International Competitiveness in Pakistan." *Oxford Development Studies* 27(1): 81–108.

Nadvi, K., and H. Schmitz. 1994. "Industrial Clusters in Less Developed Countries: Review of Experience and Research Agenda." Discussion Paper 339, Institute of Development Studies, Brighton, U.K.

OECD (Organisation for Economic Co-operation and Development). 1993. *Small and Medium-Sized Enterprise: Technology and Competitiveness*. Paris.

OTA (Office of Technology Assessment). 1990. "Making Things Better: Competing in Manufacturing." U.S. Senate, Washington, D.C.

Poon T., and J. Mathews. 1997. "Technological Upgrading through Alliance Formation: The Case of Taiwan's New PC Consortium." *Industry and Innovation* 4: 435–48.

Pyke, F., and W. Senbenberger, eds. 1992. *Industrial Districts and Local Economic Regeneration*. Geneva: International Institute for Labor Studies, International Labour Organisation.

Pyke, F., G. Becattini, and W. Sengenberger, eds. 1990. *Industrial Districts and Inter-Firm Co-operation in Italy*. Geneva: International Institute for Labor Studies, International Labour Organisation.

Rabellotti, R. 1997. *External Economies and Cooperation in Industrial Districts: A Comparison of Italy and Mexico*. Basingstoke: Macmillan.

Radosevic, S. 1999. *Technology Transfer and Catch-up in Development.* Cheltenham: Edward Elgar.

Romijn, H. 1998. "Technology Support for Small and Medium Industries in Developing Countries: From 'Supply-Push' to 'Nine-fold C'." Queen Elizabeth House, Oxford. Draft.

Rothwell, R., and M. Dodgson. 1993. "SMEs: Their Role in Industrial and Economic Change." *International Journal of Technology Management* 8(1): 22.

Schmitz, H. 1992. "On the Clustering of Small Firms." *IDS Bulletin* 23(3).

Schmitz, H. 1995. "Collective Efficiency: Growth Path for Small-Scale Industry." *Journal of Development Studies* 31(4): 529–66.

UNCTAD (United Nations Conference on Trade and Development). 1994. *Technological Dynamism in Industrial Districts.* Geneva: United Nations.

———. 1999. *World Investment Report 1999.* Geneva: United Nations.

Van Dijk, M. P., and R. Rabelloti, eds. 1997. *Enterprise Clusters and Networks in Developing Countries.* London: Frank Cass.

Van Houtte, J. 1997. "The Role of Small and Medium-Size Enterprises in the Economy and of Their Support Systems." World Bank, Private Sector Development Department, Business Environment Unit, Washington, D.C. Draft.

Wong, Poh-Kam. 1995. "Competing in the Global Electronics Industry: A Comparative Study of the Innovation Networks of Singapore and Taiwan." *Industry and Innovation,* 2(2): 35–62.

Wood, E. 1998. "Small Firms in the Innovation Process: An Empirical and Theoretical Perspective." In A. D. Cosh and A. Hughes, eds., *Innovation: National Policies, Legal Perspectives and the Role of Smaller Firms.* London: Edward Elgar.

CHAPTER 9

Support Services and the Competitiveness of Small and Medium Enterprises in the MENA Region

Antoine Mansour

Governments in industrial and developing countries are giving special attention to the promotion of small and medium-size enterprises (SMEs), since they provide the bulk of employment, and in some cases, they are substantial contributors to exports and innovative activity. Governments are investing considerable effort and resources in supporting SME growth and upgrading. However, the competitiveness of SMEs in the Middle East and North Africa (MENA) region is still relatively limited.

This chapter assesses the competitiveness of SMEs as well as the support services provided by SME-support institutions in the MENA region, with emphasis on five countries: the Arab Republic of Egypt, Jordan, Lebanon, the Syrian Arab Republic, and Bahrain. The study is based on the results of the survey conducted by the Economic and Social Commission for Western Asia (ESCWA) in 1999 entitled "Small and Medium Enterprises: Strategies, Policies and Support Institutions."[1] The sample was selected randomly, but due consideration was given to enterprises that operate in various branches of the manufacturing industry.

The databases of manufacturing firms provided by the chambers of industry or the ministries of industry in the selected countries were also used. It is worth mentioning that this chapter is also based on relevant literature findings and results of field visits to agencies concerned with SME development in the above-mentioned countries.[2]

The chapter is organized as follows: (a) discussion of the relative importance of SMEs in the national economy; (b) analysis of the entrepreneurial profiles in this sector; (c) discussion of the problems faced by SMEs because of macroeconomic policies, market distortions, and government regulations; (d) assessment of the business development services provided by SME-support institutions; and (e) discussion of the competitiveness of SMEs in the context of economic globalization. The final section offers some recommendations, which concentrate on the discussion of important criteria that SME-support institutions need to follow in order to enhance the competitiveness of SMEs and hence their role in stimulating economic growth in the MENA region.

Relative Importance of Small and Medium Enterprises in the National Economy

SMEs play a major role in most of the five countries under study. However, table 9.1 shows that oil-producing countries exhibit a different trend, where large industries are dominant in terms of their contribution to total employment and total manufacturing output. In fact, the government was the main economic actor, undertaking large investments in oil-related industries, while the involvement of the private sector has only recently emerged. For example, in Bahrain, as in the other Gulf Cooperation Council (GCC) countries, the contribution of large firms to total manufacturing employment and output is relatively high, when compared with non-oil Arab countries (State of Bahrain 1993).

At the national level some differences in the relative importance and characteristics of SMEs exist. In this respect, it is worth mentioning that the data presented in table 9.1 are based on national sources, and comparison between countries should be undertaken carefully, in view of the difference in the definitions used, and the fact that some countries do not include enterprises employing fewer than five employees in their statistics. In our analysis we shall consider an SME to be an enterprise employing fewer than 50 workers.

Now that we have established that SMEs play an important role in most of the Arab countries, we turn to compare their importance in the five selected MENA countries. Our comparison includes examining the number of establishments, their contribution to employment, and their output.

The 1994 Industrial Census of Lebanon found that most industrial firms were micro- or small enterprises. In fact, 73 percent of firms were *microenterprises* (defined as an enterprise employing four or fewer workers), while around 27 percent were *SMEs* (defined as an enterprise employing between 5 and 49 employees). *Large firms* (defined as firms employing 50 or more employees) accounted for only 1 percent of total industrial establishments.

In the Syrian Arab Republic the Industrial Census of 1993 covers only the private sector; industrial establishments employing fewer than nine workers represented 98 percent of total private industrial establishments.

TABLE 9.1 DISTRIBUTION OF INDUSTRIAL ESTABLISHMENTS BY SIZE, AND
CONTRIBUTION TO TOTAL MANUFACTURING EMPLOYMENT AND OUTPUT
(percent)

Country	Size according to employment	Share of SMEs in number of establishments	Share of SMEs in employment	Share of SMEs in output
Bahrain	1–4	47.4	9.4	2.5
	5–49	48.6	21.6	12.9
	> 50	4.0	60.9	84.6
Jordan	5–49	92.5	40.8	
	> 50	7.5	59.2	
Lebanon	1–4	72.6	39.8	23.5
	5–49	26.5	38.7	43.1
	> 50	0.9	21.5	33.4
Egypt, Arab Rep. of	10–49	76.0	11.0	9.0[a]
Syrian Arab Rep.	1–9	98.3	90.6	84.2
	> 10	1.7	9.4	15.8

a. In percentage of manufacturing value added.
Source: State of Bahrain 1993; Hashemite Kingdom of Jordan 1997; Lebanese Republic 1995; Syrian Arab Republic 1996; Egyptian Small and Micro Enterprise Association 1997.

In Jordan 93 percent of establishments are SMEs; this high percentage stems from the fact that microenterprises are not taken into consideration in the national statistics, so are not counted by Jordan.

As was previously mentioned, a totally different trend is found in Bahrain. According to the Industrial Survey carried out by the Bahraini Central Statistics Organization in 1992, 47.4 percent of total manufacturing establishments were microenterprises and 48.6 percent were SMEs. Only 4 percent of total industrial establishments were large. The concentration of manufacturing output and employment is high in Bahrain. Three establishments have more than 1,000 employees; they contribute around one-fifth of total manufacturing employment and more than one-third of total manufacturing output. This high concentration can be explained by the existing large petrochemical complex and aluminum industry in Bahrain.

While SMEs in terms of number of firms dominate the four non-oil MENA countries under consideration (that is, Egypt, Jordan, Lebanon, and the Syrian Arab Republic), their contribution to employment and output differs. For example, in Egypt employment in SMEs represents 11 percent of total employment in the manufacturing sector, 9 percent of total manufacturing value added, and a mere 0.4 percent of total manufacturing exports.[3] In Lebanon micro- and small enterprises employed around 80 percent of the total work force in the manufacturing industry, while contributing 66 percent of total manufacturing value added. In the Syrian Arab Republic establishments with fewer than nine workers employ 91 percent of the total industrial work force and contribute 84 percent of total gross output in the private sector. In Jordan, where, as noted above, national statistics do not take into consideration microenterprises, SMEs employ 41 percent of total employment in manufacturing. Large enterprises contribute approximately 59 percent to total manufacturing employment.

From this analysis we conclude that the contribution of SMEs differs from country to country. They have only a minor role in Bahrain's economy, a notable position in Egypt's and Jordan's economies, and are most significant in the Syrian Arab Republic's and Lebanon's economies.

Comparing the relative importance of SMEs in MENA countries with industrial and developing countries (table 9.2) reveals that their contribution in industrial and East Asian countries is higher than in Arab countries. For example, the share of SMEs in total manufacturing employment reaches 74 percent and 78 percent, respectively, in Thailand and the Republic of Korea, 66 percent in Germany, and 91 percent in Greece, compared with 31 percent in Bahrain and 41 percent in Jordan. At the same time, the number of SMEs is greater in industrial and East Asian countries compared with most of the selected Arab countries.

TABLE 9.2 ROLE OF SMES IN SOME DEVELOPED AND EAST ASIAN ECONOMIES (percent)

Country/economy	Share in number of enterprises	Share in employment
Hong Kong (China)	97	63
Korea, Rep. of	99	78
Taiwan (China)	96	68
Thailand	98	74
Japan	99	79
Germany	99	66
France	99	57
Greece	99	91
United States	99	53

Source: Van Houtte 1997.

Another important difference between SMEs in MENA and industrial countries is that in the latter SMEs tend to be in "modern" manufacturing and services, often in the field of cutting-edge technology, with strong entrepreneurial bases, vibrant export sectors, and a large base of educated and technical manpower. In contrast, in developing countries, including countries of the MENA region, SMEs are concentrated in labor-intensive and traditional activities with low levels of productivity and poor quality products. There is little or no technological dynamism in this group, and few graduate into larger sizes or modern technologies. In Egypt, Lebanon, Jordan, and the Syrian Arab Republic, activities of SMEs are concentrated in labor-intensive industries, particularly in food processing, textiles and wearing apparel, wood products and furniture, and nonmetallic mineral products. In Bahrain SMEs can be found involved in downstream aluminum product manufacturing. Very few, however, are involved in industries such as machinery, transport equipment, or electronics products.

Based on the previous analysis, it seems that the role of SMEs in economic growth is not fully exploited, since their contribution to employment and output is limited and they are mainly concentrated in traditional activities. In the following sections we analyze what is constraining the growth and dynamism of this sector.

Profiles of Entrepreneurs in the Small and Medium Enterprises

Entrepreneurs in the selected countries share common characteristics, though some differences exist in entrepreneurial traits among these countries. The profiles of entrepreneurs in the SME sector are numerous, but we shall limit our assessment in this chapter to the most pertinent of them.

Family Background

Most SMEs are family businesses, and many entrepreneurs come from a traditional business family background. Business family relations are important for new start-up businesses, particularly in countries characterized by a relative absence of institutional support for entrepreneurs. The family has a dominant role in business continuity and survival, providing the financing (instead of banks), the moral support, and the networks within the country and with the world.

In the selected countries many entrepreneurs inherit their businesses from their father and grandfather, or from close relatives. This group of owner-managers has a strong entrepreneurial background, and their businesses are part of a family tradition. In newly established enterprises the majority of entrepreneurs declare that one or more of the family members had a private business. In this connection, it is worth mentioning that entrepreneurs who inherited their businesses from a parent—or who were from families where another family member owned a business—were generally encouraged to work in the same business or start a new one in the same specialty.

Those who were discouraged to start a new business come, in most cases, from families who did not have any business experience. People of such background still prefer their children to have a secure job and steady income (working as a government employee, for example).

Reliance on Personal Savings

The formal banking system does not play any significant role in the provision of financial support to start-ups or to existing enterprises. Entrepreneurs must search for informal sources of finance. The capital needed to establish the business in the selected countries is usually raised through personal savings accumulated in previous jobs, or by borrowing money from family and relatives.

Lack of Innovation

SME entrepreneurs in the five selected countries have shown little innovation. The newly established businesses are typically a repetition of existing enterprises, with little or no innovation in business ideas, production processes, or targeted markets. The same applies to established businesses. The marketing constraints, which are considered by most of the entrepreneurs to be the major problem, are, in fact, related to the product itself, which does not satisfy customer needs in terms of quality, taste, design, and price.

Owner-Managers

Most of the enterprises are owned and managed by one person who takes charge of all management aspects of a firm: organization, marketing, production, accounts, and so on. The heavy load on the owner-managers prevents that individual from preparing strategic plans for the company, because he is very busy with the daily routines of the work.

It was also found that most entrepreneurs started their businesses without a business plan or feasibility study. Only in a very few cases did entrepreneurs undertake a full business study prior to the start-up of their company. Existing enterprises do not keep records, prepare financial statements, or carry out the preparation of business plans when expanding their enterprises. Business plans are, in fact, one of the major instruments that help the entrepreneurs understand market needs and therefore generate new products, but they are mostly lacking in SMEs in the countries considered.

Educational Background

The educational background of entrepreneurs is diverse. The younger the entrepreneur, the higher his or her level of education tends to be. In Lebanon and Jordan entrepreneurs are generally well educated, with high school or university degrees. In Bahrain the educational background of entrepreneurs varies widely, ranging from university degrees to illiteracy. Usually small entrepreneurs learn the business from experience and practice, rather than from formal training.

The activities undertaken by entrepreneurs are not necessarily related to their educational background. This is due to the fact that entrepreneurial people take advantage of opportunities where they exist, even if they are not related to their specialization. The surveys show that several entrepreneurs do not work in the field of their specialization.

Relative Absence of Trust among Entrepreneurs

The lack of cooperation and trust among entrepreneurs of different families is common to all selected countries, but it is more pronounced in Lebanon. Most entrepreneurs talked about dominating the competition rather than about cooperating with each other to achieve a common goal of success. Entrepreneurs are reluctant to share information with their competitors for fear that others will use their "secrets" in the same business. The tough competition among small industrialists and the small size of the markets in these countries have made cooperation a difficult option. Without cooperation, small entrepreneurs will have great difficulty competing with large firms, particularly during the globalization of the world economy.

In view of the prevalence of distrust, entrepreneurs prefer to select their business partners from among family members rather than from outside the family. Business partners belonging to the same family have stronger social incentives to honor promises, follow the norms, know each others' limits, and protect each others' interests.

Problems Facing Small and Medium Enterprises

Based on the survey results, there are a number of problems that place SMEs at a disadvantage compared with large firms: biased economic policies in favor of large enterprises; market distortions and access to inputs; isolation and size of the firm; and the administrative procedures, to name a few examples. SMEs in the MENA region find the regulatory and institutional framework lacks transparency, and is inconsistent and inefficient, thus inhibiting further development, rather than acting as a mechanism for sustained growth. Low education and low literacy rates among SME entrepreneurs make these problems especially difficult to overcome. While large corporations can alleviate some of these obstacles by producing needed services internally, SMEs do not have the organizational capacity or the resources to cope with such problems. In what follows, we discuss the details of these problems.

The Biased Macroeconomic Policies

Despite widespread privatization efforts and increased attention to the promotion of the private sector and particularly to the SME sector, macroeconomic policies are still biased in favor of large enterprises. Monetary, financial, trade, and fiscal policies discriminate against new and existing small firms through the imposition of considerable entry barriers.

In most Arab countries the policy incentive systems have been devised to encourage large rather than small enterprises through providing them with various privileges and advantages. Investment laws provide various incentives and exemptions from income tax and customs duties, but only to projects with a high level of capital investment. For example, in the Syrian Arab Republic the Encouragement of Investment Law (Law 10/1991) provides various benefits to Syrian, Arab, and foreign investment in approved economic and social development projects in agriculture, industry, transport, and other approved areas, provided that the fixed assets of the project exceed Syrian pound (SP) 10 million (equivalent to about $200,000).[4] Small and medium projects do not, therefore, enjoy the privileges of the law. In Jordan the Investment Promotion Law of 1995 provides various incentives to projects in agriculture, industry, transport, and services. A project is an "industry," however, when it has a registered capital exceeding Jordanian dinar (JD) 30,000 (equivalent to about $44,000). Any project with less than JD 30,000 is considered to be a handicraft, and therefore does not enjoy the various exemptions and incentives. In Egypt profits of an industrial company employing 50 or more persons and established after the enactment of the Income Tax Law was passed are exempt from income tax for a period of five years from the date of commencement of business. In order to lessen such imbalances, the government of Egypt passed a new Investment Law (Law 8/1997) in 1997, giving those projects financed by the Social Fund for Development the same incentives granted to large enterprises.

The other main problem inhibiting SMEs is the tax system. Small entrepreneurs generally do not keep accounting records, so government authorities impose taxes arbitrarily and (often) unfairly. SMEs tend to feel that the taxes are not proportioned to their profit, and that tax administration officials apply inconsistent criteria. Such pressure on small firms has had the double effect of discouraging people from starting businesses and encouraging existing formal activities to practice informal operations or underground activities in order to evade the increased tax pressure. By not keeping accounting records, entrepreneurs also lose the ability to accurately estimate their costs and profits. Necessary accounting details such as depreciation of machinery or other indirect costs may be excluded from margin calculations. This may ultimately affect their profits and impede their growth.

Because of difficulties in accessing resources and in taking advantage of the incentive system available to large enterprises, many small businesses operate in the informal sector and practice informal operations in order to compete in the market. Profit margins are such that avoiding the payment of taxes and social charges can make the difference between success and failure. While gaining several advantages by operating informally, SMEs lose many of the benefits of being formal, such as the access to credit, government services, and other facilities.

Market Distortions

In contrast with large firms, SMEs face problems with accessing inputs, credit, information, and technology markets. Providers of services, in fact, find it easier and cheaper to deal with a few large customers than with a large number of dispersed small enterprises. The cost of SMEs' enforcement of contracts, for example, would be disproportionately large in relation to the size of the transaction.[5]

SMEs traditionally encounter problems when trying to access credit. Access to banking and credit facilities is often limited by unreasonably high collateral requirements. Banks generally concentrate on financing large corporations and state-owned enterprises. No specialized SME counters are available at bank outlets, for instance, and administrative fees are sometimes excessive.[6] Loan conditions are prohibitive to most SMEs, particularly in the Syrian Arab Republic where the banking system is not yet prepared to finance small businesses, and in Lebanon where interest rates are very high and collateral requirements excessive. In Egypt and Jordan there are credit guarantee companies that provide up to 50 percent of collateral to a bank loan. In Lebanon the government is planning a credit guarantee scheme for SMEs. Several credit schemes have been put in place in the countries of the region, but most of them are serving microenterprises. Recently, several schemes of microfinance have been established in a number of Arab countries, particularly in Egypt, Jordan, and Lebanon. However, the ceiling of loans is limited, generally not exceeding $15,000. Only a few small enterprises can benefit from such a financial scheme.

In addition, SMEs are isolated with respect to information about competitors, suppliers, new technology, and export markets. They also lack the resources to access new technologies and skills, and are not aware of the existence of such technologies. The isolation from information is a more significant problem than the size of individual SMEs.

Complexity of Administrative Procedures

Entrepreneurs complain about the bureaucracy of the "state machinery." The registration or licensing of businesses is another constraint for SMEs. In fact, entrepreneurs find that registration is a lengthy procedure which involves too many different administrations and which is often costly. To avoid the complexity of administrative procedures and the registration fees, which the entrepreneurs considered to be excessive, many businesses operate informally. In doing so, as discussed above, SMEs lose potential benefits of registration, such as better access to credit or government support services.

Entrepreneurs involved in importing goods also complain about long delays at customs, inconsistent tariffs, and lengthy procedures. Moreover, some entrepreneurs find that the same rules do not apply for everyone; licenses with import permissions are illegally traded and personal connections can affect the application of relevant laws. SME entrepreneurs usually rely on experienced importers because of complicated administrative requirements.

Assessment of Business Development Services

The business development services (BDS) provided by support institutions to SMEs will be assessed in the following areas: training services, advisory and counseling services, information services, and marketing services.

Training Services

Training for start-ups and existing businesses is being delivered by various agencies in the region: government agencies, chambers of commerce and industry, business associations, training institutions, nongovernmental organizations (NGOs), credit agencies, and private sector organizations. Training for SMEs is almost nonexistent in the Syrian Arab Republic and exists to an even lesser extent in Lebanon. The few institutions that offer relevant training courses are mainly private consultancy firms that prefer to address the needs of larger firms. In Jordan and Egypt there are several institutions that deliver business training to start-ups as well as to existing small enterprises, but most of them address either microenterprises or large firms.

The survey showed that most agencies providing training programs are not effectively reaching the SME entrepreneur. Training programs are often prepared without serious identification of problems faced by entrepreneurs, though there is increasing awareness of the importance of needs assessment as a prerequisite to the delivery of courses. Entrepreneurs interviewed in the four selected countries have displayed common views regarding the training offered by development agencies. Few entrepreneurs have participated in any training courses, and even fewer have taken management courses. Entrepreneurs are interested more in technical training related to production. They are not aware of the importance of management in the success of an entrepreneurial venture. A survey carried out in 1996 of 56 SME industrial firms in the 10th of Ramadan City, Egypt, revealed that most of the entrepreneurs indicated that they did not benefit from the training that was offered by government institutions or other NGO or private sector institutions.[7] Even though most of the training courses are provided free of charge or at nominal fees, they have not attracted participants.

Training is often delivered at times convenient to the organizers of the course rather than to the entrepreneurs, who need more flexibility. However, a more innovative approach has been introduced by the International Labour Organisation (ILO)–United Nations Development Programme (UNDP) project at the Vocational Training Corporation (VTC) in Jordan, carrying out the courses at enterprises' locations, and at times convenient to the business owners who are their targeted clients.

Even though they promote these programs as being addressed to SMEs, most trainers have difficulty reaching the small entrepreneurs. Their programs are more oriented to medium and large firms. This is the case of the European Business Centres in Egypt, Jordan, and the Syrian Arab Republic; the Centres attract firms with more than 50 employees. The beneficiaries of the VTC in Jordan are also enterprises with more than 20 employees. Entrepreneurs of small companies, in most cases, are not aware of the existence of training courses and programs, or of the institutions providing the support services.

Entrepreneurs consider "learning by doing" as their most important training, and more useful than formal education and learning in classrooms. To them, the importance of training is linked to how training responds to their real needs. They regard their own personal work experience in previous jobs and in their current occupation as the prime source of their skills.

Learning and knowledge acquired from the environment have been more effective than formal education and training. In fact, an entrepreneur's learning process is based on daily work and experience; the reality and the environment; lessons from success and failure; contacts with relatives, friends, peers, and the market; feedback from customers; relations with competitors and suppliers; lessons from problems solved; and difficulties faced, particularly during times of stress.

Advisory and Counseling Services

Advisory services, known also as extension or counseling services, comprise technical assistance and management advisory services. In most countries of the region, with the exception of private consultancy offices, there are very few specialized agencies devoted to the provision of advisory services.

With the support of the ILO, the VTC in Jordan provided extension services during the period 1992–97 to SME industries employing between 5 and 100 employees. Most problems solved by VTC experts were in the management of production. After the completion of the ILO assistance, VTC was not able to continue its assistance, despite the establishment of a specialized Institute for Small and Medium-Scale Industries; one reason for the failure of this service to be self-supporting is that entrepreneurs were reluctant to pay nominal fees (5 Jordanian dinars for one hour of advice or technical assistance). The failure of VTC to attract clients after the completion of the project can also be attributed to the very bureaucratic nature of VTC.

The Outreach Consultation Project at the University of Jordan has been quite successful in linking the Industrial Engineering Faculty with SMEs through seminars, as well as through consultation services. The approach used by faculty members with business owners is more of a teacher-to-student relation, however, than an effort to build the capacity of the enterprise.

In Bahrain, Lebanon, and the Syrian Arab Republic the ministries of industry do not have specific units to provide systematic business advice to those wishing to start or expand businesses. The business support services provided by the European Community to SMEs in Egypt, Jordan, and the Syrian Arab Republic are provided upon request, but these services benefit the large enterprises more than the SMEs.

Entrepreneurs interviewed in the four countries consider the advisory services to be almost nonexistent; they rarely find agencies that provide them with support. As an example, the entrepreneurs in the 10th of Ramadan City in Egypt indicated that although they are members of business associations, they never receive assistance or support from those associations.[8] In countries where business advisory services are available, entrepreneurs may not be aware of their existence, because support institutions do not sufficiently advertise their services and the services offered tend to address the needs of large enterprises. Entrepreneurs rely more on advice from their suppliers and from other providers of services in the private sector.

Business Information Services

Various sources of business information are available at the country level in the region;[9] they are scattered, incomplete, at times inconsistent, and difficult to access, however. They do not provide all the relevant information in one integrated package. The public sector is the main provider of business information, while the private sector has not yet developed databases on business information. This is due to the fact that businesses, particularly SMEs, are not yet ready to pay appropriate fees for information.

Market-related information is also not easily available. The survey showed that SME managers experience many difficulties related to the absence of business information. Most of them are not aware of the availability of needed information, or how to access it. In addition, existing information providers do not advertise their services effectively. Entrepreneurs need information about their competitors' products and prices, domestic and foreign suppliers, and so on. This survey showed that brochures and catalogues produced by foreign suppliers seem to be an important source for local entrepreneurs to keep up-to-date on new trends and technologies.

Small entrepreneurs usually rely on friends and relatives, as well as on suppliers and business journals, magazines, and catalogues to obtain the needed information, or else they rely on exhibitions and fairs that they visit. Networks, including relatives outside the country, enable many entrepreneurs to obtain some of the latest information regarding new technologies, new products, and new market trends. In contrast to small entrepreneurs in most countries of the region, Lebanese entrepreneurs indicated that they are not facing serious problems in obtaining needed information to start or run a business. Most of the surveyed entrepreneurs in other countries expressed the need to obtain accurate and clear business information.

Efforts have been made by support institutions in the region to provide business information. European Union business support services in Egypt, Jordan, and the Syrian Arab Republic include information and data on companies and market potentials in Europe. Information services, however, are more readily available to large firms than to the SMEs. The Trade Information Centre in Lebanon and Trade Points in Egypt have databases that can be used by entrepreneurs, and access is possible through the Internet, or directly by phone, fax, or visits in person. Very few enterprises are aware of the existence and benefits of these sources, however.

The Chamber of Industry in Jordan has already created a database on registered companies; others such as the Association of Lebanese Industrialists and the Damascus Chamber of Industry are making serious efforts to compile the same records. The most-developed databases on industrial firms can be found in Egypt at the Credit Guarantee Corporation for Small Scale Enterprises and at the General Organization for Industrialization. Databases on exporters are available at the Jordan Export Development and Commercial Centres Corporation as well as at the Egyptian Export Development Centres; small industries do not benefit from such services, since most of them are not exporters. Most exporters consist of enterprises that employ more than 40 or 50 employees.

One main opportunity to improve communication and information flows is the use of the Internet. The Internet offers the opportunity to make information relevant to SMEs easily accessible. It also offers new marketing and networking opportunities for SMEs. Many SME managers expressed a desire to know more about the relevance of Internet applications in business.

Marketing Assistance

In general, SMEs are most concerned with effective marketing, a problem outweighing even financing. Entrepreneurs, particularly in Jordan, Lebanon, and Bahrain, consider the limited size of the local market, the competition from local and imported products, and government policy with regard to protection of local industries as the most important marketing constraints. The real problems, however, can be attributed to the inability of enterprises to expand the market base beyond the local community and close neighborhood, as well as to the product itself, which does not meet local standards including quality standards, or satisfy the tastes and needs of customers.

On the other hand, entrepreneurs find difficulties in formulating an adequate marketing strategy. They have insufficient experience. For most of them trade fairs are an important forum for exchange of information and marketing of products, but setting up a stand at such a fair is often prohibitively expensive.

Marketing assistance to small firms is relatively scarce in the selected countries, since existing marketing services are available more for large firms. Support programs for SMEs are limited to assisting them in displaying their products in fairs and exhibitions, and in offering entrepreneurs training courses within the framework of management courses, dealing with such marketing issues as methods of costing and pricing, and techniques of promotion and sales.

Market assistance includes support of entrepreneurs in the local market and the export market. The support for export is being organized by specialized government agencies, such as the Egyptian Export Promotion Centre and the Jordan Export Development and Commercial Centres Corporation. These agencies provide support to exporters in the fields of market information and research, trade statistics, product promotion, product design and development, information on procedures and regulations for export in foreign countries, information on international exhibitions and fairs, and so on. Although these agencies state that they are giving particular attention to SMEs, the main beneficiaries are, as indicated above, mostly the large firms, and to some extent the medium ones. This may be explained by the fact that most small firms have no exportable products, and no serious efforts are being made to assist small producers who have growth and export potentials to adapt their production to customer needs.

The support provided by chambers of commerce and industry is confined to informing members about domestic or international fairs and to organizing awareness seminars on marketing and international regulations and procedures with regard to export in the European and North American markets, as well as with regard to the impact of World Trade Organization (WTO) agreements and international standards (such as International Standards Organization 9000).

Among the countries considered in the study, Egypt has the most developed marketing support infrastructure for small entrepreneurs. The Small and Micro Enterprise Project of the Alexandria Business Association (ABA) organizes exhibitions on a regular basis for products of borrowing firms; these firms can also display their products in the showroom established on the ABA's premises. The Social Fund for Development and the Industrial Bank also provide market support to their clients through the organization of fairs and exhibitions, and through participation in the Cairo International Fair.

A survey carried out in 1996 in Egypt on organizations and agencies supporting microenterprises and small enterprises—34 NGOs, private agencies, and government agencies—indicated that only 13 percent of assistance programs are specialized in marketing support and product development, and that only 22 percent of these programs are specific to a branch or a subsector. Thirty-three percent of the programs charge subsidized fees, and only one organization covers its costs completely.[10]

International experience in industrial and developing countries confirms the importance of sectoral manufacturers associations specializing in export promotion. Chile's small woodworking industry sector, which served only the domestic market, was able to enter the export markets, thanks to the support provided by the association of SMEs and the export manufacturers association. The association of SMEs assisted the wood products sector in attending international fairs, and in establishing links with local and international technical institutes. The growth of the size of the export market for a specific product encourages small firms to cooperate to meet the needs of the market, and also promotes specialization.

The Competitiveness of Small and Medium Enterprises in the Context of Globalization

SMEs are facing challenges because of globalization and increased competition. Protecting them from foreign competition through trade barriers was an easier task than enhancing their competitiveness in the world market. In order to help SMEs in facing the challenges of globalization, there is a need to assist them in forming networks, clusters, and sectoral associations, as well as facilitating subcontracting arrangements with large companies. Several factors impede, however, the creation of networks in the selected countries. With few exceptions, industries are scattered geographically and sectorally. Very little interfirm cooperation exists, as trust between entrepreneurs is relatively absent.

Globalization: A Threat or a Business Opportunity?

The development of SMEs will be seriously affected by economic globalization. For some SMEs globalization will open new opportunities for growth and expansion in the international market. For most small firms, however, the entry of imported competitive products in the local market will constitute major threats, unless SMEs introduce major changes in their management practices and in the quality of their products. Protecting SMEs from foreign competition through trade barriers was an easy task; enhancing their competitiveness in the world market is a more difficult task.[11]

Trade liberalization under the WTO agreement will provide opportunities for small firms to enter new export markets and to improve their access to production technologies and to other input materials. In fact, information technology and communications will allow SMEs to operate at the global level. Trade liberalization will also constitute real threats for enterprises that are not able to compete against imports, particularly those with lower prices. Since SMEs are an important source of employment generation, the national economy would be severely affected if SMEs lose their competitiveness; steps must be taken to assist SMEs in this regard.

The Benefits of Clustering and Other Preglobalization Tactics
International experience in both industrial and developing countries has proved that the geographic or sectoral clustering of firms contributes to enhancing their competitiveness, and provides the appropriate vehicle for intervention of the support institutions. Benefits of such concentration for individual firms can be derived from external economies. Concentration of firms on a sectoral basis, in fact, will encourage suppliers, marketing agents, and other providers of services to establish themselves in the cluster. It will enhance interaction between small firms and lead to a certain division of labor, thus increasing specialization and innovations. The existence of clusters will provide increased opportunities for SMEs to work together and cooperate in various areas.

In Brazil the existence of the Sinos Valley footwear cluster has been beneficial for the local producers of footwear because of the intervention of two actors: (a) the Brazilian Service for Small Enterprises, which pays half of the exhibition cost for small firms wishing to participate in trade fairs organized by the public sector, and (b) the export agents of the private sector who facilitate the connection between the cluster and the export markets.

It is important to note that the emergence of clusters and industrial districts in Europe and even in the developing countries was spontaneous, and not the result of a planned action by government agencies or private sector institutions. There was no overreaching industrial strategy, even though the public and private sectors played a role in the growth of clusters.[12] In the Italian industrial districts real services have been provided to small firms by local development agencies, on a sectoral basis (knitwear, clothing, shoes, and so on) and in specific specialized areas (export promotion, quality upgrading, information on international market trends and technological developments, subcontracting opportunities, technical and managerial training, and so on).

Networks among small firms would also provide mutual benefits through active cooperation and joint action. They are a cost-effective solution to the absence of geographic and sectoral clusters. Networking would contribute to improving the competitiveness of SMEs and to preparing them to deal with globalization through the development and marketing of new products. It would also contribute to cooperation in the establishment of agents and distributors in new markets.

An interesting example of a small firm network is the government-subsidized Danish Networking Program. The program consists of requesting enterprises to form networks and cooperate in a number of areas. Networking was promoted with the aim of improving SME competitiveness, and to prepare them to deal with globalization, through the development and marketing of new products, and through cooperation in the establishment of agents and distributors in new markets. It is interesting to note that the program succeeded in inducing SMEs to cooperate, although interfirm cooperation was not part of the industrial culture in Denmark.

In Chile the government agency for SME promotion assisted SMEs in a specific locality to establish networks of small groups, usually between 10 and 30 firms per group. The establishment of such a network faced difficulties, in view of the fact that entrepreneurs in Chile are usually individualistic and resist government intervention. The aim of the network is to facilitate the delivery of support services by various support institutions that prefer to deal with groups rather than with small individual firms. The network also tries to promote interfirm cooperation through the development of better relations between the participating firms in the network. Such cooperation enables SMEs to raise their competitiveness and focus on the areas of product design and standardization, process innovation, and human resource management.

Constraints for Interfirm Collaboration in the Selected Countries
Several factors impede the creation of networks and cooperation between firms in the selected MENA countries. With few exceptions, industries are scattered geographically and sectorally; it is rare to find a concentration of small firms in one location or on a sectoral basis. Very little interfirm cooperation exists, competition is dominant among firms, and trust among entrepreneurs is relatively absent. Moreover, industries are generally isolated: their market is limited to the area in which they are located. Two significant reasons for the relative absence of networks of entrepreneurs are the distrust that exists among owner-managers and the absence of programs promoting interfirm collaboration.

Most of the support institutions and agencies dealing with SMEs in the region are devising special programs to support SMEs, concentrating their activities on improving the performance of individual firms through advisory services, provision of credit, and training for upgrading technical and managerial skills. They also focus on recommending policies that are likely to improve the macroeconomic environment for SMEs, through liberalization measures and facilitation of bureaucratic and administrative procedures. However, very few programs emphasized interfirm cooperation and interaction, or self-help groups, as a means to improve the competitiveness of small firms and assist them in facing the challenges of globalization.

Competitiveness of small firms can also be achieved through the promotion of subcontracting arrangements with large firms or among each other. However, in several countries, the markets lack linkages among small businesses and large corporations. In modern market economies, large corporations play a pivotal role as SMEs cluster around these companies to act as subcontractors. SMEs offer specialized inputs since they enjoy greater flexibility and cost-efficiency. Incentives could be offered to large enterprises to subcontract some of their activities to SMEs.

Conclusions

SME-support institutions, also called Business Development Services (BDS) organizations, need to introduce major changes in their management, structure, approach of work, level of expertise, and so on, in order to effectively meet the real needs of small entrepreneurs. The experience of support institutions in the region is relatively new, starting mostly in the early 1990s. It is therefore important to benefit from international experiences in SME support. This can provide BDS organizations with effective systems, mechanisms, values, and approaches to assist them in the delivery of services to SMEs, in the hope that SMEs can increase their competitiveness and face the challenges of globalization.

Regional and international experiences[13] on support to SMEs suggest the following criteria for successful programs:

Specialization

Activities of BDS organizations generally lack focus; they are scattered and non-integrated in a comprehensive framework or program, and with little follow-up mechanism and activities.

Programs that provide nonfinancial support exclusively have proved to be more cost-effective. When programs combine credit with nonfinancial support instruments, clients are more interested in the financial services than the nonfinancial component of the program. Specialization can be in one of the following areas: technical training, managerial training, counseling, marketing assistance, or information.

BDS organizations should not overdiversify their activities, but should focus on what they can do most effectively. Specialization will raise the technical capability and capacity of the organization; it will also lead to increased capacity of the organization in innovation and design of new services, within the scope of the specific services provided.

Sector-Specific Approach

Services provided to clients in one specific sector are of a higher technical value. Most of the BDS organizations, including the service delivery organizations and business associations, provide services to several sectors at the same time: trade, industry, agriculture, and so on. Many of the business associations, particularly those in the industrial zones or cities, do not represent a specific subsector, but instead represent several industrial branches. The existing business associations or syndicates representing a subsector in the region are particularly active in the areas of food industries, textiles, leather, and garments. These associations and syndicates rarely devise programs of assistance to help members to improve efficiency and competitiveness.

Scale
Programs should reach significant numbers of clients in order to be effective. The scale of operation of most BDS organizations is very limited, reaching at most a few hundred beneficiaries, while thousands of entrepreneurs within the same area start or run their businesses with no support at all. Information technology now provides good opportunities for BDS organizations to operate on a large scale through various possibilities such as the conversion of training materials into CD multimedia and the use of the Internet.

Sustainability
Fees should be charged for services rendered to clients. This makes the services more valuable in the eyes of clients, thereby making them more likely to access and subsequently use the service, and enables the organization to sustain its activities. For firms to achieve social objectives of certain services and at the same time operate as a private profit maximizing firm, SMEs need the support and help of governments and donors. The problem of sustainability is also caused by the low salary of staff in these institutions, when compared with the salaries of staff in the private sector. Low salaries encourage the staff to look for other jobs, thus reducing the ability of these organizations to effectively sustain their activities.

Demand Assessment
There is a need to identify the real demand of the target group through needs assessment surveys or other mechanisms before providing the services to entrepreneurs. Training courses and advisory services should be tailored to the specific conditions and needs of the entrepreneurs. BDS organizations should be in continuous close communication with their clients, to better understand their needs and to conceive and implement programs that respond better to real needs.

A Businesslike Approach
The best BDS organizations to support SMEs are those operating on a commercial basis, similar to the way SMEs operate. They are also similar to SMEs in terms of their personnel, systems, and values.[14] The "social" approach is still dominant in the region in the provision of services. The government organizations and the nonprofit organizations in the region have proved to be more charity-oriented than businesslike. The bureaucratic nature of these organizations is another constraint keeping them from being cost-effective.

Notes

1. The structured interviews of the sample of manufacturing SMEs (25 to 45 enterprises) were conducted in four MENA countries: Bahrain, Jordan, Lebanon, and the Syrian Arab Republic (ESCWA 1999).

2. Based on studies such as Egyptian Small and Micro Enterprise Association 1997.

3. See Mansour 1998.

4. All dollar amounts are U.S. dollars.

5. See Lall 2000.

6. One bank in Lebanon started charging $200 yearly administrative fees in 1999 without prior notice to its SME customers.

7. El Mahdi and El Said 1996.

8. El Mahdi and El Said 1996.

9. See ESCWA 1997, 1998.

10. Egyptian Small and Micro Enterprise Association 1997.

11. OECD 1997.

12. Schmitz 1995.

13. Committee of Donor Agencies for Small Enterprise Development 1998.

14. Committee of Donor Agencies for Small Enterprise Development 1998.

Bibliography

Committee of Donor Agencies for Small Enterprise Development. 1998. "Business Development Services for SMEs: Preliminary Guidelines for Donor-Funded Interventions." Summary of the Report to the Donor Committee for Small Enterprise Development. Washington, D.C. January.

Egyptian Small and Micro Enterprise Association. 1997. "Marketing and Micro-enterprise in Egypt." Friedrich Ebert Stiftung, Cairo. September.

El Mahdi, Alia, and Hala El Said. 1996. "Small Industries Complex in the 10th of Ramadan City: Needs and Potentials—A Target Group Analysis." Study conducted under the auspices of the Federation of Egyptian Industries and the Chamber of Engineering Industries in cooperation with the Friedrich Ebert Stiftung and the Association of Promoting Small and Medium-Sized Industries in the New Cities.

ESCWA (Economic and Social Commission for Western Asia). 1997. "Review and Assessment of Sources of Information in the Industrial Sector in the ESCWA Region." (In Arabic). E/ESCWA/ID/1997/8.

———. 1998. "Trade Efficiency in ESCWA Member Countries: A Comprehensive Study 'Business Information.'" In Seminar on Trade Efficiency in the ESCWA Member States, 30 November–2 December 1998, Beirut. (E/ESCWA/ED/1998/WG.1/8).

———. 1999. "Small and Medium Enterprises: Strategies, Policies and Support Institutions." Lebanon.

Hashemite Kingdom of Jordan. 1997. "Employment Surveys for Establishments Engaging 5 Persons or More, 1995." Department of Statistics No. 49.

Lall, S. 2000. "Strengthening SMEs for International Competitiveness." Paper presented during the Third Mediterranean Development Forum, held in Cairo, on March 5–8.

Lebanese Republic. 1995. "Report on Industrial Census—Final Results." Ministry of Industry and Petroleum, Directorate of Industry. December.

Mansour, Hosam. 1998. "Towards a Policy for Promotion of Small Industries." (In Arabic). Paper presented to the First Arab Meeting on "The Role of Small and Medium-Sized Industries in Industrial Development," organized by Arab Industrial Development and Mining Organization (AIDMO) and others. February.

OECD (Organisation for Economic Co-operation and Development). 1997. "Globalization and Small and Medium Enterprises (SMEs)." Vol. 1. Synthesis Report. Paris.

Schmitz, Hubert. 1995. "Collective Efficiency: Growth Path Small-Scale Industry." *The Journal of Development Studies* 31(4/April): 529–66.

State of Bahrain. 1993. "Industrial Survey Results." Central Statistics Organization, Directorate of Statistics.

Syrian Arab Republic. 1996. "Results of the Industrial Survey for the Private Sector of 1993." Central Bureau of Statistics, Damascus. February.

Van Houtte, J. 1997. "The Role of Small and Medium-Sized Enterprises in the Economy and of Their Support Systems." World Bank, Private Sector Development Department, Business Environment Unit, Washington, D.C. Draft.

CHAPTER 10

Beyond Credit—A Taxonomy of Small and Medium-Size Enterprises and Financing Methods for Arab Countries

Mahmoud A. El-Gamal
Nihal El-Megharbel
Hulusi Inanoglu

Small and medium-size enterprises (SMEs) have traditionally been confined to economic development studies that focused on their role in poverty alleviation and employment creation in poor countries.[1] Economic writings that focused on the positive role of small-scale firms, such as Schumacher (1973), were viewed by most economists as mere curiosities that went against the common wisdom that economic growth and development implied capitalization on economies of scale in industry. However, the link among SMEs, economic growth, entrepreneurship, and international competitiveness has begun to play an important role in economists' perceptions of their role in advanced as well as in developing economies.[2]

SMEs play a significant role in Arab countries, both in terms of the total number of enterprises and in terms of their contribution to employment levels. The Arab Development Agency reported that the number of SMEs in the Arab world increased from 114,000 in 1990 to 130,000 in 1995, and that the number of workers in such enterprises increased from 1,845 million workers to 2,397 million workers. During that same period the output of SMEs increased from $35 billion[3] to $60 billion (or from 25 percent to 28 percent as a percentage of total manufacturing output), their exports increased from $14.6 billion to $17.9 billion, and their imports increased from $24.4 billion to $26.9 billion.[4]

This clear indication that SMEs play an important role in economic growth and export promotion, as well as in employment creation, is the motivation for this chapter. Looking beyond traditional SMEs, which are considered strictly as developmental tools for poverty alleviation and employment creation, this study concentrates on the other types of SMEs that are more capable of helping Arab countries to attain higher rates of economic growth in the short, medium, and long terms.

To this end the study first considers how SMEs are currently affecting the growth rates in Arab economies in terms of overall economic growth. After establishing the significant influence SMEs have on growth rates, we propose a taxonomy of SMEs that differentiates between the diversity of enterprises included under this umbrella term: traditional SMEs, market-niche-finding SMEs, and avant-garde SMEs. We next discuss how each type functions in the general economy, evaluate whether each contributes more to short- or long-term growth, and cite ideal characteristics for the financial support systems they require. We then discuss specific financing schemes that are suggested for each SME type based on the general characteristics described in the previous section. Finally, we conclude the chapter by summarizing the study's proposals.

The Economic Role of Small and Medium Enterprises in the Arab World

The fundamental obstacles to raising the growth rates in Arab countries are the low levels of domestic savings and investment, coupled with a significant gap between the two. Figure 10.1 illustrates this fact by comparing the rates of savings and investment in the Middle East and Eastern Europe with those of the Asian countries that experienced much faster rates of growth during the 1990s. Even during the Asian crisis of the late 1990s, the rates of savings and investment in those countries remained significantly higher than their counterparts in the Arab countries. The higher rates of savings and investment are largely responsible for fueling the current Asian recovery and expectations of higher rates of growth into the early 2000s. Figure 10.1 highlights two fundamental problems: (a) the need to increase Arab domestic savings and investment and (b) the need to close the gap between them through inflows of foreign savings.

There are numerous methods for closing the gap between domestic savings and investment in developing countries. In recent years the most prevalent of those methods has been foreign direct investment (FDI), which is preferred by most developing countries due to its other externalities in the areas of technology transfer and export promotion.[5] Unfortunately, as figure 10.2 illustrates, flows of FDI to the region have lagged behind FDI inflows to other emerging markets, even during the golden opportunity of the Asian crisis when flows to those countries slowed down.

Small and Medium Enterprises and Economic Growth
It must be noted that the size of SME activity in an economy is not necessarily a direct contributor to economic growth. For instance, early empirical analyses of

FIGURE 10.1 SAVINGS AND INVESTMENT IN ASIA, 1980–2005

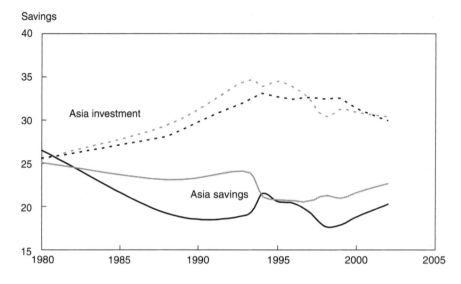

Source: International Monetary Fund 1999.

FIGURE 10.2 FDI INFLOWS TO EMERGING MARKETS BY REGION

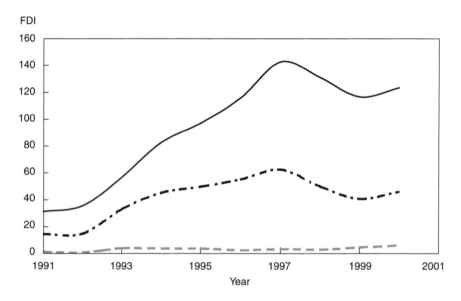

Source: International Monetary Fund 1999.

the relationship between firm-size distribution in certain sectors and productivity growth (measured as total factor productivity [TFP]) show a negative relationship (Acs, Morck, and Yeung 1999). However, as the authors point out (Acs, Morck, and Yeung 1999, p. 393), the effect of SMEs on growth seems to be a catalyst. SMEs tend to generate more innovations and develop an entrepreneurial class with the requisite managerial skills, thus making larger firms in the economy significantly more productive.[6]

Despite the invigorated interest in SMEs, there is a scarcity of data in all countries. Unfortunately, this lack of data is most extreme in the countries that need it most to formulate coherent policies toward SME promotion—the developing countries. In what follows, we use the very limited information we could find on SMEs, and the SMEs' role in the Arab countries to make comparisons with other developing regions.

When comparing the relative numbers of SMEs to total enterprises across a group of Arab and Asian countries, the relationship between the size of the SME sector and GDP growth rates appears to be slightly negative, as shown in table 10.1 and figure 10.3.

This negative relationship is preserved (and indeed strengthened) if we use another source—the official country statistics reported in Mansour 2000—together with matched average GDP growth rates (table 10.2). There are some dramatic

TABLE 10.1 SMALL- AND MEDIUM-ENTERPRISE SHARE IN TOTAL ESTABLISHMENTS AND THEIR CONTRIBUTION TO EMPLOYMENT (percent)

Economy	SME share	SME contribution to employment	Average GDP growth rate
Egypt[a]	90	75	4.5
Syria[b]	90	62	2
Lebanon[c]	84	—	3
Jordan[d]	93	32.9	5.7
Tunisia[e]	84	—	3.5
Brunei[f]	90	70	−1
Hong Kong, China[f]	98	60	−5
Japan	99.1	78	1.5
APEC[f]	90	(32–84)	—
Member countries	—	—	—

— Not available.
Note: APEC = Asia Pacific Economic Cooperation.
a. Giugale and Mobarak 1996.
b. Shahin 1999.
c. Hamdan 1995
d. Karmoul 1995.
e. Bechri, Najah, and Nugent 1999.
f. Global Information Network for SMEs Web site: http://www.gin.sme.ne.jp/.

FIGURE 10.3 SHARE OF SMES IN TOTAL ESTABLISHMENTS VS. GROWTH RATE

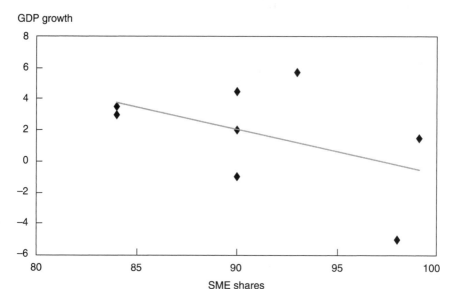

Source: Giugale and Mubarak 1996; Hamdan 1995; Karmoul 1995; Bechri, Najah, and Nugent 1999; Global Information Network for SMEs Web site: http://www.gin.sme.ne.jp/.

discrepancies between the figures presented in Mansour's data and those in table 10.1, however. Contribution to employment in Egypt, for example, is reported at 75 percent in table 10.1 and at 11 percent in table 10.2. This difference can be attributed to the general poverty of data on SMEs, as well as the wildly different definitions used by different data collecting agencies.

Nonetheless, we can see in Figures 10.4 and 10.5 that the negative relationship between the share of SMEs in the total number of establishments is preserved. Moreover, we can see that SMEs' contribution to overall employment is also negatively correlated to GDP growth rates.

Small and Medium Enterprises and Export Growth

Evidence from the fast-growing Asian countries of the 1990s suggests that the relationship between SME activities and overall export growth is rather complex. As illustrated in table 10.3 and figures 10.6 and 10.7, there seems to be a negative relationship between the percentage of total exports that are attributed to SMEs and overall export growth. On the other hand, there is a positive relationship between the contribution of SMEs to manufacturing and overall export growth. Those two relationships confirm the catalytic role played by SMEs that we have already seen in the area of economic growth. The direct influence of SMEs is seen in both

TABLE 10.2 SMES' SHARE IN TOTAL ESTABLISHMENTS AND THEIR
CONTRIBUTION TO EMPLOYMENT
(percent)

Economy	SME share	SME contribution to employment	Average GDP growth rate
Bahrain[a]	96.0	31.0	–2.0
Egypt[a]	76.0	11.0	4.5
Syria[a]	98.3	90.6	2.0
Lebanon[a]	99.1	78.5	3.0
Jordan[a]	92.5	40.8	5.7
Tunisia[b]	84.0	—	3.5
Brunei[c]	90.0	70.0	–1.0
Hong Kong, China[c]	98.0	60.0	–5.0
Japan[c]	99.1	78.0	1.5
APEC[c]	90.0	32–84	—
Member countries	—	—	—

— Not available.

a. Mansour 2000, based on official figures.

b. Bechri, Najah, and Nugent 1999.

c. Global Information Network for SMEs Web site: http://www.gin.sme.ne.jp/.

FIGURE 10.4 SHARE OF SMES IN TOTAL ESTABLISHMENTS VS. GROWTH RATE

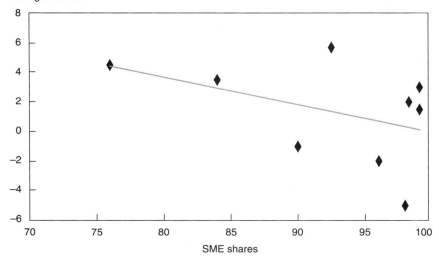

Source: Mansour 2000, based on official figures; Bechri, Najah, and Nugent 1999; Global Information Network for SMEs Web site: http://www.gin.sme.ne.jp/.

FIGURE 10.5 SHARE OF SMES IN TOTAL EMPLOYMENT VS. GROWTH RATE

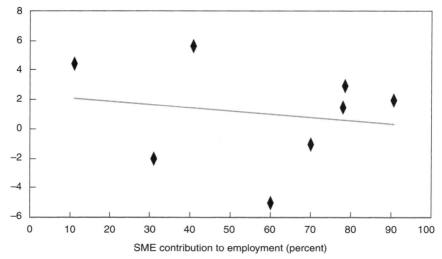

GDP growth rate

SME contribution to employment (percent)

Source: Mansour 2000, based on official figures; Bechri, Najah, and Nugent 1999; Global Information Network for SMEs Web site: http://www.gin.sme.ne.jp/.

TABLE 10.3 SMALL- AND MEDIUM-ENTERPRISE CONTRIBUTION TO OUTPUT IN MANUFACTURING, 1990S, AND EXPORTS, 1991–92
(percent)

Economy	SME contribution to manufacturing output	SME contribution to exports	Export growth rate
China	—	40–60	23
Japan	52	—	12
Korea, Rep. of	44	40	30
Singapore	19	16	22
Malaysia	—	15	26
Taiwan, China	39	56	—
Indonesia	30	11	14
Myanmar	71	—	9
Thailand	—	10	21
Vietnam	40–70	20	—

— Not available.
Source: U.N. 1998.

FIGURE 10.6 SMALL- AND MEDIUM-ENTERPRISE ROLE IN PROMOTING
EXPORT GROWTH (a)

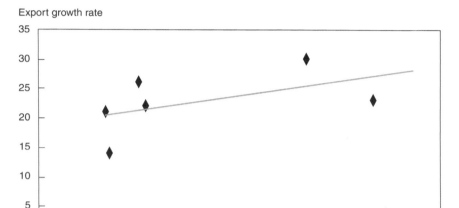

Source: U.N. 1998.

cases to be paradoxically negative, but the positive externalities they generate for
larger firms are undeniable, both in achieving higher rates of growth and in enhancing the export orientation of the growth path.

This suggests that macroeconomic policymakers must target SMEs carefully.
SMEs that contribute directly to exports (for example, artisan-sector production
of quilts, rugs, leather products, and so on—highlighted as a success story in
Bangladeshi microfinance) are not necessarily the types of SMEs that contribute
to GDP, and overall export, growth. The types of SMEs that contribute significantly to the growth of economic activity and exports seem to be enterprises that
function through subcontracting with the main industrial sectors of developing
countries. The policy implications of this relationship throw into question the
traditional microfinancing methods and target enterprises, and recognize the more
dynamic types of SMEs that could nurture the Arab world's emerging entrepreneurial class.

Small and Medium Enterprises, Foreign Direct Investment, Exports, and Economic Growth

There is no available evidence on inward SME foreign direct investment (FDI)
flows for any developing countries, and raw data from which such data may be

FIGURE 10.7 SMALL- AND MEDIUM-ENTERPRISE ROLE IN PROMOTING
EXPORT GROWTH (b)

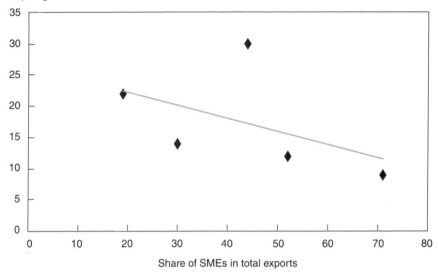

Export growth rate

Share of SMEs in total exports

Source: U.N. 1998.

generated are not readily available. An attempt was made to construct estimates of
SME FDI by using home country data on outgoing FDI by host country, and defining all such investments of $1 million or less as SME FDI inflows (U.N. 1998).
The resulting series is reported in table 10.4, along with GDP and export growth
rates intended for a preliminary analysis.

It has long been maintained that inflows of FDI funds to firms, especially
SMEs, contribute substantially to the development of human capital, both in
terms of higher levels of skills and productivity and in terms of managerial and
entrepreneurial skills. Unlike other sources of funding, incoming SME FDI is
likely to be an effective source of technology transfer, thus having a much more
dramatic impact on overall productivity in the economy. Figures 10.8 and 10.9
clearly illustrate that there is a positive relationship between SME FDI and GDP
growth, as well as export growth. In this regard, SME FDI seems to be a more
appropriate catalyst for bringing into effect the classical growth and export-
enhancing advantages discussed in the FDI literature.[7] While acknowledging the
severe limitation of traditional SME microfinance, these data seem to suggest

TABLE 10.4 SELECTED ASIAN ECONOMIES: INWARD FDI FLOWS WITH
RESPECTIVE EXPORT AND GDP GROWTH RATES, 1995

Economy	Inward FDI flow (percent GDP)	Export growth rate (percent)	GDP growth rate (percent)
China	0.04	23	7.8
Japan	0.003	12	−2.6
Republic of Korea	1.1	30	−6.8
Singapore	24.6	22	1.3
Taiwan, China	2.7	—	4.8
Indonesia	6.5	14	−13.7

Source: U.N. 1998.

FIGURE 10.8 SMALL- AND MEDIUM-ENTERPRISE FDI INFLOWS' ROLE
IN PROMOTING GROWTH

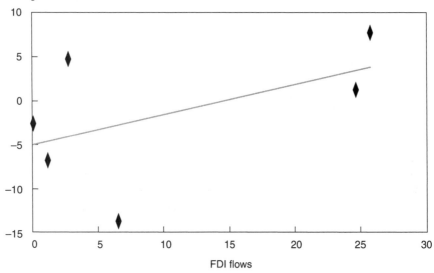

Source: U.N. 1998.

FIGURE 10.9 SMALL- AND MEDIUM-ENTERPRISE FDI INFLOWS' ROLE
IN PROMOTING EXPORT GROWTH

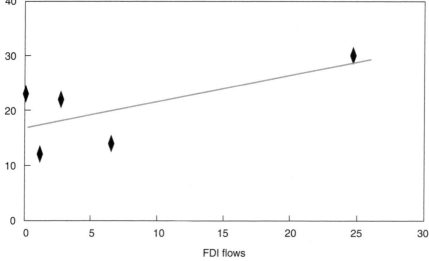

Source: U.N. 1998.

that more innovative types of SME should be the primary targets of macroeconomic policymakers.

A Taxonomy of Small and Medium Enterprises and Their Economic Role

As mentioned before, although SMEs have become a popular topic of discussion in recent years, a very limited amount of critical thought has been applied to them to date—particularly in terms of the methodology most often used to approach them. Economists have traditionally discussed SMEs only in terms of size, distinguishing among micro, small, and medium-size enterprises. However, proposing that such categories are not particularly conducive to study, this analysis presents a new taxonomy of SMEs that distinguishes among three main types: (a) SMEs in traditional production areas, (b) SMEs that identify an emerging market niche, and (c) SMEs in avant-garde (high-tech and other "new economy") industries. All three types share some key features: small size in terms of total employment and total capital stock, a low capital-labor ratio, high responsiveness to market conditions, and unsuitability of the SME credit-risk structure for conventional bank financing. Moreover, all three types of SMEs offer similar economic advantages for growth and development, including employment creation, promotion of an entrepreneurial class, the creation of a more skilled labor force, and enhanced economic dynamism.

Despite these similarities, however, there are fundamental differences among the three types of SMEs that render certain alternative sources of financing appropriate for some but not for others. In this section we provide a more detailed taxonomy of the three SME types. In all three cases our focus will be on the factors that render such enterprises "small or medium-size," their significance to the economy, whether they contribute more to short- or long-term growth, and ideal characteristics for the financial support systems they require.

Traditional Small and Medium Enterprises

SMEs in traditional areas of production fit the classical stereotype of small-scale industry. Such enterprises specialize in producing goods and services, or components thereof, with technologies and managerial processes that do not exhibit economies of scale. This lack of economies of scale and the low-skilled, labor-intensive aspects of their production and management technologies render them an ideal vehicle for employment creation and poverty alleviation. Such enterprises survive on direct production to the market, or subcontracting with larger enterprises that produce goods for a larger market. In either case, they draw on labor in the vicinity of a specific market or firm location. In the latter case, they rely on a flexible pool of unskilled workers that can flow between the SME and traditional sectors during various phases of the business cycles.

Such enterprises are expected to produce low rates of return on capital, and tend to be staffed and managed by relatively unskilled workers and entrepreneurs. In most cases, entrepreneurs in these types of enterprises in Arab countries lack access to bank credit for reasons similar to those faced by similar entrepreneurs all over the world:

- Lack of efficient credit ratings systems, as well as lack of local financial institutions with direct knowledge of the borrowing agent

- Agency problems and associated credit risk perceived to be too high

- Fixed cost of establishing an information network or local branches too high for commercial banks to undertake, given the low rates of return expected to be earned by such enterprises.

This class of SMEs is the traditional class considered at length by economic development agencies, and for which a variety of financial solutions have been

220   GLOBALIZATION AND FIRM COMPETITIVENESS

provided in theory and practice. Such financial solutions tend to concentrate on
government-led efforts to encourage public banks to extend low-interest loans to
such entrepreneurs, together with cooperative efforts from nongovernmental organizations (NGOs) and international economic bodies.

Despite the concerted efforts of Arab governments, NGOs, and international
economic bodies, there is still a significant classical credit gap for SMEs (Stiglitz
and Weiss 1981) in the Arab world. Table 10.5 illustrates the size of this gap.

Consequently, existing SMEs rely mostly on personal or family funds. The
resulting dependence on individual—and family—wealth gives rise to the familiar situation in other contexts wherein success of SMEs depends crucially on
individual wealth and human capital (Evans and Jovanovic 1989; Black, de Meza,
and Jeffreys 1996; Cressy 1996). Table 10.6, which reveals the sources of funding of 173 surveyed SMEs in Egypt (representing 66 percent of the active borrowers in the region [Brandsma and Chaouali 1999]), illustrates the excessive
dependence on private funds that is, without exception, more pronounced for
smaller enterprises.

This study (Nathan Associates 1997) also sheds light on the fact that traditional SME entrepreneurs are not a homogeneous group. By evaluating the bimodal
distribution of educational levels of the 173 surveyed SME entrepreneurs (table
10.7), we can see that SME entrepreneurs in Egypt are a heterogeneous group,
with a resulting heterogeneity of the type of SME they run.

This empirical evidence seems to suggest that there is a vicious circle for financing the first type of SMEs in the Arab world. "Type 1" SMEs are of primary
importance, since they employ relatively poor and low-skilled (low human capital)
workers and entrepreneurs. However, theory and evidence suggest that the government and NGO-sponsored "microfinance" plays a minor role for such enterprises,
a role that becomes more insignificant the more "micro" the finance tends to be.

TABLE 10.5 CREDIT GAP FOR SMALL AND MEDIUM ENTERPRISES
IN THE ARAB WORLD

Economy	Outreach gap (number of borrowers)	Microfinancing gap (millions of dollars)
Egypt, Arab Rep. of	1,475,000	371
Jordan	145,000	54
Lebanon	36,000	37
Morocco	485,000	194
West Bank and Gaza	33,000	17
Yemen, Rep. of	649,000	97

Source: Brandsma and Chaouali 1999.

TABLE 10.6 SOURCES OF INVESTMENT CAPITAL FOR 173 SURVEYED EGYPTIAN
SMALL AND MEDIUM ENTERPRISES
(percent)

	Enterprise		
Firm size	Micro	Small	Medium
Personal savings	87	69	64
Family and friends	4	3	0
Bank loan	8	27	36
NGO loan	1	0	0
Supplier loan	0	1	0

Source: Nathan Associates 1997.

This result is not surprising, given the fact that the previously discussed classical
problems with financing SMEs (higher credit risk and asymmetric information,
together with profit margins that are too low to justify the initial investment in
local branches, and information and monitoring agencies) are particularly acute
for microenterprises.

As recent studies[8] have shown, of the 60 surveyed microfinance programs in the
region, only two are sustainable, with eight others approaching sustainability; the
balance are considered to be unsustainable. An ideal solution for this vicious circle

TABLE 10.7 EDUCATIONAL LEVEL OF ENTREPRENEURS OF 173 SURVEYED
EGYPTIAN SMES
(percent)

	Enterprise		
Educational level	Micro	Small	Medium
Postgraduate	0	3	4
University graduate	20	39	52
Technical	20	19	8
High school	6	8	4
Basic education	18	6	16
Can read and write	23	23	12
Can read	4	0	0
Illiterate	9	2	4

Source: Nathan Associates 1997.

may be for Arab countries to implement group-lending microfinance agencies (such as, for example, Grameen Bank in Bangladesh). Concentrating microfinance operations on group lending to the most traditional SMEs can help alleviate many of the sustainability problems facing NGOs and other funding agencies.

Market-Niche-Finding Small and Medium Enterprises

The second type of SME entrepreneurs we consider are dynamic businessmen who discover unexploited market niches in the domestic or world markets, and move quickly to capitalize on them. The small size of this type of SME is dictated by the dynamic nature of the operations, shifting from one focus to another as competitors fill market-niches and new niches are identified. This type of SME is not suited for microfinancing or any other traditional form of financing administered by conventional bank loan officers. Attempting to finance such dynamic businesses through traditional loans is impractical for at least two reasons. First, loan officers are accustomed to evaluating projects based on experience in the area of business and the performance of comparable competitors. However, by the very nature of the market-niche finders, they are pioneers in new markets, where neither they nor others have an established track record for the loan officer to analyze. Second, the monitoring costs in such dynamic areas are very high, and the types of group lending and agent-monitoring that are prescribed for traditional microfinance are also inapplicable. Therefore, agency problems prevail for such SMEs, rendering them unattractive candidates for any type of conventional loan financing.

Two fundamental problems result from this mismatch between conventional bank lending institutions and our "type 2" SMEs. First, because banks are reluctant to lend to such entrepreneurs, we expect excessive reliance on the entrepreneur's wealth as well as informal financing through family and friends. Second, the only entrepreneurs in those types of SME sectors who will be able to obtain loans from conventional financial sources are the ones who seem to have low levels of credit risk due to such individual and family wealth. Those two factors, in turn, give rise to two sources of market distortion. First, active entrepreneurs in those sectors will not necessarily be the most talented in the economy, but rather the ones with the appropriate initial level of wealth. Second, the ability of those mediocre entrepreneurs to leverage their initial capital through access to conventional loans amplifies the riskiness of those sectors artificially, compounding the initial agency problems.

Thus, in order to allow the best entrepreneurial talents in the economy to participate in this sector and maximize economic efficiency, we need to develop a set of financing alternatives for this type of entrepreneur. In general, the form of financing we seek for type 2 of SMEs must:

- Require little knowledge of the industries in which the SME will venture

- Minimize agency problems and credit risks which are borne by the financial institution, and consequently

- Be readily available at low cost to entrepreneurs with no initial wealth or track record.

Avant-Garde Small and Medium Enterprises

The final type of SME we consider is the "path-finding" type. The entrepreneurs involved in this type of enterprise are highly skilled risk takers. While the small size of the first type of SMEs was dictated by lack of economies of scale, and that of the second type was dictated by the dynamism and shifting emphasis on different markets, the "smallness" of this third type of SMEs is dictated by its riskiness. The first two types of SMEs had little to no scope for utilizing economies of scale. In contrast, type 3 SMEs are predicated on taking substantial risks precisely because of the potential existence of significant economies of scale. The entrepreneur risks losing a substantial portion of the capital put into this type of enterprise, and therefore attempts to sink the minimum possible initial investment into it before increasing the size of the enterprise to capitalize on its significant economies of scale, if successful.

Like type 2 SMEs, this type of SME exhibits features (lack of a track record and so on) that render dependence on conventional financial means impractical and distortionary. However, it lacks the second type of SME's emphasis on dynamism, which encourages investment in forms of fixed capital with multiple uses (for example, vehicles, real estate, and so on). Such forms of capital are easy to finance through lease contracts, since the agency risks are largely reduced by the financing agency's ability to inspect the leased capital goods periodically, and to seize possession in case of default. In the case of avant-garde enterprises, however, the capital investment can be largely in human capital (for example, software firms, Internet-based commerce, and so on) or unconventional forms of capital (for example, manufacturing prototypes of a new machine and so on). Such forms of capital are difficult to inspect and virtually impossible to seize if the circumstances dictate such actions. Moreover, conventional financial institution employees (loan or lease officers) would need to acquire substantial amounts of human capital in the area in question to determine the feasibility and probabilities of success and failure of the enterprise.

These limitations suggest that the financial institutions that cater to this type of SME must possess two main properties. First, they must have substantial information on the specific sector within which the new SME is venturing. Second, they must rely on equity-based financing, since monitoring is virtually impossible and the capital in which funds are invested is difficult to recover if such an action (that is, to recover the capital) is needed. Knowledge of the industry minimizes the initial cost of assessing the success probability of the SMEs, while equity investment allows the funding agency to share in its potential capitalization on economies of scale. The ideal institution for funding this third type of SME would therefore consider a large number of potential investments in a specific sector, and diversify the high risks of each such investment by investing in a large number of relatively small enterprises. This is the venture capital financing model, which is credited for the "new economy," which is based on high technology, and which is spreading throughout much of the industrial world.

As we shall see, establishing a reliable and transparent system of intellectual and physical property rights is crucial for the existence of such a venture capital sector that undertakes significant risks, and relies for profitability on the security of equity stakes in highly profitable enterprises. Similarly, the lease financing approach advocated for the second type of SMEs requires security of property rights and transparency of the legal and regulatory system, which allows the leasing agency to seize its assets if the SME were to shirk its responsibilities. Any additional credit or legal risk would render such institutions inoperable, and limit the ability to create a thriving sector of SMEs of the second and third types. The SMEs of type 2 and 3 are the ones most conducive to economic growth, while the type 1 SME is—at best—an indirect form of socioeconomic welfare subsidization. Therefore, most of our policy suggestions would pertain to the creation of an enabling environment for the latter two types of financing.

A Taxonomy of Matched Financing Sources for Small and Medium Enterprises

Based on the outlines given in the previous section, we shall now suggest appropriate alternative sources of financing and government policies that can enhance the utilization of the three types of SMEs.

Group Lending to Traditional Small and Medium Enterprises
The best means for funding the traditional type of SME is largely in place in many Arab countries and constitutes traditional microfinance. This type of finance is mostly conducted by conventional bankers, who undertake it reluctantly to satisfy government requirements. Thus, the largest active parties in this form of finance in the Arab world have tended to be state-owned banks, as well as NGO-financed operations.

However, as we have previously stated, most of those microfinance operations in the region are not financially sustainable (see Brandsma and Chaouali 1999). The reasons for this unsustainability are the same ones that discourage private bankers from engaging in microfinance: (a) lack of information about potential borrowers, (b) low profit margins earned by the SMEs seeking microloans, and (c) lack of collateral. The last two factors make microloans risky (due to adverse selection and moral hazard problems associated with the one-sided incomplete information), while the low profitability factor makes it difficult for banks to compensate for this risk through higher interest rates. As a result, microfinance of SMEs continues to be an NGO- or government-subsidized industry, which renders it a form of transfer to the poor rather than a bona fide financing operation.

Such transfers to the poor are indeed warranted, and microfinance may provide a more useful enabling environment to the poor than a simple welfare transfer. To help this emerging industry become more sustainable, it is important to solve the adverse selection and moral hazard problems outlined above. The tendency to date seems to have concentrated on government- and NGO-backed guarantee corporations intended to encourage private financial institutions to participate in microfinance. However, it is well known (Adams and Vogel 1984) that government- and NGO-sponsored credit programs for the poor have extremely low repayment rates (below 25 percent). In the Egyptian experience, which constitutes the lion's share of microcredit in the Arab world, with the exception of Egypt's National Bank for Development (NBD), which reports a repayment rate of 97 percent, most other banks in the Arab world seem to have experienced much lower repayment rates (Nathan Associates 1997).

An alternative and complementary method that seems to have been largely ignored in the Arab world is the concept of group lending (Adams and Landman 1979), popularized in recent years by the perceived success of the Grameen Bank in Bangladesh (Hossein 1988). The theoretical foundations for using groups' abilities to apply moral suasion, which can be viewed as a form of "social collateral" (Besley and Coate 1995), have been well established. The basic idea is that moral hazard problems, and the associated agency costs incurred by the microlending institution, can be reduced significantly through a system of "agents monitoring other agents" (Varian 1990). While the idea of group lending has been associated mainly with rural lending in rural Bangladesh (and earlier in Egyptian agricultural cooperatives of the 1960s), the theoretical arguments for the alleviation of agency costs apply to other environments (for example, groups of artisans, guilds, unions, and so on). To the extent that microlending to traditional SMEs continues to be a major part of NGO and government economic development policies, coupling this strategy with a group-lending approach may improve the sustainability of the lending institutions and assist in achieving the goals of the sponsoring agencies.

Leasing to "Niche-Finding" Small and Medium Enterprises
We have argued that the recently emerging class of Arab entrepreneurs is concentrated in dynamic enterprises, where they aim to capitalize on short- to medium-term domestic or international market niches. Those entrepreneurs are very competitive and thus may not be expected to exercise moral suasion on one another. Therefore, they are very poor candidates for group-lending institutions. Moreover, because of their dynamism, their geographic and sectoral affiliations are constantly shifting, which renders those of them who lack substantial collateral poor candidates for any form of lending. As we have argued previously, the need for collateral limits this sector somewhat to those entrepreneurs who already have access to funding sources through individual wealth, family, and friends. Lending to those individuals is tantamount to allowing them to exercise

excess leveraging of their initial capital, thus amplifying the risks associated with the sector, and increasing the agency costs of lending to those without such initial sources of capital. The result, it was argued, is an inefficient allocation of resources toward already established entrepreneurs, limiting the desired potential for this sector to provide nourishment for a growing entrepreneurial class, and encourage innovation.

For this class of entrepreneurs, the bulk of their capital needs may be office spaces and equipment, warehouses and storage spaces, transportation vehicles, and so on. While the types of businesses in which these SMEs engage may be in constant flux, the forms of capital they require are by necessity traditional and thus can be monitored. This suggests that lease and lease-purchase financing can be a very successful source of funding for entrepreneurs in this sector. The advantage of lease financing is that lease payments are calculated to ensure that the value of the asset after normal market depreciation remains above the balance needed for the lessee to purchase the object from the lessor. The leased object thus becomes a *de facto* collateral that the lessor may seize in case of default or if signs of abuse of the leased object are detected. Thus, the agency costs associated with moral hazard are reduced from the costs of monitoring the activities of the agent to the much lower costs of inspecting the leased object. Because of the general use of the capital goods thus leased, it is not difficult for funding agencies to have in-house experts who can monitor the depreciation of this collateral.

The leasing vehicle is also useful due to its ease of securitization, which would allow the leasing companies to reduce the risk they bear. While Arab financial markets remain largely underdeveloped in the areas of asset-based securitization, some advances have begun, starting in the mid- to late-1990s. For instance, the Saudi National Commercial Bank (NCB) first introduced asset-backed securities (ABSs) in 1994, through its Corporate Finance Group division. The activities in such securities have been increasing within Saudi Arabia and mobilizing intraregional financial flows.[9] The increased emphasis of international banks on using ABSs as a vehicle for investing in emerging markets, and in particular in the Middle East and emerging European markets, suggests that growth in the leasing industry and associated securitization can provide a valuable source of foreign investment funds.[10] New developments in the area of reducing sovereignty risk through international insurance companies[11] also promise that this sector may continue to grow in the future, provided that the Arab countries continue to liberalize their financial markets and develop a stable and transparent legal and regulatory framework.

Venture Capital Financing of Avant-Garde Entrepreneurs

The class of SMEs we labeled "avant-garde" in section II is perhaps the largest potential contributor to effecting the type of economic growth needed for Arab countries. This type of SME is more likely to attract FDI flows, cultivate managerial and entrepreneurial skills, and increase productivity in different parts of the economy. Unfortunately, the very advantages that make avant-garde SMEs attractive to a developing country also make traditional financing methods inapplicable to them.

The avant-garde SMEs are high-risk, high-return ventures. This is not in the domain of conventional banks, which provide low-risk, low-return financial intermediation. Thus, conventional banks are limited to dealing with traditional SMEs, where low risk implies low return, both at the enterprise and at the economic levels. The riskiness of the projects undertaken by SMEs is further exacerbated by the novelty of the sectors in which they operate. Another source of risk is the unconventional nature of avant-garde SME capital, a substantial portion of which takes the form of "inalienable" human capital which cannot be repossessed by a funding agency (Hart and Moore 1994), thus rendering avant-garde SMEs poor candidates for lease financing.

The ideal financing method for high-risk, high-return avant-garde enterprises, judging from historical experiences of advanced industrial economies, seems to be the venture capital model (Doerflinger and Rivkin 1987). This model is predicated on the existence of groups of investors who are willing to invest in a number of small enterprises with high probabilities of complete failure and great success. They provide funds to SMEs in exchange for a claim to a share of the enterprise's equity. If the enterprise is successful, the venture pays the investors handsomely. Venture capital firms attempt to reduce risks in a number of ways. First, they specialize in a specific industry, thus maximizing their ability to formulate good ex ante expectations of potential losses and gains for any potential enterprise. Second, they diversify the risk by investing simultaneously in a number of competing SMEs, thus increasing the chance that at least one of their investments will pay, compensating them for the many losses they may incur. Third, by staging their investment expenditures in each enterprise, they minimize agency risks induced by one-sided asymmetric information (Gompers 1995).

This staging of investment also guards against the firms' renegotiation of the investors' claim at a later stage (Neher 1999). Sahlman (1990) provides a methodical treatment of the means by which venture capital firms monitor and exercise some control over the actions of entrepreneurs until such time that the entrepreneurs' human capital is embodied in the enterprise. The value added by entrepreneurs is determined by their managerial abilities. Often, once an enterprise reaches that point of its development, when human capital is embodied in the enterprise, the avant-garde entrepreneurs receive compensation for their earlier efforts, and the enterprise is turned over to traditional managers who seek traditional means of debt and equity financing of the firm. If an avant-garde SME reaches this stage of development, the firm makes a transition out of the SME category into the mainstream sectors of the economy, carrying with it the advantages of increased productivity growth and possible access to FDI inflows and export markets.

Conclusion

The preceding taxonomy of SME types and their appropriate means of financing suggests that the government's role in encouraging SME growth and financing should be less direct than it seems to be in the Arab world. This involves limiting the role of NGO- and government-sponsored microcredit to the poor, and concentrating instead on creating an enabling environment for private financial institutions to take the lead. This enabling environment requires a transparent legal structure of property rights and repossession procedures to assure leasing companies that the costs of re-possessing leased capital goods are manageable. Such a legal structure will also make it easier for venture capital firms to form and finance the most innovative SMEs, while ensuring the safety of their claims to equity in the emerging firms. The role of the government and NGOs in poverty alleviation and employment creation is likely to continue focusing on welfare-motivated transfers through microcredit. It is advisable to take a longer-term view of the problems of development and poverty, however, recognizing that those welfare goals may best be met if SMEs play a piv-otal role in achieving a sustainable path of economic growth.

In summary, our three types of SMEs can be ranked in terms of their contribu-tion to economic success, as well as their regulatory and legal requirements:

- Traditional SMEs contribute very little to long-term growth and develop-ment. The best financial vehicle for funding such SMEs is group lending through conventional banks and NGOs. In their ability to attract money through international NGOs and development funding agencies (for ex-ample, International Finance Corporation [IFC], United States Agency for International Development, and so on), this class of SMEs may assist in enhancing the inflow of foreign savings into Arab countries, through official and semi-official debt. Historically, this form of capital inflow has had the lowest correlation with economic growth and development. The main advantages of this type of SMEs and associated financing meth-ods are the ability to meet short-term needs of poverty alleviation and employment creation, together with the fact that the regulatory frame-work for such financing is already in place in all Arab countries.

- Market-niche-seeking SMEs contribute more to long-term growth and development, and can serve as a vehicle for channeling private foreign savings through ABSs of leasing company accounts receivable. The dis-advantages of this type of SME are that it relies on the exploitation of market imperfections which are likely to disappear in the long term, as well as its limited potential for increasing FDI inflows. On the other hand, the existing class of entrepreneurs engaged in this sector has contributed to recent growth trends, and this class of SMEs may serve as a nurturing environment for more enterprising entrepreneurs to emerge. Moreover, the regulatory framework for meeting the financial needs of this sector is quickly taking shape in many Arab countries. As the market matures, traditional sources of development financing can contribute further to the maturity of this sector. Indeed, the IFC and other agencies have played a major role in enhancing the potential for ABS financing to play a larger role in the region.[12]

- In the long term, the third class of SMEs is the only one in our taxonomy that promises to serve as an engine of private sector–led export-oriented growth. It is also the class of SMEs best positioned to play a major role in enhancing the inflow of managerial and technology-transferring FDI. Unfortunately, the venture capital financial institutions best suited for funding such SMEs are very scarce in the Arab world, and the financial regulatory framework necessary for their viability remains largely under-developed there.

Notes

1. See, for instance, the literature review in Admiraal 1996, and the references therein.

2. See Acs 1996, and the references therein.

3. All dollar amounts are U.S. dollars.

4. As reported in Cairo Chamber of Commerce 1999.

5. For a brief survey of the pros and cons of FDI and means of attracting its flows to Arab countries, see El-Erian and El-Gamal 1997.

6. See Carson and others 1995, pp.74–76, for a discussion of the role of SMEs in developing such skills.

7. See El-Erian and El-Gamal 1997 for a brief survey of those advantages as they pertain to the Arab world.

8. Brandsma and Chaouali 1999.

9. See Al-Jifri 1998 for a discussion of the increased volume of ABS trading in Saudi Arabia. There is also evidence that some Egyptian companies have used the National Commercial Bank's (NCB's) services to securitize some of their own accounts receivables.

10. Chase Bank of America and other international banks have begun paying more attention to the ABS market in the Middle East (*Asset-Backed Security Week* 1997).

11. See *Asset Sales Report* 1999.

12. Starting in 1997 the IFC played a leading role in pioneering ABS finance in Lebanon and Morocco (*Asset Sales Report* 1996).

Bibliography

Acs, Z. 1996. *Small Firms and Economic Growth*. Cheltenham: Edward Elgar.

Acs, Z., R. Morck, and B. Yeung. 1999. "Productivity Growth and Firm Distribution." In Z. Acs, B. Carlsson, and C. Karlsson, *Entrepreneurship, Small and Medium-Sized Enterprises and the Macroeconomy*. Cambridge, U.K.: Cambridge University Press.

Adams, D., and J. Landman. 1979. "Lending to the Poor through Informal Groups: A Promising Financial Market Innovation." *Savings and Development* 2: 85–94.

Adams, D., and R. Vogel. 1984. "Rural Financial Markets in Low-Income Countries: Recent Controversies and Lessons." *World Development* 14: 477–87.

Admiraal, P., ed. 1996. *Small Business in the Modern Economy*. Oxford: Basil Blackwell.

Al-Jifri, A. 1998. "ABS Products Gain Popularity in the Kingdom." *Saudi Gazette*, July 5, 1998.

Asset-Backed Securities Report International. 1999. "OPIC Offers Political Insurance Coverage for ABS." August 9.

Asset-Backed Securities Week. 1997. "B of A Opens an ABS Shop in Europe." May 19.

Asset Sales Report. 1996. "ABS on the Horizon for Middle East/North Africa." December 9.

Bechri, M., T. Najah, and J. B. Nugent. 1999. "Anatomy of an Institutional Failure: Tunisia's Lending Program to SMEs MENA Countries." Economic Research Forum (ERF) Sixth Annual Conference, Egypt, October.

Besley, T., and S. Coate. 1995. "Group Lending, Repayment Incentives, and Social Collateral." *Journal of Development Economics* 46: 1–18.

Black, J., D. de Meza, and D. Jeffreys. 1996. "House Prices, the Supply of Collateral, and the Enterprise Economy." *Economic Journal* 106: 60–75.

Brandsma, J., and R. Chaouali. 1999. *Making Micro-Finance Work for the Arab World*. Washington, D.C.: World Bank.

Cairo Chamber of Commerce. 1999. "Periodic Report." Research Department. February.

Carson, D., S. Cromie, P. McGowan, and J. Hill. 1995. *Marketing and Entrepreneurship in SMEs: An Innovative Approach*. London: Prentice Hall.

Cressy, R. 1996. "Are Business Startups Debt-Rationed?" *Economic Journal* 106: 1253–70.

Doerflinger, T., and J. Rivkin. 1987. *Risk and Reward: Venture Capital and the Making of America's Great Industries*. New York: Random House.

El-Erian, M., and M. El-Gamal. 1997. "Attracting Foreign Direct Investment to Arab Countries: Getting the Basics Right." Working Paper #9718, Economic Research Forum (ERF), Cairo.

Evans, D., and B. Jovanovic. 1989. "Estimates of a Model of Entrepreneurial Choice under Liquidity Constraints." *Journal of Political Economy* 97: 808–27.

Giugale, Marcelo, and H. Mubarak. 1996. *Private Sector Development in Egypt*. Cairo: The American University in Cairo Press.

Gompers, P. 1995. "Optimal Investment, Monitoring, and Staging of Venture Capital." *Journal of Finance* 50: 1461–89.

Hamdan, K. 1995. "The Informal Sector in Lebanon: General Overview." Economic Research Forum (ERF) Workshop on "The Dynamics of the Informal and Small-Scale Enterprises Sector," Egypt.

Hart, O., and J. Moore. 1994. "A Theory of Debt Based on the Inalienability of Human Capital." *Quarterly Journal of Economics* 109: 841–79.

Hossein, Mahabub. 1988. "Credit for Alleviation of Rural Poverty: The Grameen

Bank in Bangladesh." International Food Policy Research Institute Report 65, February.

International Monetary Fund. 1999. *World Economic Outlook.* Washington, D.C.: IMF.

Karmoul, A. 1995. "The Dynamics of the Informal and Small-Scale Enterprises Sector in Jordan." Workshop on "The Dynamics of the Informal and Small-Scale Enterprises Sector," Egypt.

Mansour, A. 2000. "Competitiveness of SMEs and Support Services." Paper prepared for MDF 2, Cairo, March.

Nathan Associates. 1997. "Financial Reform for Small Business Development in Egypt." Prepared for the Government of Egypt. Contract #: 263-C-00-96-00001-00.

Neher, D. 1999. "Staged Financing: An Agency Perspective." *Review of Economic Studies* 66: 255–74.

Sahlman, W. 1990. "The Structure and Governance of Venture-Capital Organization." *Journal of Financial Economics* 27: 473–521.

Schumacher, E. 1973. *Small Is Beautiful.* New York: Harper and Row.

Stiglitz, Joseph E., and A. Weiss. 1981. "Credit Rationing in Markets with Imperfect Information." *American Economic Review* 71(3): 393–410.

U. N. (United Nations). 1998. *Handbook on Foreign Direct Investment by SMEs: Lessons from Asia.* New York.

Varian, H. 1990. "Monitoring Agents with Other Agents." *Journal of Institutional and Theoretical Economics* 146: 153–74.

CHAPTER 11

The Competitive Position of the Tourism Industry in the MENA Region

Sahar Tohamy

Broadly defined, tourism is regarded as the world's largest and fastest growing industry, accounting for over one-third of the value of the total worldwide services trade. Highly labor-intensive, it is a major source of employment generation in industrial as well as in developing countries. Tourism demand, both domestic and international, is directly related to income levels, and therefore has prospered as global wealth has increased.

The World Tourism Organization ranks tourism in the top five export categories for 83 percent of countries, notably in Europe, the Middle East, and the Americas. Furthermore, tourism is the leading source of foreign exchange in at least one in three developing countries. According to World Travel and Tourism Council (WTTC) estimates, tourism worldwide employed 8.2 percent of workers in 1999, and general travel accounted for 11 percent of worldwide gross domestic product (GDP) in 1999. For developing countries, it is one area where they run consistent trade surpluses, widening steadily from \$4.6 billion[1] in 1980 to \$63.1 billion in 1997. In addition, tourism's role in the world economy is expected to grow even further in the next couple of decades, with predictions that travel and tourism will add 5.5 million new jobs per year until 2010.

With a view on utilizing tourism's growth potential for the benefit of Middle East and North Africa (MENA) countries, and with the complexity of developing sector policies for tourism, this chapter raises the following questions:

a. What is the current position of MENA in world tourism?

b. What are the strengths and weaknesses of the region?

c. How can we enhance the region's tourism prospects?

The chapter is organized as follows. First we summarize global industry trends, recent developments, and industry prospects and highlight the MENA region's tourism-related indicators. Next we use four country-level cluster analyses from MENA to highlight common strengths and weaknesses. These analyses are studies of Egypt, Tunisia, Jordan, and the Palestinian territories. Finally we focus on marketing strategies (demand side) and human resource development (supply side), which are the two policy areas necessary for enhancing tourism's potential in the region.

The Current Position of Middle East and North Africa in World Tourism

In the 10 years from 1989 to 1998 tourist arrivals worldwide grew at an average annual rate of 4.9 percent. International receipts (excluding transport) increased by a corresponding 7.9 percent annually during the same decade. In 1997 tourism receipts accounted for a little over one-third of total exports of services and slightly over 8 percent of the total world exports of merchandise (table 11.1).

In contrast to trade and current account deficits for developing countries, travel account balance has been persistently in surplus, widening steadily from $4.6 billion in 1980 to $63.1 billion in 1997. Developing countries' surplus in travel almost doubled in the second half of the 1980s, a doubling attributed to a sharp widening of surplus in Asia and Pacific (excluding Japan, Australia, and New Zealand) and Africa. In 1997 developing countries' travel surplus was $63.1 billion, offsetting more than two-thirds of their current account deficit.

Despite the growing importance of tourism activity in developing countries, the top 10 tourism destination and earner countries remain dominated by the United States (7 percent of international tourist arrivals and 16.5 percent of tourism receipts), France (11 percent of arrivals and 7.5 percent of receipts), and Spain (8

TABLE 11.1 IMPORTANCE OF TOURISM IN WORLD TRADE, 1995–97

Indicator	1995	1996	1997
International tourism receipts (billions of dollars)	403	438	438
Share of tourism in exports of commercial services (percent)	34	34	34
Share of tourism receipts in merchandise exports (percent)	8	9	8

Source: World Tourism Organization 2000.

TABLE 11.2 TOP 10 TOURISM DESTINATIONS AND EARNERS, 1999

Country	Dollars (millions)	Share in world (percent)	Country	Dollars (millions)	Share in world (percent)
France	71,400	11	United States	73,000	16.5
Spain	51,958	8	Spain	33,572	7.6
United States	46,983	7	France	32,876	7.5
Italy	35,839	5	Italy	31,000	7
China	27,047	4	United Kingdom	20,972	4.8
United Kingdom	25,740	4	Germany	16,406	3.7
Mexico	20,216	3	China	14,099	3.2
Canada	19,556	3	Austria	11,259	2.6
Poland	17,940	3	Canada	10,282	2.3
Austria	17,630	3	Mexico	7,850	1.8
Subtotal	335,036	51	Subtotal	251,316	57
World total	656,933	100	World total	441,255	100

Source: http://www.world-tourism.org.

percent of arrivals and 7.6 percent of receipts) (table 11.2). Regionally, Europe dominates the market with close to 60 percent of total tourism receipts and arrivals. The corresponding shares for the MENA region are between 2 and 3 percent for receipts and arrivals, respectively (figure 11.1). Within MENA the main tourism players in 1999 were Tunisia with 4.9 million arrivals, Egypt with 4.4 million arrivals, and Morocco with close to 4 million arrivals. On the receipts side, Egypt dominates with close to $4 billion, followed by Morocco and Tunisia, $1.9 billion and $1.6 billion, respectively. Turkey and Israel represent the other non-Arab main players in the Middle East region, with Turkey receiving 6.8 million tourists and Israel 2.2 million for 1999 (table 11.3).

As for the importance of tourism to hosting economies in the MENA region, WTTC estimates that tourism contributed 7.3 percent of the Middle East's GDP (6.8 percent for North Africa), 7.1 of total employment (6.1 percent for North Africa), and 9 percent of gross investment (6.1 percent for North Africa). Tourism plays a more important role in economies of all other regions, with the exception of South Asia and Latin America (table 11.4).

Strengths and Weaknesses of Selected MENA Countries and Economies: Egypt, Jordan, Tunisia, and the Palestinian Territories

In spite of the fact that each of the countries and economies studied has its own unique features in terms of the size of tourism in its respective economy and the

FIGURE 11.1 REGIONAL DISTRIBUTION OF RECEIPTS IN 1998
AND ARRIVALS IN 1999

Regional Distribution, Receipts, 1998

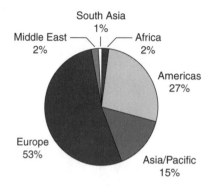

Regional Distribution, Arrivals, 1999

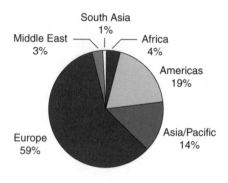

Source: http://www.world-tourism.org/.

nature of its tourism assets, there are general strengths and weaknesses that cut across all four regions.[2] Tourism represents a primary source of foreign currency in all of these four entities. In 1997, for example, receipts for Egypt, Jordan, and Tunisia represented 40 percent, 45 percent, and 56 percent of total service exports, respectively. Tourism receipts account for around 5 percent of GDP in Egypt, 8 percent of Tunisia's GDP, and 12 percent of Jordan's GDP. The following sections highlight the common strengths and weaknesses in these four economies.

Strengths

Geographical, historical, and economic development features lend themselves to some natural points of strength for the region. The most important among these are abundant natural and historical endowments, the region's proximity to Europe, and the potential for a substantial increase in domestic growth from the region's own countries.

NATURAL AND CULTURAL ENDOWMENTS

Many people rank the Middle East region's attractions among the most important places to visit in the world. The opportunities for expansion of cultural tourism given the region's concentration of religious and historic sites can hardly be over-estimated, especially when the Middle East itself was for centuries the strategic land bridge for the trade routes between the Orient and Europe. As the spiritual

TABLE 11.3 TOURIST ARRIVALS AND RECEIPTS BY COUNTRY IN THE MENA REGION, 1995–99

Country	Tourist arrivals (to United States)					Tourism receipts (millions of dollars)				
	1995	1996	1997	1998	1999	1995	1996	1997	1998	1999
Tunisia	4,120	3,885	4,263	4,718	4,880	1,402	1,451	1,414	1,557	1,608
Morocco	2,602	2,693	3,072	3,243	3,950	1,304	1,674	1,449	1,745	1,850
Turkey	7,083	7,966	9,040	8,960	6,800	4,957	5,962	8,088	7,809	5,000
Egypt, Arab Rep. of	2,872	3,528	3,657	3,213	4,489	2,684	3,204	3,727	2,564	3,815
Israel	2,215	2,100	2,010	1,942	2,240	2,964	2,955	2,836	2,656	3,050
Saudi Arabia	3,325	3,458	—	—	—	1,210	1,308	—	—	—
Syrian Arab Rep.	815	830	891	1,267	1,393	1,338	1,206	1,035	1,190	1,360
Jordan	1,068	1,096	1,116	1,248	—	661	743	774	853	—
Northern Africa	7,305	7,248	—	—	—	2,600	2,864	—	—	—
Middle East	13,465	14,084	—	—	—	7,115	7,739	—	—	—
World total	567,381	599,035	619,718	636,676	656,933	407,317	437,938	439,896	441,255	—

— Not available.

Note: Northern Africa = Algeria, Morocco, Sudan, and Tunisia. Middle East = Bahrain, Egypt, Iraq, Jordan, Kuwait, Lebanon, Libya, Oman, Qatar, Saudi Arabia, Syria, United Arab Emirates, and the Republic of Yemen. Total includes Middle East, North Africa, Turkey, and Israel.
Source: World Tourism Organization 1998.

center for three of the world's major religions—Christianity, Islam, and Judaism—much of MENA countries' past is shared or related—with common traditions and beliefs. Egypt alone is said to have nearly two-thirds of the historical monuments in the world (Fawzy 1998). This diverse and rich tourism asset base presents a huge opportunity for better utilization. At the same time, there are tremendous opportunities in leisure tourism development that capitalize on the region's superb climate and other natural gifts.[3]

PROXIMITY TO EUROPE

Geographically speaking, the MENA region is a neighbor to one of the most important areas in exporting tourism. Europe accounts for around 60 percent of world tourists. Even with over 90 percent of these tourists traveling within Europe, it remains the largest exporting region, accounting for close to 40 percent of total world tourism (figure 11.2).

Already countries such as Egypt, Morocco, and Tunisia receive a large share of their tourists from Europe. European tourists constituted 64 percent, 83 percent, and 56 percent of Tunisia's, Morocco's, and Egypt's arrivals in 1998, respectively. Tourism practitioners in these countries are familiar with Europeans' demands and

TABLE 11.4 TRAVEL AND TOURISM ECONOMY, 1999
(percent of total)

Region	GDP	Employment	Investment
Caribbean	20.6	16	25.7
Other Western Europe	15.4	15.8	16.1
Oceania	14.7	15.6	15.8
European Union	14.1	14.5	13.9
North America	11.8	11.9	11.7
Sub-Saharan Africa	11.2	11.7	9.8
Central and Eastern Europe	11.1	7.4	9.7
Southeast Asia	10.6	7.4	9.5
Northeast Asia	10	7.3	9.1
Middle East	7.3	7.1	9
North Africa	6.8	6.1	6.1
Latin America	5.6	6	6.1
South Asia	5.3	5.4	5.5

Source: WTTC 1999.

FIGURE 11.2 SHARE OF SAME-REGION TOURISM IN TOTAL OUTBOUND, 1996

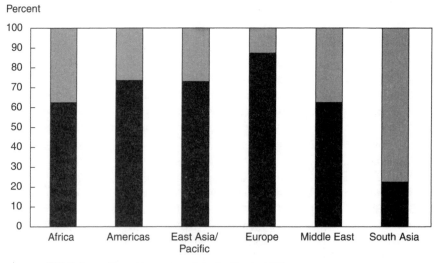

Percent

☐ Outbound travel by region of destination in 1996
■ Same continent/region

Source: World Tourism Organization 1998.

languages. Despite the large share of Europeans in main tourism destinations in the Middle East, the share of MENA in total outbound tourism is 2.5 percent of the total of Europe's outbound tourism, hence the unexploited potential for the Middle East and North Africa.

In addition to representing an unutilized tourism source for the Middle East, Europe is a major destination for travelers from the Americas and the Far East; over 22 million Americans traveled to Europe in 1996. This number is larger than the total number of arrivals to the Middle East and North Africa region combined for the same year. Another 13 million Far Eastern tourists arrived in Europe in 1996. Similarly, travelers to Israel from the Americas accounted for 26 percent of Israel's arrivals in 1997. This compares with a mere 7 percent of arrivals from the Americas to a tourism-leading Arab country such as Egypt. The actual share does not represent the potential. Research has to identify whether poor marketing or supply is constraining the MENA region's ability to share this huge tourist supply from these three high-income regions.

DOMESTIC TOURISM

The MENA region is one of the fastest growing regions with a young and growing population. In addition, many MENA countries are embarking on structural adjustment and economic reform programs that are producing sustainable economic growth. The region also boasts countries with per capita GDP that is among the highest in the world.[4] Based on a sample of tourist establishments, the following are the percentages of foreign-domestic distribution of tourism activities (foreign to domestic):

- Hotels: 50–50

- Travel agencies: 60–40

- Restaurants: 30–70

- Bazaars: mostly foreigners.

In Tunisia, it is estimated that close to 20 percent of tourism activity caters to the Tunisian tourists.

Higher standards of living for the population should produce trends in Arab outbound tourism similar to those which have developed globally in the past two decades. Efforts to tap this "latent" growth potential must be strengthened with policies to employ domestic tourism as a complement to foreign tourist demand and not a substitute in times of shocks or low seasons.

Looking at domestic demand in the regional sense (for example, Arab tourism demand for travel in the region as a whole), we find that cultural bonds, which Arabs share, have made other Middle East countries the natural destination for "outbound" Arab tourism. In 1996, close to 70 percent of Middle East outbound tourism poured into the Middle East region, for example, Arab's international travel is predominantly within the region (table 11.5). While a natural strength, efforts must be made to efficiently allocate resources between Arab and non-Arab tourism demand. Familiarity with non-Arab tourist demands, tastes, and expectations may be weakened if Arab tourism service suppliers rely too heavily on this "captive" Arab tourism demand.

Weaknesses

This section addresses some common weaknesses for tourism in MENA countries and economies in general, and in Egypt, Jordan, Tunisia, and the Palestinian territories in particular. A thorough evaluation of each entity's weaknesses and recommendations to improve them must underlie a comprehensive tourism development strategy for each.

LACK OF A COMPREHENSIVE TOURISM DEVELOPMENT STRATEGY

Increasingly nations are realizing the potential tradeoff between extensive tourism activity and historical, cultural, and (depletable) natural resources. This realization has developed into an awareness that tourism development cannot be left to pure market forces. "The concept implies protecting the environment, maintaining cultural identity and integrity and achieving a high level of tourist satisfaction, while still generating substantial economic benefits."[5]

Most MENA tourism plans focus on tourist numbers, revenues, and length of stay.[6] Tunisia lacks a strategy to reach the objective of moving from mass tourism to targeting higher niche markets. The Office National du Tourisme Tunisien (ONTT) has, however, initiated marketing policies to rely on the Internet and other marketing tools to promote Tunisian tourism.

The Jordanian case presents its tourism strategy as focused on more tourists, higher spending, and longer stays. The plan aims at making Jordan one of the top tourist destinations, yet there is no clear mechanism by which the Jordanian Tour-

TABLE 11.5 SHARE OF MENA IN OUTBOUND TOURISM, BY REGION, 1996
(percent)

| Destination | \multicolumn{6}{c}{Country of origin} |
	Africa	Americas	East Asia and Pacific	Europe	Middle East	South Asia
Middle East	5.8	0.6	1.2	1.3	62.5	23.4
North Africa	9.4	0.1	0.1	1.2	7.6	0.1
Middle East and North Africa	15.2	0.7	1.3	2.5	70.2	23.4

Source: World Tourism Organization 1998.

ism Board appears to be achieving this goal (Zuraikat 2000). Zuraikat argues that public-private cooperation in all aspects of tourism future strategy is lacking. These issues include, among others, promotion, marketing, human development, infrastructure development, and tourist attraction development. Palestinian tourism suffers from the obvious dependence on the Israeli tourism strategy.

Recently the Egyptian Ministry of Tourism announced a strategy that sets, in addition to arrival, expenditure, and number of establishment growth goals, four pillars upon which the next tourism strategy is built.[7] These four pillars are:

a.   Sustainable growth in tourist arrivals from targeted markets to reach 9.5 million tourists and 66.5 million tourist nights in 2005.

b.   New markets, while maintaining marketing efforts in existing markets. Emphasis is being placed on groups with high incomes and a higher propensity to spend.

c.   New types of tourism such as conference tourism, health tourism, and desert tourism, in addition to specific-sport tourism, such as golfing and car racing.

d.   Specific events such as cultural, sport, festivals, and so forth.

This strategy is complemented by presidential decrees in 1999 that focused on developing airport services at major Egyptian airports, allowing foreign airlines to provide direct flights to domestic tourist destinations, and improving road transportation relevant in tourist areas, as well as a comprehensive effort to facilitate tourism-related services. While the current Egyptian tourism development strategy is more comprehensive and pragmatic than previous five-year plans, an example of a more complete tourism strategy appears in the Nova Scotia strategy in appendix 11A.

INADEQUATE SUPPLY OF INFRASTRUCTURE
The important role that infrastructure plays in tourism policy cannot be ignored: tourists arriving in Egypt spend around 10 percent of their total expenditure on transportation alone. The second-highest complaint from tourists coming to Egypt stems from domestic transportation quality. The studies on Jordan, Tunisia, and the Palestinian territories also cite infrastructure as a weak area in their cluster evaluations.

MENA as a region exhibits varying qualities and costs of infrastructure, power, and telecommunication services, all of which are relevant services in the tourism product. Yet, generally speaking, telephone lines per 1,000 people in cities are one-half to two-thirds the number of the world average, let alone tourism high-achievers. Mobile phone use, computers per capita, and cost of international telecommunications all present the region with a competitive disadvantage (table 11.6).

TABLE 11.6 PHYSICAL INFRASTRUCTURE: POWER, TELECOMMUNICATIONS, AND INFORMATION

Indicator	Electric power			Telephone main lines			International telecommunications		Information age		
	Consumption per capita (kwh), 1996	Production annual percentage growth, 1980–96	Per 1,000 people, 1997	In largest city (per 1,000 people), 1997	Waiting time (years), 1997	Cost of local call ($ per 3 minutes), 1997	Outgoing traffic (minutes per subscriber), 1997	Cost of call to U.S. ($ per 3 minutes), 1997	Mobile telephones (per 1,000 people), 1997	Personal computers (per 1,000 people), 1997	Internet hosts (per 1,000 people), 1997
Egypt	924	7.4	56	..	3.9	0.01	37	6.82	0	7.3	0.31
Algeria	524	7.2	48	55	7.9	0.02	113	4.78	1	4.2	0.01
Tunisia	674	6.2	70	80	1.3	0.06	147	5.7	1	8.6	0.07
Morocco	408	5	50	112	0.2	0.08	109	6.3	3	2.5	0.2
Jordan	1,187	11	70	178	4.8	0.03	216	..	2	8.7	0.8
Syria	755	8.7	88	132	>10	0.05	69	33.41	0	1.7	0
Lebanon	1,651	1.2	179	..	..	0.05	107	7.29	135	31.8	5.56
Libya	3,579	10.2	68	84	..	0.03	93	..			
Saudi Arabia	3,980	9.8	117	178	5.8	0.02	351	6.41	17	43.6	0.15
Kuwait	12,808	4.8	227	..	0.2	0	389	5.44	116	82.9	32.8
World	2,027w	4.7w	118w	254w	0.9m	0.05m	116m	5.16m	40w	58.4w	75.22w
Middle income countries	1,222	8.2	87	235	1.3	0.04	90	5.16	24	32.4	10.15
High income countries	7,941	3.1	506	..	0	0.08	165	2.63	188	269.4	470.12
Latin America and the Caribbean	1,347	5.1	110	192	0.9	0.04	82	4.42	26	31.6	9.64
Middle East and North Africa	1,166	8.4	75	153	2.9	0.03	111	6.02	6	9.8	0.25

Note: w = weighted average; m = median values.
Source: World Bank 2000.

POOR HUMAN CAPITAL, EDUCATION, AND ILLITERACY INDICATORS

Even apart from tourism education per se, the region's human development indicators are not competitive when compared with other developing country regions such as Southeast Asia. For example, male and female illiteracy rates for youth between 15 and 24 years old in Egypt are 25 and 40 percent, respectively (table 11.7). For both Egypt and Jordan *The Global Competitiveness Report* (World Economic Forum 1998) judges poor training and productivity of workers as among the two countries' competitiveness "liabilities" (table 11.8). Poor education quality in general, and in tertiary and vocational schools in particular, inevitably affects the supply of labor entering into tourism, its foreign language skills, its ability to benefit from training, and its ability to accumulate job-specific human capital. Detailed and up-to-date information on these indicators is a must for assessing the specific weaknesses in each country, despite the fact that labor quality is mentioned as a weak area in all four-cluster cases.

Human resources present tourism with a challenge: A continuously changing environment needs to stay on top of technological developments and information technology developments, and needs to remain flexible. While detailed analysis of the region's specific weaknesses is not available yet, all four case studies cite poor quality of labor, training programs, and so on, as among the main areas where the "cluster" exhibits weak links. For now, it is sufficient to mention that in all four

TABLE 11.7 EDUCATION PARTICIPATION AND YOUTH ILLITERACY IN MENA

	Net enrollment ratio		Youth illiteracy rate	
Indicator	Primary (percent of relevant age group), 1996	Secondary (percent of relevant age group), 1996	Male (percent ages 15–24), 1997	Female (percent ages 15–24), 1997
Egypt	93	68	25	41
Tunisia	98	—	4	15
Morocco	74	—	26	47
Jordan	—	—	2	0
Syria	91	38	5	25
Saudi Arabia	61	42	6	12
Kuwait	54	54	9	8
Middle East and North Africa	87	61	*14*	*27*
Middle income	94	—	4	6
High income	97	91	—	—

— Not available.

Source: World Bank 1999.

TABLE 11.8 LABOR COMPETITIVENESS BALANCE SHEET

Assets	Rank	Liabilities	Rank
Egypt			
Minimum wage regulations	1	Primary education enrollment indicator	41
Unemployment insurance	1	Employee training	45
Collective bargaining power	4	Worker productivity	46
Labor force	5	Child labor	51
Labor market flexibility	8		
Labor regulations	16		
Labor force participation	16		
Jordan			
Collective bargaining power	5	Child labor	40
Labor regulations	8	Secondary education enrollment indicator	40
Hiring and firing practices	12	Worker productivity	41
Unemployment insurance	14	Employee training	42
Minimum wage regulations	14	Primary education enrollment indicator	49
Labor market flexibility	18		

Source: World Economic Forum 1998.

cases the issue about low-level labor quality arises, albeit with different degrees of severity. For Jordan, Zuraikat (2000) argues that the lack of enforceable codes of ethics and the lack of enforceable requirements for licensing for tour guides have resulted in Jordanian tour guides having a bad reputation; many foreign groups rely on their native tour guides for trips to Jordan. Private sector practitioners lack the confidence in competing with international players in hotel management, travel agencies, and other services, and therefore lobby for protection from foreign competition. Fawzy (1998) echoes the same "cluster weakness," and emphasizes that human resource skills are weak in most cluster elements, especially in the fields of hotel management, tour guides, and marketing. She further recommends reliance on international expertise in designing education and training programs for these categories of labor.

DOMINANT ROLE OF THE GOVERNMENT

Socialist policies adopted by many MENA countries during the 1950s and 1960s resulted in a dominant role for governments in economic activity.[8] This general trend in Arab countries has produced similar patterns, including favoring industry at the expense of services and agriculture; lack of flexibility in decisionmaking and excessive reliance on planning; and most important, lack of principles such as consumer sovereignty and emphasis on customer satisfaction. These features appear magnified in tourism, with overlapping and sometimes contradictory policies and jurisdictions in tourism policies in the Egyptian case (Fawzy 1998). Similarly, in Tunisia the three relevant entities in tourism development are the Agence Financière Touristique (AFT), ONTT, and Tunis Air—all of which are public sector. Furthermore, AFT has a de facto monopoly over land development in tourist areas.[9]

Privatization drives and the perception of a new "role for the state" to play in economic activity are creating changes in the traditional government-tourism industry partnership and creating an increasing need for self-reliance within the tourism industry. Pursuit of efficient resource allocation in the economy in general and in tourism in particular will have to set new modes of cooperation between public and private tourism entities. The role of government in developing and maintaining public sector museums, parks, and historic sites will remain intact. Thus reevaluation of expenditure policies on these assets and their limits under "hard budget" constraints will have to be considered. Pressures on public sector budgets will continue to erode their capacity to develop, attract, and serve tourists if ways are not found to overcome these problems, and new means found to finance expenditure on public tourist assets. Tourism sector organizations and members of the industry must work at strengthening their capabilities and must work together in true and effective partnerships.

The financial pressures confronting our governments will make it increasingly difficult for them to provide direct financial support for tourism initiatives. As a result, governments and industry together will have to ensure that all activities to develop tourism are cost-effective. At the same time, the industry itself will have to enhance its own effectiveness in working together on product and market development.

PERCEIVED POLITICAL INSTABILITY

The success of achieving comprehensive peace between Israel and the Palestinians is a crucial factor in reducing the image of political instability in the region. Yet despite its natural and cultural resources, particularly in the European market, the Middle East is viewed as prone to terrorism by American markets. Collaboration efforts among countries of the region is needed to dilute this negative perception. In addition to efforts to speed up the peace process, MENA countries must utilize statistics on crime rates, the limited magnitude of organized crime and violent crimes in general to portray the region as a "safe" part of the world where the statistics for a "safe" tourism experience work for and not against the region. Information of this kind can be found in country-specific reports originating from industrial countries' consulates and advisories for their travelers. These types of statistics are, however, underutilized by MENA countries as points of strengths rather than weakness in their tourism efforts.

Enhancing the Region's Tourism Prospects: Marketing and Human Resource Development

The previous section highlights the main strengths and weaknesses for tourism development in the MENA region. This section takes a closer look at two main areas:

tourism marketing (demand side) and human resource development (supply side). The reason the study focuses on these two variables is twofold: First, these are two areas where countries (both industrial and developing) need to work constantly, especially given the increasingly competitive international tourism market.

Second, in terms of their possible payoff, marketing and human resource development are areas where the tourism sector's initiative can produce short- to medium-term results. Other weak areas such as infrastructure and transportation, while having a huge (negative) influence on tourism, will have to be addressed in the context of general macroeconomic policy for each country as whole. Setting indicators for human capital development and marketing strategies is more important than going by the numbers of arrivals, the revenues, and other short-term indicators, which are highly volatile and are sometimes misleading as outcomes of a specific policy.

Marketing

Countries with highly sophisticated tourism sectors and countries enjoying a large share of world tourism—such as France, Spain, Canada, and the United States— recognize the increasingly competitive tourism market, and consequently the increasingly important role that marketing is going to play in their respective tourism industries. This section analyzes some of the main patterns of a successful marketing strategy, its components, its challenges, and its "en vogue" marketing angles.

A crucial prerequisite for any marketing strategy is the information set upon which such a strategy depends. The higher the level of detail, the higher the frequency and promptness of collecting information, and the more diligent the analysis is of each and every piece of information, the more the marketing team will be able to utilize opportunities and new markets. This applies both for the macrolevel— marketing the country as a whole—and for the microlevel—where individual establishments rely on official data to enhance their establishment-marketing strategy.

Egypt, as well and some other Arab countries, has adopted the standard World Tourism Organization foreign tourist expenditure survey. The survey produces information on tourist sources, their education levels, purpose of visits, lengths of stay, and other indicators. In addition, projections about the number of tourists, regional growth patterns, main tourist exporting regions, and so forth are readily available through the World Tourism Organization. These can be used as the starting point for a more comprehensive tourism dataset which includes accurate employment numbers and structure, value added, output, import-component, links with other sectors, investment, contribution to tax revenue, and so forth (see www.wttc.org).

Other data which are needed include client satisfaction information, detailed expenditure information, repeat visits, quality of services, and so on. Extensive tourist establishment surveys must be conducted to give a detailed picture of these firms' needs, potential shortage in their inputs, and so forth. Data on trends and patterns in international tourism markets, patterns in major competing markets, and patterns of growth of particular tourism types must be collected, collated, and periodically analyzed.

INTERNET AND E-COMMERCE

Increasingly, technological innovations are used to create awareness about travel destinations, to provide information, and to sell the product.[10] There is a risk that destinations not ready to embrace these technological changes will lose business. At the same time, however, these innovations are creating new global opportunities to sell tourism products. Again the general level of adoption of these technologies in a country creates the right environment for efficient utilization of such resources (table 11.6). Elements such as widespread use of credit cards, the prevalence of automated media of exchange, and so forth facilitate tourism transactions. For international chain hotels and travel agencies, the infrastructure is there, including on-line reservations, frequent flier services, and client account services. For other hotels efforts must be intensified to remove barriers on utilizing such services.

Both Tunisia and Egypt already have competitive tourism sites on the Internet. These include the ONTT site for Tunisia and the Ministry of Tourism site for Egypt. In addition, Egypt has just set up a site with the Information and Decision Support Center. The focus of these sites, however, could use more diversification. Other services, such as global distribution systems, where airline and hotel reservations can be made directly through these clearinghouses, are key to boosting the tourism industry.

MARKET DIFFERENTIATION STRATEGIES

The biggest challenge facing tourism is the constant need for change in products and services. These changes are creating new challenges for traditional tourism suppliers. The marketplace is becoming more competitive, with destinations continuously expanding marketing efforts and becoming more sophisticated in marketing techniques. Tourism resources rely less on the traditional tourism assets and more on new techniques of targeting growth niche markets.

Emphasis on concepts such as "quality tourism" is increasing. This concept refers to tourism that has a good price-quality combination. The development of such concepts presents tourism practitioners with opportunities and challenges to compete effectively.

All these developments require that the tourism industry find ways to use its information about market opportunities and for this information to be communicated effectively through the domestic industry. Without coordination and mechanisms to utilize such scarce resources, however, the industry will be wasting valuable resources and missing out on opportunities. Without partnerships that are incentive-compatible where all participants can benefit, any attempt to "foster cooperation" will result in vague and ineffective efforts.

Two experiences (from Switzerland and Australia) provide focused and targeted tourism marketing. Switzerland, in what is known as the Key Account Management program, has identified key agents who are interested in investing resources to push Switzerland to cater to tourists from the affluent Japanese market. With these resources, the Swiss program helps channel the right information and gets the Japanese tourists in touch with the right Swiss partners. It also identifies key trends and develops specific products to help agents. For example, it has identified the marathon runners market from Japan as one such potential niche. Marathon runners from Japan mostly go to Hawaii and the Gold Coast, with very few going to Switzerland.

Australia, in a similar attempt to diversify its market, has shifted its marketing focus from selling Australia's magnificent nature to efforts to sell Australian cities and its unique city-life experiences. Spearheading the campaign is the "Australia—Let the Magic Begin" advertisement, which projects a sophisticated, youthful, and vibrant Australia to Asia. The campaign is targeted at the 18- to 44-year-old consumers, and is part of a $100 million global repositioning campaign.

The effective development, operation, and management of tourism require certain institutional elements. These seem to be particularly weak in all of the countries studied using the cluster analysis approach (Fawzy 1998; Zuraikat 2000).

MARKETING ON THE BASIS OF ENVIRONMENTAL CONSCIOUSNESS

Growth trends in the numbers of environmentally conscious and the increasing interest in outdoor- and nature-based activities are being reflected in the industry's initiatives to maintain environmental standards in tourism. Under the Green Globe program of the WTTC, 500 hotels in 100 countries have made commitments to environmental standards and can receive certification and awards. Through the International Hotel Environment Initiative (IHEI)—set up by the Prince of Wales' Business Leaders Forum in 1992 with 12 top hotel companies—over 8,000 hotels in 111 countries follow guidelines for environmental practices. In addition, the International Hotel and Restaurant Association works with the United Nations Environment Programme and IHEI to raise awareness and distribute the "Environmental Action Pack for Hotels" among its 700,000 member establishments in over 150 countries.

The industry itself has suggested that international bodies such as the United Nations could review these initiatives to assess their credibility, impact, and possible use as certification schemes linked to International Standards Organization (ISO) standards. In 1996 the WTTC, the World Tourism Organization, and the Earth Council jointly launched an "Agenda 21 for the Travel and Tourism Industry," based on the action plan for sustainable development adopted at the Rio Earth Summit. One proposal calls for this plan to be linked to the Local Agenda 21 programs underway in over 2,000 cities worldwide (http://www.un.org/esa/sustdev/dpif1.htm).

Another area where present trends in tourism create a golden opportunity for newcomers is ecotourism, or nature tourism. Various countries, foremost among which is Australia, developed national ecotourism strategies. Ecotourism focuses on ecologically sustainable tourism activities, which preserve the natural integrity of primitive areas.

While statistics on the accurate growth of ecotourism may not be available at the time of this writing, a quick Internet survey suggests that ecotourism is gaining in popularity, and hence is a potentially significant growth area. Ecotourism opportunities and activities may include highly specialized, small- or large-scale tourism, remote tourism, and cultural and natural combinations. It adds that conservation should apply not only to ecotourism, but also to all forms of tourism.[11]

MARKETING SPECIFIC TOURIST ATTRACTIONS

Marketing strategies at the national level must be mirrored for special tourist areas and regions. Priorities need to be made in terms of limited resources, financing developments, and so forth. Market targets by number, type, and country or region of origin, socioeconomic group, tourist groupings, length of stay, and other relevant characteristics must be set and adhered to. These targets then must be used to assess the right fees, duties, and licenses in such a way to control excessive use of the attraction.

The same exercise should be performed for new accommodations and other tourist facilities such as travel operations; restaurants; banking and money exchange; handicraft, specialty, and convenience shopping; medical and postal facilities and services; and public safety and tourist information services.

MARKETING TOURISM ACTIVITY TO THE LOCAL COMMUNITY

At the community level there is an increasing interest in developing tourism activity as the continued decline in traditional resource and manufacturing industries forces communities to consider new growth opportunities. Without programs to create public awareness of the importance of tourism to a regional or local economy, and without guarantees that tourism will not jeopardize the local community's identity, there will be a lack of support for developing or promoting tourism.

Greater efforts must be invested in building public and political support for the industry, based on an enhanced awareness of the potential for economic growth through a healthy, strong tourism industry. Preserving the identity of the tourist area has the twin benefits of addressing communities' concerns about their heritage and tradition, while capitalizing on whatever initially drew the tourist to the area in question. Thus, while a tourist may be interested in an international-chain five-star setting in Cairo, part of the attraction of an accommodation facility in Upper Egypt is its indigenous identity.

The focus on marketing tourism development locally is on lobbying government officials for tax benefits, government expenditure on tourism-related services, and so forth. While necessary, especially in a setting where the government remains the main decisionmaker in infrastructure areas, preparing the private local community for adopting tourism as a main activity on which their livelihood depends is crucial for creating effective public-private cooperation. Considerations must be given to ways to enhance and distribute the economic benefits of tourism, environmental protection measures, efforts to reduce adverse social impacts, and conservation of the cultural heritage of people living in the tourism areas.[12]

MENA countries such as Egypt, Bahrain, and others, as well as a WTTC regional study on the Middle East countries, have contributed significantly to creating this awareness. In addition to highlighting links between tourism and other parts of the economy, these studies create the necessary lobbying momentum for collective support of tourism activity.[13]

Human Resource Development

The previous sections give the essence of the increasingly complex tourism market, whose demand segmentation, constant change, and advent of new technologies pose continuous challenges for tourism practitioners. Therefore, formulating the labor requirements that fulfill the tourists' and the suppliers' demand expectations faces the same complexity, especially since the human factor constitutes one of the key elements in achieving competitiveness in tourism businesses and regions.

Two aspects of human resource development must rise to this challenge: formal tourism education and on-the-job training. For formal tourism education, in addition to the challenges it imports from education and labor standards in the economy as a whole, there are inherent difficulties that characterize tourism education in particular. Even at the conceptual level, there is a clear discrepancy between the industry's increasingly popular definition of tourism as "an activity encompassing all activities carried out by people when traveling," and the perspective of public authorities responsible for tourism education. In spite of different attempts to systematize the subject areas that should be catered to by any tourism education system, tourism does not yet constitute a methodologically ordered corpus of doctrine. The great challenge for tourism education and training, therefore, lies in constructing an educational system which avoids falling into the trap of tackling issues in an isolated, fragmentary way, dependent on the academic origin of the researcher or educator and instead aims for a more comprehensive perspective. Figure 11.3 shows the infinite number of disciplines and areas of study upon which tourism depends to meet its human resource requirements.

If we are to target tourism education that adapts human resource skills to new market needs, tourism education and training must attain standards of quality (responding to the real needs of the tourism industry) and efficiency (researching and weighing the costs and benefits of the universe of possible education processes and methods).

In addition to the young tourism worker, the industry and because of the magnitude of change that it undergoes on a regular basis, requires flexible and proactive management. People already in the tourism industry come from different backgrounds; it is very unlikely that they have acquired the comprehensive familiarity with the interdisciplinary nature of tourism during the course of their education. What is important, instead, is on-the-job education and experience. All too

FIGURE 11.3 AREAS OF KNOWLEDGE NECESSARY FOR TOURISM
HUMAN RESOURCES

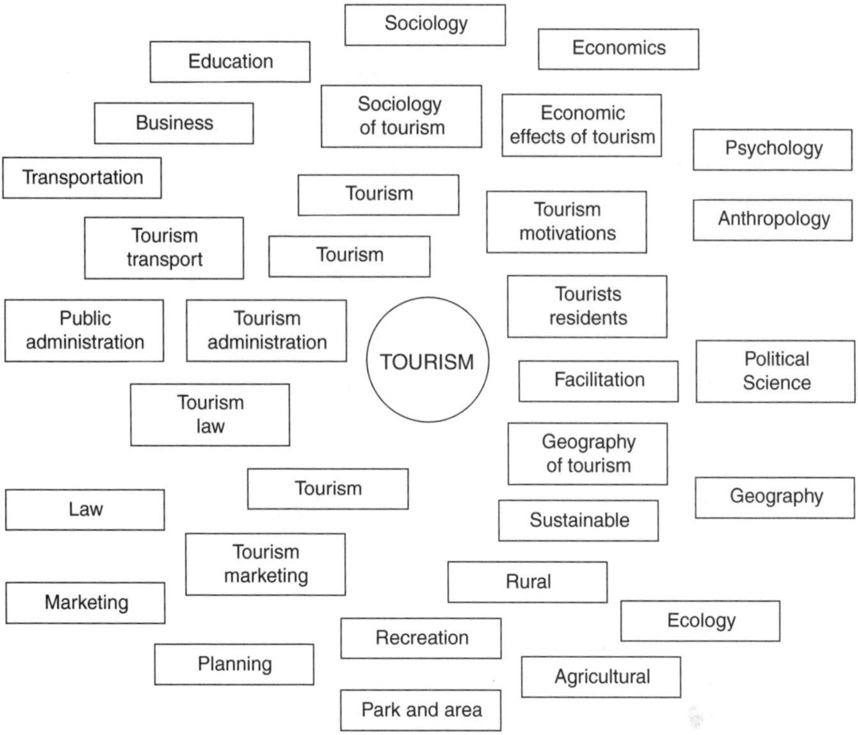

Source: World Tourism Organization 1997.

often tourism education and training have been the result of an ad hoc response to the particular needs of tourism businesses or regions, rather than a well-thought-out strategy of general tourism education.

The dispersed nature of the labor that feeds into the tourism industry brings us to conditions in the economy that are relevant for determining the strengths and weaknesses of the human resource pool (figure 11.3). Table 11.9 provides some competitiveness indicators for both labor and management conditions in Egypt and Jordan. Other Arab countries are not listed in this survey. These indicators, while they may not hinder the competitiveness of managers of the five-star-level management in tourism, can seriously hinder middle and upper management cadres of other establishments. Concerns about management and labor quality are

TABLE 11.9 EGYPT AND JORDAN: MANAGEMENT AND LABOR
COMPETITIVENESS, 1998

	Rank				Rank	
Indicator	Egypt	Jordan	Indicator		Egypt	Jordan
Management quality	45	41	Labor force abundance		5	23
Product design	47	46	Labor force participation		16	34
Production technology	40	34	Child labor		51	40
Total quality management	42	37	Average years of schooling		37	36
Marketing skills	41	46	Worker productivity		46	41
Customer orientation	38	37	Minimum wage regs.		1	14
Staff recruitment and			Hiring and firing practices		35	12
motivation	43	45	Flexibility of labor regs.		16	8
Staff training	41	42	Unemployment insurance		1	14
Willingness to delegate	37	48	Labor market flexibility		8	18
Performance-related pay	43	45	Strikes		6	9
Financial management	45	44	Industrial relations		28	21
Cost control	44	37	Collective bargaining power		4	5
Effectiveness of corporate			Primary education enrollment		41	49
boards	26	38	Labor tax wedge		39	n/a
Management education	43	47	Secondary education enrollment		34	40
Managers' international ex-						
perience and language skills	25	16				
Use of information technology	42	41				

Source: World Economic Forum 1998.

echoed in the Egyptian tourism industry, however. The Accor Hotels estimate projected labor needs for the tourism industry, areas of training and skill enhancement, and ways to go about meeting those needs in the coming few years. (The preceding is based on a phone interview with Mr. Abdel Hakim Hussein, Director of Human Resources, Accor, Egypt.)

The key to effective staff development and training is to link it to business objectives formulated by managers. Managers who have the ability to define objectives and communicate them to their staff will improve their business performance through improved standards of service, increased customer satisfaction, and more repeat business, leading to greater profitability. Thus, both groups—managers and workers—must change fundamental attitudes from one of selling what they have toward one of developing and delivering what the customer wants.

According to a 1996 survey of 100 tourism practitioners worldwide, tourism experts' dissatisfaction with the quality of labor varies from one category to the next. For example, while there are huge gaps between actual qualifications and required qualifications in areas such as market forecasting for high-level management (45 percent of respondents), upper managers' general research abilities or legal knowledge appears to pose a smaller problem (18 percent of respondents). Alarming gaps between available and required qualifications appear in frontline personnel such as waiters and receptionists and their supervisors in their interpersonal and communication, language, and computing skills (table 11.10).

Focusing on the Middle East region, we find that survey results showing that lower levels of satisfaction are more apparent for frontline personnel (33 percent) and their supervisors (11 percent), while satisfaction for management positions was around 50 percent.[14]

Another area where concern should be raised for the MENA countries is language requirements and the preferred language skills that the survey highlights

TABLE 11.10 QUALITY TRAINING GAPS AT THE DIFFERENT OCCUPATION LEVELS

Training area	Frontline personnel		Supervisory personnel		Medium-level management		High-level management	
	Priority	Gap	Priority	Gap	Priority	Gap	Priority	Gap
Basic training								
Business knowledge	39	48	49	40	56	39	47	31
Impact analysis	7	20	6	11	14	19	25	21
Knowledge of the tourism industry	24	28	34	35	45	31	41	36
Market forecasting	2	18	15	14	27	11	29	45
Legal knowledge	9	13	17	16	20	17	18	18
Administrative procedures	0	5	2	5	9	14	22	24
Management	3	18	45	54	67	69	68	39
Marketing	6	28	11	22	36	56	31	42
Multicultural knowledge	49	28	29	19	17	22	16	21
Research	1	5	6	5	18	25	14	18
Strategic planning	0	5	2	6	12	29	72	58
Technical training								
Computing	56	42	55	36	42	39	21	30
Languages	74	46	38	35	19	25	14	18
Personal skills								
Interpersonal communication	88	54	87	54	53	33	39	28

Source: World Tourism Organization 1997.

TABLE 11.11 PREFERRED LANGUAGE KNOWLEDGE
(percent)

Knowledge	Frontline personnel	Supervisory personnel	Medium-level management	High-level management
English	79	79	79	78
French	27	26	29	20
Spanish	25	26	24	17
German	23	21	22	16
Italian	6	4	4	5
Japanese	21	24	17	17

Source: World Tourism Organization 1997.

(table 11.11). Eighty percent of respondents cite the English language as a preferred skill for all job levels. That may be a challenge for the MENA region and may be a priority in terms of emphasizing the need to boost the industry as a high-profile career option for graduates of foreign language schools in the region.

Countries have addressed these weaknesses on two levels: tourism human development in their tourism strategies and private initiative efforts of international certification.[15] The United Kingdom's Tourism Strategy: Tomorrow's Tourism, published in 1998, acknowledges the paramount importance of developing a trained and motivated work force capable of delivering quality tourism service (www.open.gov.uk). The government and the tourism industry have entered into a partnership called the New Deal Initiative, which ensures that the industry manages to find the staff it needs, and that the industry is able to train them to the standards required. Tourism employers, in turn, are heavily involved in developing the education and training curricula needed and determining how to achieve these skills (www.open.gov.uk).

Other aspects of the human development plan include campaigns to challenge the negative perception and stereotypes associated with tourism and hospitality jobs; jobs in the tourism industry have the reputation of being low-paid, involving menial work, and requiring antisocial working hours. To these perceptions, in the MENA region, one can add images of not providing "a glamorous career" or "upward mobility," and especially important for young women, not providing "a socially correct" job. To counter these perceptions, the government (in collaboration with the tourism industry) has developed plans to give tourism careers a higher profile through career festivals and image campaigns.

As for on-the-job training, the strategy encourages the private sector to invest in training, especially for small- and medium-scale operators through a diverse set of courses and seminars (check, for example, www.tourism-training-scotland.org.uk). For example, a tourism training program in Scotland provides many one- or two-day seminars that focus on a specific aspect or skill. Private sector participants are encouraged to require or use such training courses as bonuses.

Other efforts are being implemented in Australia, South Africa, Canada, the European Union, and the United States, with different combinations of required licenses and accreditations, and more reliance on government to provide voluntary participation in training and education in other countries (see, for example, the International Council for Hotel, Restaurant, and Institutional Education at http://chrie.org; the Accreditation Commission for Programs in Hospitality Administration (ACPHA); and the Commission for Accreditation of Hospitality Management Programs (CAHM) at http://cbix.unh.edu/).

Conclusions

Tourism is a growing industry worldwide. The Middle East already has its undisputed strengths such as its location and its large share in world historical assets. It also has potential strength in the region's growing domestic market. Cluster analyses of Egypt, Jordan, Tunisia, and the Palestinian Territories suggest that the region shares common patterns of weaknesses such as inadequate infrastructure quality, the dominant role of the government in economic activity, and weaknesses related to human capital and marketing strategies.

While the speed to address infrastructure and privatization weaknesses will have to be determined by the speed of economywide policies of each country, tourism marketing and human development can benefit from tourism-specific policies. Other countries' experiences provide a host of options that can enhance the region's efforts to compete effectively in a vibrant and constantly changing market for tourism services. These options include industrywide human resource development programs, accreditation, licensing, and on-the-job training programs.

Appendix 11A. Strategy for the Tourism Industry of Nova Scotia

Vital Objectives

1. Having the right products for the right markets through:

- undertaking research necessary to make the best product, market development;
- developing products and experiences in which Nova Scotia has a competitive strength;
- extending the season into shoulder periods, and develop products and off-season marketing;
- developing targeted packages.

2. Providing quality of experience and value for our tourists through:

- committing to delivering quality products;
- working to enhance the standards of customer service and hospitality in the industry;
- working to provide a high standard of visitor-related services;
- cultivating a commitment among managers to management education and staff training.

3. Developing effective marketing initiatives through:

- enhancing the awareness of Nova Scotia as an outstanding travel and vacation destination;
- promoting and selling our products and experiences to identified market segments;
- developing cooperative programs to market packages;
- implementing measures to monitor market trends and measure the effectiveness of marketing programs.

Critical Examples

1. Effective leadership and partnerships among the industry stakeholders through:

- developing effective leadership and partnerships among industry stakeholders;
- establishing a task force to investigate options for tourism industry restructuring;
- working with the provincial government tourism agency to strengthen the public/private partnership within tourism.

2. A supportive business environment and an entrepreneurial, customer-oriented busienss culture within the tourism sector through:

- building a collaborative partnership relationship with other industries and non-tourism government agencies;
- working to build and strengthen partnerships at the Atlantic Canada and national levels;
- identifying and developing leaders, and encouraging them to come forward and play a role;
- improving access to market and product research and information;
- building new partnerships among public sector attractions and expand the resources available.

3. To foster a supportive business environment and an entrepreneurial customer-oriented business culture within the tourism sector through:

- fostering a supportive business environment and an entrepreneurial customer-oriented business culture within the tourism sector;
- developing a regulatory, policy, and economic environment which will support growth in the tourism industry;
- improving the level of awareness of the importance and diversity of tourism with both the general public and government;
- advocating the positioning of tourism as a key economic growth sector for Nova Scotia;
- fostering entrepreneurship;
- encouraging a willingness to accept and embrace change, and an understanding of the "big picture" and fostering professionalism in the tourism sector.

4. To improve transportation access from key markets and transportation infrastructure within the province through:

- improving our internal transportation linkages and services within the province.

5. Protection of our tourism assets—the environment, our cultures, our way of life through:

- developing and encouraging the implementation of sound environmental practices;
- developing a plan to build awareness about the importance of preserving our cultures, heritage, lifestyles, and natural environment.

Source: http://www.gov.ns.ca/ecor/pubs/tourstra.

Notes

1. All dollar amounts are U.S. dollars.

2. There are special characteristics for the Palestinian territories which highlight the importance of developments in the peace process. Progress on the Israeli-Palestinian peace process is also a factor in Egypt's and Jordan's tourism development, albeit at a much smaller level.

3. Arthur Andersen 1996.

4. Refer to World Bank, pp. 250–51.

5. World Tourism Organization 1994, p. 238.

6. A planning approach, which has received considerable attention in recent years, and is applicable to some tourism areas, is strategic planning. While outcomes of strategic and long-range comprehensive planning may be very similar, strategic planning is somewhat different. It focuses more on identification and resolution of immediate issues. Strategic planning typically is more oriented to rapidly changing future situations and how to cope with changes organizationally. It is more action oriented and concerned with handling unexpected events.

7. Based on an article in *Al-Ahram* newspaper dated February 10, 2000. Efforts are being made to acquire the full tourism strategy document.

8. In Egypt, the share of state-owned enterprises in gross domestic investment averaged 65 percent during the period 1985–90 and 13.8 percent of total employment for the same period.

9. Bechri 2000.

10. It was estimated that Internet users in 1996 ranged from 30 million to 50 million worldwide. This number is estimated to have grown significantly since then.

11. According to Egypt's foreign tourist survey, pollution and poor environment quality are the most frequently cited weaknesses in visiting Egypt. (CAPMAS 1997).

12. World Tourism Organization 1994, p. 6.

13. See, for example, KPMG Management Consulting 1996; Tohamy and Swinscoe 1999; and WTTC 1997.

14. The sample corresponds to only 10 respondents out of the hundred surveyed. These results, therefore, while they exhibit the same general patterns, may need to be interpreted with caution.

15. Multilateral efforts to address tourism training and education challenges are constantly being tackled through the World Tourism Organization initiatives such as the Global Tourism Training Community and through the WTTC.

Bibliography

Al-Ahram (Newspaper). 2000. "Egyptian Tourism between Two Years: An Interview with Minister El-Beltagui." Mamdouh February 10, issue 41338 vol. 124, Al-Ahram, Cairo.

Arthur Andersen Report. Web site: http://www.hotel.online.com/Neo/Trends/Andersen/Middle East Hospitality Industry-Winter1996.htm/

Bechri, Mohamed. 2000. "The Tourism Cluster in Tunisia." Third Mediterranean Forum, Cairo.

CAPMAS (Central Agency for Public Mobilization and Statistics). 1997. "Tourism Sample Survey." Cairo.

Fawzy, Samiha. 1998. "Egypt: The Tourism Cluster." A study prepared for The Ministry of Economy, March.

http://cbix.unh.edu/.

http://chrie.org.

http://www.open.gov.uk.

http://www.tourism-training-scotland.org.uk.

http://www.un.org/esa/sustdev/dpif1.htm.

http://www.world-tourism.org/.

KPMG Management Consulting. 1996. "Bahrain Tourism Strategy: Economic Impact Analysis." Directorate of Tourism.

Nova Scotia, Canada "Strategy for the Tourism Industry of Nova Scotia." Web site: http://www.gov.ns.ca/ecor/pubs/tourstra.

Tohamy, Sahar, and Adrian Swinscoe. 1999. "The Economic Impact of Tourism in Egypt." The Egyptian Center for Economic Studies, Working Paper 40, Cairo.

United Kingdom. 1998. "Tourism Strategy: Tomorrow's Tourism." United Kingdom. Web site: http://www.open.gov.uk.

World Bank. 1999. *World Development Indicators*. Washington, D.C.: World Bank.

————. 2000. *Entering the 21st Century—World Development Report 1999/2000.* New York: Oxford University Press.

World Economic Forum. 1998. *The Global Competitiveness Report.* World Economic Forum. Geneva: World Link Publications, January.

World Tourism Organization. 1994. *National and Regional Tourism Planning: Methodologies and Case Studies.* London: Routledge.

————. 1997. *World Tourism Education and Training Series. An Introduction to TEDQUAL: A Methodology for Quality in Tourism Education and Training.* Madrid.

————. 1998. *Yearbook of Tourism Statistics 1998.* Madrid.

————. 2000. *Tourism Highlights 1999.* Madrid.

WTTC (World Travel and Tourism Council). 1999. " The Liberalization of Egyptian Aviation Policies: The Benefits for Tourism and the National Economy." http://www.wttc.org/.

Zuraikat, Gaith. 2000. "Hashemite Kingdom of Jordan: The Tourism Cluster." Third Mediterranean Forum, Cairo.

Index

A

accounting
    International Forum for Accounting Development, 134
    standards, 141
administration
    business costs, 70–71
    procedures, 195
advisory services, 197
    consultation fees, 179
agriculture, 24
    tariffs, 19, 20
    trade, 18–19
Alexandria Business Association, 200
Algeria, surveys, 75
alliances, 52
amins, 83
Antibribery Convention, 146
Arab Development Agency, SMEs, 208
Arab Free Trade Area (AFTA), 20, 24–25
arbitrary power, limiting, 92–93
arbitration, 108
    Indonesia, 108

arbitrators, 96
Asia
    East Asia, 139, 160, 190
    savings and investment, 209, 210
Asian Newly Industrialized Economies, SMEs, 168–173
asset-backed securities, 226, 229
Australia, tourism, 248
auto industry, 47, 51–52
automation, 180
avant-garde SMEs
    economic role, 223–224
    financing, 226–227, 229

B

Bahrain, SMEs, 189
Bangkok Conference, 145, 148–149
    recommendations, 149–152
banking, 133, 192, 222
    systems, 124
bankruptcy law, 89–92
    Korea, 106
    Thailand, 107
benchmarking index, U.K., 166–167
bias, macroeconomic policies, 193–194
board of directors, 123, 141
    essential information, 147
    responsibilities, 127, 143
Brazil
    clustering, 201
    judicial reform, 107
    property rights, 106
Bubble Act, 136–137
bureaucracy, risk guide, 27
business
    constraints, 71–74
    corporate governance reform, 150–151
    development service organizations, 203
    development services, 195–200
    incubators, 168
    information services, 198–199
    leaders, 148–152
business environment, 66, 166, 228
    reform, 63–64

regional, 63–75
SMEs, 173
business link program, 166, 167–168
businesslike approach, 204

C

Cadbury Commission, guidelines, 140
Cairo International Fair, 200
California Public Employees' Retirement System, 144
can companies, 56
Canada
    small firms, 53–57
    tourism strategy, 256–257
capability focus, 174
capacity building, 131
capital
    markets, 164
    providers, 121
    see also credit; financing
carrot-and-stick approach, 176
casino capitalism, 142–143
Center for European Policy Studies, 144
Center for Export Requirements (CENTREX), 26
Center for International Private Enterprise, 138, 152
chief inspector, 35
Chile, 139, 200
    networks, 202
China, 53
    see also Hong Kong; Taiwan
city-centered development, 53
civil law
    countries, 106–107
    property rights, 106
clothing industry, 54–55
clustering, 163
    benefits, 201–202
    development, 176
    promoting, 165
    Spain, 180–182
collectivity, 174
Colombia, industrial restructuring, 39–40
commercial services, regional trends in import and export, 32
common-law countries, 107

competence, 175
competition
  global, 46
  new, 158, 161
  SMEs and, 161–165
competitiveness
  constraints, 78–82
  definition, 1–2
  impediments, 64–67
  indicators, 67–71
  international, 39, 67–71
  measure, 52–53
  MENA and, 2–3
complementarity, 174–175
Comprehensive Development Framework, 134
computerization, 34
computers, 35
  access, 69
  industry, 56
concentration, 175
confidence, 133
conglomerates, family-owned or -managed, 128
constitution, 109
consultation fees, SMEs, 179
consumers' preferences, 47
contestable markets, 124
context, 174–175
control market, 124
control premiums, 123
coordination, 175–176
corporate governance, 6–7, 119–137
  application, 145
  basic rules, 141–142
  benefits to society, 145–146
  central issues, 133
  challenge in emerging markets, 128–133
  defined, 121–122, 140–141, 142, 149, 151
  framework, 122–128
  global forum, 135–136
  history, 119, 136–137
  model, 125–126
  model procedures, 144
  principles, 126–127
  support for reform, 134–135
  voluntary measures, 127–128

corporations
    external architecture, 122, 124–127
    instant, 128–129
    internal architecture, 122, 123
    ownership, 128
    ownership structure, 123
corruption, 146
cost, 51
    judicial reform, 94–95
Costa Rica, property rights, 88
counseling services, 197
credibility, 9
credit, 219
    bureaus, 96
    competition for, 124
    gap, 220
    markets, 164
    see also loans
cumulativeness, 174
customer orientation, 174
customs administration and reform, 25–26

D
debt-equity swap, 90–91
decentralization, 34
delays, 70–71
demand assessment, 204
Denmark, networking, 202
deregulation, Mexico, 38
design, Hong Kong, 172–173
developed countries
    obstacles to business, 80, 81
    SMEs, 159–160, 190, 191
    technology-based exports, 177–178
development projects, 168
diamond of national competitiveness, 52–53
    virtual, 54
differentiation, 50, 51, 52
directors. *See* board of directors
disclosures, 127, 143
dispute resolution, 76–115
    access, 82
    cost reduction, 86–100
    delay, 105, 106

demand for, 84–85
evolution, 83–85
imperfect, 85–86
transaction costs and, 83–86
dispute resolution, alternative, 86, 95–100, 108
advantages, 95
costs, 96, 97
disadvantages, 97–98
encouraging development and use of, 99–100
distortions in markets and institutions, 163–164, 194–195

E

East Asia
financial crisis, 139
SMEs, 160, 190
Eastern Europe, 21, 139
e-commerce, tourism, 247
Economic Freedom Rating, 79, 104
economic growth, SMEs and, 209, 211–212
economies of scale. *See* scale
economy, importance of SMEs in national economy, 188–191
ecotourism, 248–249
education, 192–193, 250–251, 258
tourism, 243–244
see also training
efficiency, 22, 63
Egypt
business information services, 198
dispute resolution, 80, 82
educational level of entrepreneurs, 221
investment capital, 221
law, 84
macroeconomic policies, 193–194
management and labor competitiveness, 252
marketing assistance, 199, 200
SMEs, 189, 190
tariffs, 40
tourism, 241, 246, 247, 258
trade facilitation, 30
Egyptian Export Promotion Centre, 199
El Salvador, judicial independence, 93
electric power, tourism, 242
Electronic System for Exports (SIEX), 26

emerging market economies, corporate structure, 128–129
employment, SMEs, 211–212, 213, 214
England, corporate governance, 136–137
enterprise environment. *See* business environment
enterprises
    constraints, 67
    surveys, 64–67
entrepreneurs, 220, 222–223
    educational level, 221
    Egypt, 221
    profiles, 191–193
environmental consciousness, tourism marketing, 248–249
Europe, 41
    proximity to, 237, 239
    travel and tourism economy, 238
European Union (EU), 21, 47
    SMEs, 182
Europe-Mediterranean agreements, 20, 21–24
    costs and benefits, 22
    exporting firms, binding constraints, 26
exports
    SMEs, 212–216, 218
    to industrialized countries, 64, 65

F

factor markets, 163–164
family
    background, 191–192
    business, 146
    conglomerates, 128
    funds, 220
feasibility studies, 168
financial discipline, enforcing, 130
financial institutions, 30
financial sector, 39, 129
financing, 223–224
    methods, 208–232
    microfinancing, 220–221, 222
    sources, 224–227
firms
    actions, 47–48
    competitiveness, 55
    constraints for interfirm collaboration, 202–203

corporate governance and risk, 145
    role, 8–9
    small, 4–5, 53–58
Focus Technical, 168
follow-up, 30
food importers, 19
foreign direct investment, 105
    inflows, 15, 209, 210
    SMEs, 215–218
France, 56
free trade
    agreements, 4, 23
    area, 22

G

GDP growth, 215–217
    Asia, foreign direct investment, 217
    SMEs and, 212, 213, 214, 228, 229
General Agreement on Trade in Services (GATS), 19
General Motors, guidelines, 144, 152
Global Corporate Governance Forum, 135–136
globalization, 45–46, 57
    competition, 48–49
    defined, 46–48
    firms, 49, 50
    industries, 48–49
    levels, 48
    national markets, 48
    SME competitiveness and, 200–203
    strategies, 49–52
global rules for business, 3–5
goods, trends in export and import, 33
governance issues, 27
    see also corporate governance
government
    business community and, 65, 73
    corporate governance reform, 149–152
    financing, 228
    hands-off policy, 51
    policies, SMEs and, 164–165
    role, 9, 46, 50–52, 77, 142–143
    SMEs, 173, 179
    tourism, 244–245
Green Globe program, 248

group-lending, 224–225
Gulf Cooperation Council (GCC), 20, 25, 41

H

harmonization, 126
health products, disposable, 55–56
high-risk ventures. *See* avant-garde SMEs
Hong Kong, SMEs, 171–173
Hong Kong Design Innovation Company, 172–173
Hong Kong Productivity Council, 171–172
human resources
    development, 250–255
    tourism, 243–244, 250–255

I

import
    card, 34
    duties, 68, 69
importing firms, binding constraints, 26
imports, 23–24
incentive systems, Arab, 194
Index of Economic Freedom, 79, 102–103
Indonesia
    arbitration, 108
    bankruptcy law, 91
    dispute resolution, 100
industrial countries, SMEs, 158, 160
industrial restructuring, 30–31
    Colombia, 39–40
    Mexico, 38–39
Industrial Technology Research Institute (ITRI), 169
industry, 24
inter-industry trade, 15
    structure, 47
    tariff rates, 19, 20
    trade, 18–19
inflation, 71–72
information
    age, tourism, 242
infrastructure, 37
    providing, 30
    sharing, 74
    see also networking

infrastructure
    privatized, 131
    tourism, 241–242, 255
    trade-related, 27–28
innovation, 192
    counselors, 168
    support, 181
instability, 00
    political instability, perceived, tourism, 245
integration, 16, 17, 51, 52
interest groups
    dispute resolution, 101
    resistance from, 131–132
internal control, 141
International Finance Corporation (IFC), 133–134
International Hotel Environment Initiative, 248
International Labour Organisation, 196, 197
International Standards Organization, 149
internationalization, patterns, 14–15
Internet, 69
    tourism and, 247, 258
interstice markets, 57
investment
    capital, Egypt, 221
    laws, 194
investors, 125
Iran, dispute resolution, 100

J

Japan, 47
    tourism, 248
Jordan
    advisory and counseling services, 197
    business information services, 198
    macroeconomic policies, 194
    management and labor competitiveness, 252
    marketing assistance, 199
    reforms, 105
    registration, documentation, and customs procedures, 34
    SMEs, 189
    tourism, 240–241
    training, 196, 197
Jordan Export Development and Commercial Centres Corporation, 199
judicial reform, 86, 92–95, 100–101, 107

Brazil, 107
cost benefit, 94–95
judiciary
access to, 92, 94
budget, 93
consistency, 82, 85, 92, 94
independence, 92–93
speed and efficiency, 92, 93
system, 131

K

Key Account Management program, 247–248
knowledge indicators, 70–71, 74
Korea
bankruptcy law, 106
GDP, 105
SMEs, 170

L

labor. *See* work force
language skills, 253–254
Latin America, 146, 153
law, 80
ambiguity, 87
commercial, 139
compliance and, 119–120
corporate governance reform, 151–152
Egypt, 84
enforcement, 92
imperfect, 66
inconsistency, 82
investment, 194
Islamic, 105
Korea, 170
national, 56–57
rule of, 74
Law of Economic Activity, 142
leasing, to niche-finding SME, 225–226
Lebanon
business information services, 198
registration, documentation, and customs procedures, 34–35
SMEs, 188, 189, 190
tariffs, 23

legal systems
    multiple, 83–84
    reform, 86–92, 100–101, 107, 131
LINK scheme, 166
literacy, tourism, 243–244
litigation, 82
loans, 222
    guarantee schemes, 167
    Korea, 170
    see also credit

M

macroeconomy, biased policies, 193–194
Malaysia, 28
management systems, 148
manufacturing, SMR, 22
    see also SMEs
market
    competitive, establishing, 130
    differentiation strategies, tourism, 247–248
    distortions, 163–164, 194–195
    failure, SMEs, 165
    new, 29
market-based learning, 157
marketing, 255
    assistance, 199–200
    tourism, 246–250
market-niche-finding SMEs
    economic role, 222–223
    financing, 225–226, 228–229
media, corporate governance reform, 151
mediators, 96
merchandise exports, 15, 16
Mexico, industrial restructuring, 38–39
microfinancing, 220–221, 222
monitoring, 24, 133
Morocco, 16, 23, 40
multifocal strategy, 52
multination corporations, Singapore, 170, 171

N

national responsiveness, 52
networking, 69–71, 201–202

niche-finding SME, leasing to, 225–226
nontariff barriers (NTBs), 18
    eliminating, 22
Nova Scotia, tourism strategy, 256–257

O

obstacles to business, 78–82
oil-producing countries, SMEs, 188
opportunism, 51
Organisation for Economic Cooperation and Development (OECD)
    corporate governance reform, 134–135
    guidelines, 140
    principles of corporate governance, 126–127, 143–145
oversight, 34, 133
owner-managers, 192
ownership, 87
    with due diligence, 132–133
    see also property rights

P

pension funds, 144, 146
Peru, dispute resolution, 91
Philippines, 28
Poland, 142
policies, 141
    macroeconomic, 193–194
    SMEs, 173–176
political instability, perceived, tourism, 245
population growth, 76
port reforms, Mexico, 39
practices, 141
principal-agent problem, 121
private sector, 24, 31
    development, 77
    Global Corporate Governance Forum and, 136
    SMEs, 181
privatization, 76–77, 128–129
    drive for, 139
    tourism, 245, 255
Product Development Assistance Scheme, Singapore, 171
product lines, new, 29
production sharing, 14
property rights, 85–86, 87–89, 107, 224
    civil law, 106

public, corporate governance reform, 149–150
public-private
   cooperation, 140
   partnership, 30, 31

Q
quality tourism, 247

R
R&D
   Korea, 170
   SMEs, 179, 180
reform
   fundamentals, 130–131
   World Bank Group strategy, 133–136
regional focus
   agreements, 20–25
   business environment, 5–6, 63–75
   development, 53
   selective assistance, 167
regionalism, revival, 40–41
registration, documentation, and customs procedures
   Jordan, 34
   Lebanon, 34–35
regulations, 66, 78–80
   business costs, 70–71
   existing, 91–92
reputation, 95–96
reputational agents, 125, 137
restrictions, 78–80
rule of law, 140

S
safety, tourism, 245
Saudi Arabia, financing, 229
savings and investment, 209
   Asia, 210
scale, 46, 204, 219
   SMEs, 162
sector-specific approach, 203–204
securities market, 125, 129
   fostering, 130–131
self-assessment, 134

service centers, SMEs, 180–181
service sector, 182
services trade, 15–16
    commitments to open market, 21
shareholders, 125, 141
    minority, 145
    rights, 127, 142
    role, 127
    treatment, 127, 143
Singapore, SMEs, 170–171
size, small, disadvantages, 161–163
small- and medium-size enterprises (SMEs), 7–8
    advantages, 158–159
    Asian Newly Industrialized Economies, 168–173
    challenges, 160–165
    competition and, 161–165
    competitiveness, globalization and, 200–203
    economic role, 209–218, 218–224
    employment, 211–212, 213, 214
    export growth, 212, 214, 215
    GDP growth, 212, 213, 214
    government role, 173
    Hong Kong, 171–173
    Korea, 170
    policies, 173–176
    problems, 193–195
    profiles of entrepreneurs, 191–193
    role in selected countries, 160
    significance, 158
    Singapore, 170–171
    strengthening, 157–186
    support policies, 165–173
    support services and competitiveness, 187–207
    Taiwan, 169–170, 178–180
    United Kingdom, 165–168
Small Industry Technical Assistance Scheme, Singapore, 171
small, peripheral firms, 53–58
Smart Scheme, 168
social approach, 204
Sonakul, M. R. Chatu Mongol, 139–140
South Sea Company, 136–137
southern Mediterranean (SMR) countries, 22
Spain, clustering, 180–182

specialization, 203
SSEA, obstacles to business, 80, 81
stakeholders, role, 6
standardization of products, 29
standards, explicit, 144
state-owned enterprises (SOEs)
    economic activity, 68
    Mexico, 38
stereotypes, tourism jobs, 254
subcontracting, 163, 176
support services, SMEs, 187–207
sustainability, 204
Switzerland, tourism, 248
Syria, 194
    SMEs, 188, 189, 190

T
Taiwan, SMEs, 169–170, 178–180
Taiwan New PC Consortium, 169
talent, 139
tariff bindings, Uruguay Round and, 19
tariffs, 41
    bound, before and after Uruguay Round, 20
    by region, 14
    common, postponing, 41
    reduction, 18
taxation, 66, 71, 80, 82, 83–84, 131, 164, 166, 194
Technology Development Center, Singapore, 171
technology-based activities and products, 161, 162
    exports, developing countries, 177–178
    Hong Kong, 172
    Taiwan, 169, 178–179
technology counselors, 168
technology transfer, 180
telecommunications, 28–29, 35, 69
    indicators, 36
    tourism, 242
    see also networking
Thailand
    bankruptcy law, 91, 107
    property rights, 88
think tanks, role, 9–10
time, dispute resolution, 82

tourism, 8, 233–260
    development strategy, 240–241
    domestic, 239–240
    enhancing prospects, 245–255
    human resources development, 250–255
    importance in world trade, 234
    infrastructure, 241–242
    knowledge necessary, 251, 254
    marketing, 246–250
    marketing to the local community, 249–250
    MENA's current position, 234–235
    outbound by region, 240
    receipts and arrivals, by country, 237
    receipts and arrivals, by region, 236
    same-region, 238
    strategy, 258
    strengths and weaknesses, MENA countries, 235–245
    top 10 tourism destinations and earners, 235
tourist attractions, marketing, 249
toy manufacturing, Spain, 180–182
trade
    facilitation, 29–31
    infrastructure, 35
    liberalization, 39, 201
    patterns, 16–17
traditional SME
    economic role, 219–222
    financing, 224–225, 228
training, 196–197, 250, 252–255, 258
    Hong Kong, 172
    initiatives, 167
    quality training gaps, 253
    see also education; work force
transaction costs, 73–74, 77
    dispute resolution, 85–86
    reducing, 86–100
    SMEs, 165
transition economies, corporate structure, 128–129
transition periods, 31
transparency, 125, 127, 143
    government-business, 138–154
    requiring, 130
    weakness, 141

Treaty on Intellectual Property Rights (TRIPS), 89
trust, 133
    entrepreneurs, 193
Tunisia
    industrial restructuring, 30
    obstacles to business, 80
    surveys, 75
tourism, 239, 240, 247
trade, 22–23, 40, 41

U

uniform standards, 126
United Arab Emirates, 41
United Kingdom, SMEs, 165–168
United States
    alternative dispute resolution, 108
    differentiation, 55–56
    GDP, 105
universities, role, 9–10
Uruguay Round. *See*   World Trade Organization Uruguay Round Agreement

V

valuation of a good, 34
    Jordan, 34
venture capital financing, 226–227
    Singapore, 171
verificateur, 35
Vienot Commission, guidelines, 140
virtual diamond of competitiveness, 54–56
Vocational Training Corporation, 196, 197

W

Work force
    costs, 22–23
    labor regime, 39
    low-skilled, 219
    see also training
World Bank Group strategy, reform programs, 133–136
World Business Environment Survey, 74–75
    inflation, 75
World Trade Organization
    post-Seattle environment, 19–20
    Uruguay Round Agreement, 18–19